THOMAS HARDY, ARCHITECT

THE WESSEX PROJECT

KESTER RATTENBURY

LUND HUMPHRIES

First published in 2018 by Lund Humphries
Office 3, Book House
261A City Road
London
EC1V 1JX
UK

www.lundhumphries.com

Supported by a Publications Grant from the
Paul Mellon Centre for Studies in British Art

PAUL MELLON CENTRE
for Studies in British Art

Designed by Crow Books
Printed in Slovenia

CONTENTS

ACKNOWLEDGEMENTS

I am hugely indebted to a great number of people who have helped this book into print. Simon Gatrell has given an unreasonably generous amount of his time and attention to assist these arguments and speculations towards publishable form and I am entirely in his debt. Many others have also given time, help, advice and expertise: notably John Bold, Lindsay Bremner, Murray Fraser, Maarten Delbeke, Adrian Forty, Richard Difford, Leon van Schaik, and at the Dorset County Museum, Helen Gibson and Andrew Leah, who has also patiently assisted the unreasonable demands for photography in architectural publications. Gregory Stevens Cox and Toucan Press have also been exceptionally helpful. The Dorset County Museum have been extremely supportive of this work throughout, and I, like all other Hardy students, cannot thank them enough. Other forms of advice, support, discussion, ideas, accommodation, creative suggestions and criticism have been provided by many others, notably Katrin and Mark Russell, Jamie Telford and Jane Gifford, Camilla Wilkinson, Anastasia Christakou, Steve Larkin, Michael McGarry, Anna Joynt, Katharine Heron, Robert Kennett, Iona Foster, Sarah Wigglesworth, John Morgan, Harry Charrington, Susannah Hagan, Daire Moffat and most especially Tim Dobbs who has had to suffer this project for the whole of this century, and who remains its strongest critic, supporter and proofreader. In the huge work of bringing this to publication I am (once again) entirely indebted to Clare Hamman, a steadfast creative enabler who seems able to make impossible things happen. Wonderful alternative cover designs (which I certainly plan to use elsewhere) were done and discussed by Laurence Deane, Arthur Mamou-Mani, Ali Musa and Eddie Blake, and images of their own work were generously provided by Bernard Tschumi and Mike Webb. At the publishers I would like to thank Val Rose, Sarah Thorowgood, James Piper and Tom Furness, as well as Jacqui Cornish. I hope that in publishing such a personal and speculative reading, I can give grounds for other, and more knowledgeable, writers to demolish or consider my suggestions.

This book is dedicated to Tim and Alfrey,
and to my mother, Jay Rattenbury

ILLUSTRATION CREDITS

The reproduction of illustrations on the pages listed below is courtesy of the following copyright holders:

PART 1

VISION

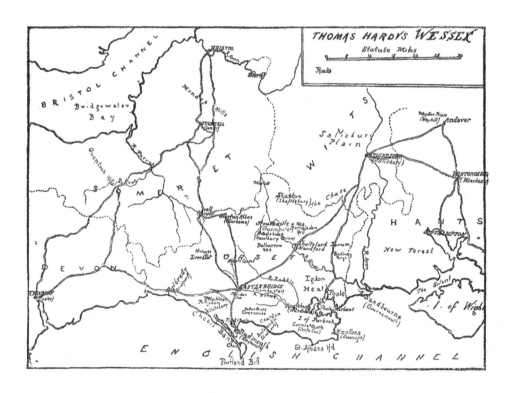

Overleaf: The first map of Hardy's Wessex, published in 1891.

1

NOT MUCH OF AN ARCHITECT

A Different Perspective

The 'shocking' Max Gate in 1885.

Thomas Hardy has not been seen as much of an architect. His best known building is Max Gate, the suburban house which he designed and built for himself and his first wife Emma on the outskirts of Dorchester, long after he had given up working as an architect and become a famous novelist, and it was described, for almost a century, with derision or dark, psychic suspicion. 'Appalling', Margaret Drabble called it: 'an almost perfect negation of the ideal country home, being ugly, uncomfortable, and in Hardy's day administered with a meanness for which apologies were by all accounts all too necessary.'[1]

Its design – unremarkable but for its imaginative context – was part of a gloomy myth of Hardy's domestic life: a masochistic self-immolation in which he tormented himself and both his wives, wilfully abrogating the thatched rural past he immortalised in poetry and prose. But with the benefit of a peculiar kind of architectural hindsight, this view is a big mistake. Despite the normality of the few buildings he actually built, there is a good case for listing Hardy amongst the greatest of all *conceptual* architects – the prophet, well before the fact, of a particular type of speculative, imaginary architectural project – a form with long roots in high architectural culture, but of a type which would boom a century later.

Architectural projects are curious things and not quite the same as buildings. A project begins *before* a building is built, in imaginary and drawn form, to allow architects to test their ideas. The project, literally, is what the architect projects from his or her mind. It is a form of coherent alternative reality and exists in an active form for other architects – whether the building is built or not.

It is not limited to building proposals, either. Masterplans, furniture, art exhibitions and books may all be classed as 'projects' by architects and their critics. Books, and particularly illustrated books, play a special role in how 'experimental', 'speculative' or 'conceptual' projects are made and shared – and they are often seen as 'projects' in their own right. These speculative architectural projects are often unknown outside the profession, but they incubate many big shifts in architectural thinking. Freed from the demands of building, 'conceptual projects' can test, illustrate, discuss and publish ideas which have not yet been built. Architects use them for many things: as advertisements for clients; to experiment with new media; to invent new building types; to challenge 'normal' architectural practices; and to work things out, realistically, before building. Some projects are meant for publication only while some remain unbuilt by chance. And (for better or worse) many of those projects (by Palladio, Le Corbusier or Archigram, for example) have gone on to change the world, by reshaping the imaginations of those designing it.

Comparing Hardy's Wessex to famous, latter-day conceptual projects may sound curious, but finding odd comparisons is a key part of architectural criticism. Having experienced the architectural critic's initial, uneasy sense of the *similarity* of Hardy's work to other architectural works, which were apparently poles apart, I discovered a flood of evidence to support it in the substance of the novels themselves: in their rich, detailed, technical and unusually analytical descriptions; in their content, vision and polemic; in the architectural theories within and surrounding Hardy's work; and in the intriguing, accretive qualities of his buildings.

Most striking to an architectural critic were the *images* which Hardy made or used. These included maps, drawings, sketches, diagrams, details, models, photographs and stage designs, sometimes of very remarkable types. Pictures and artefacts are (to

Hardy's birthplace at Higher Bockhampton.

architects) lucid, fundamental parts of architectural work: they are both process and product; both method and content. Approaching Hardy's work as though it were any other body of architectural work meant assembling the material and *imagining* (as a critic must) what it adds up to. Doing this, some remarkable arguments began to emerge. Not only that Hardy's Wessex was drawn from the architectural ideas of his time, but that it *predicted* some of the most inventive architectural work of our own age. It became apparent that not only could we see Wessex as an architectural project, but that Hardy himself had already done so.

*

It is easy to get lost in the rambling woodlands of literature on Hardy and Wessex. He attracts anyone from high theorists to Sunday walkers. He immerses you in another time and place so completely that it is hard to see the experimental methods he is using to do it. Critics and biographers have to keep pointing out that Hardy is a modernist whose work overturned conventions; who supported divorce, free love and women's rights; whose techniques prefigured a cinematic vision; and whose stories were so shocking that the Bishop of Wakefield burnt *Jude the Obscure* and wrote to *The Yorkshire Post* to say so.[2] Paradoxically, Hardy's Wessex was both an elegy for a vanishing world and a condemnation of its cruelties. But paradoxes are just where Hardy is at his most potent.[3]

He has never, until now, been seen as *architecturally* radical. Even his most careful critics have tended to treat his architecture as a problematic, unsorted job lot. Max Gate, which he designed at the height of his creative powers while in his forties and where he lived until his death aged eighty-seven, was seen as bewildering: a raw piece of suburban, aspirational modernism, inexplicably generated by the great chronicler of the vanishing rural world. Another great Dorset writer, John Fowles, says:

> There is, I think, no greater shock in English literary biography than to go round that far from distinguished villa just outside Dorchester, set on its rather bleak upland. It neither matches that environment, which he has made so vivid in words, nor any conception of Hardy gained from his books; and can conform rather painfully to almost every prejudice we may have against late Victorian taste and the middle class ethos behind it.
>
> To stand inside Max Gate and remember what came out of it – *Tess of the d'Urbervilles, Jude the Obscure, The Dynasts*, the countless poems ... that is when most of us feel we should give up trying to understand great writers. We come expecting the palace of the maker of a fabulous kingdom and we are faced with a brick mediocrity, more suitable to a successful local merchant of his time than anything else.[4]

Fowles is doing something so common that we overlook how curious it is. He is going somewhere *real*, to imagine somewhere partly *imaginary*. Novels depend on this curious suspension of spatial disbelief and countless authors are famous, powerful operators in this field. But architects are trained to develop imaginary places in a very particular way. They use specialised language, pictures, technical knowledge, theories and instincts both learned and unlearned to do so. And they have their own ways of reading all this information together as though it were a real working place. Hardy, an architect himself, had a very particular set of tools at his disposal: the obvious, technical, practical skills of working architectural practice; and those lesser-known to the public – the experiments in representation; the speculations, visions and polemics; and the complex, imaginary constructions of how the world is, or might be made.

Wise critics are wary of writing off any Hardy paradox. Fowles suggests the house was a 'kind of neutral matrix where his masterly power of close and particular recall functioned best'.[5] Others agree that it is more comfortable and less pretentious than its early critics suggest. Hardy, and even Florence Hardy, lived out their lives there, and all three of its later tenants left reluctantly. It has aged – a great deal, and gracefully: its raw, red brick grown with lichen to the colour of flint. When Hardy extended it, he left the walled-up windows and doors visible, so that his strong sense of time was worked into the building.

Just as Hardy's novels have unexpected grains of perverse black comedy folded into their tragic sweep, Max Gate has definite jokes. These are hidden in the faint, common architectural references: cottage, country house, castle; the minor Latin riddle carved on the sundial;[6] and the name.

That name immortalises the demolished tollhouse on the site, kept by Mr and Mrs Henry Mack. Mack's Gate was 'Latinised' on an early drawing, perhaps when 'Romano-British' (actually Paleolithic) graves were found on site. Hardy once called it Maxima Porta: 'Great Gate'. Further corruptions (which Hardy used for place names himself) might make it 'Long Walk' or 'Great Stride', echoing the epic walks of Hardy's famous characters; and it is a social step from his rural childhood home, itself just a walk away through the fields.

Max Gate has a peculiar, uncomfortable relationship with the Arts & Crafts movement, its unavoidable architectural context. It is not unlike Pugin's own, much-criticised house, St Marie's Grange, and its one really distinctive feature – an intriguing double staircase – is right in the Arts & Crafts heartland. But it isn't precious, or pretty, as we now casually assume the Arts & Crafts to be. It seems to us, now, cussedly *normal*, name and all.

But that is important. Generations of architects and critics have turned their noses up at the suburban mix – the aspirational, referential, well-serviced idyll – as the fascinating book *Dunroamin* describes.[7] It is still only the most radical architects who overtly argue *for* the suburbs, and hardly any of them are to be found actually living there. But Hardy *did* choose modern houses himself: rented houses in Sturminster Newton, Hook, Surbiton, Tooting ('for such utter rustics as ourselves, Tooting seemed quite town enough to begin with'[8]) and Wimborne Minster preceded Max Gate. Hardy *was* one of those rare architects who argued for such comfortable, aspirational houses. 'How are the mighty fallen!' says one of his architect-heroes, visiting the erstwhile lord of an ancient castle in his new suburban villa:

> It was almost new, of streaked brick, having a central door and a small bay window on each side to light the two front parlours ... On the neat piers of the neat entrance gate were chiselled the words 'Myrtle Villa'. Genuine roadside respectability sat smiling on every brick of the eligible dwelling ...

But immediately, the cynical architect is surprised by his reaction:

> Perhaps that which impressed him more than the mushroom modernism of Sir William de Stancy's house was the air of healthful cheerfulness which pervaded it ... a canary singing welcome from a cage in the shadow of

the window, the voices of crowing cocks coming over the chimneys from somewhere behind, and sun and air riddling the house everywhere.[9]

That is a real comparison to the cottage life of *Tess*, *Jude*, or *The Woodlanders* – which is hardly idyllic. Hardy was present at the start of a vast battle between the profession and the public over the suburbs – and he was on the layman's side. He once said 'architects do get above themselves; even today when they have had so many lessons'.[10] Even that name, Max Gate, acts as Hardy's curious, camouflaged colours nailed to the mast, signalling the *normality* of this unremarkable house. He knew it was an irritant. But he meant it.

It is not exactly visible, but to an architectural visitor, Max Gate (the front rooms; the original house) – first faintly, then insistently – recalls the layout, orientation and setting of his parents' house at Higher Bockhampton, with its simple plan, central entrance and stair and its living rooms to each side. (Albert Richardson, the architectural historian, must have felt this too: he said it was 'built to the traditional Dorset plan with a central stairway!'[11]) Then there is its similar, south-western orientation; its rising ground; its asymmetrical, part-hipped roof. Conquer Barrow lies to the South, rather as Rainbarrow lies to Bockhampton. The much-maligned, dark trees that half-buried the house by the end of his life were planted by Hardy, just as his grandfather planted trees behind his own new house. Looking at older photographs you can see the open views, the ancient landscape and the time before the ring road. You can even read Hardy's earliest poem 'Domicilium' against it, describing his grandmother's account of the Bockhampton house:

> It faces west, and round the back and sides,
> High beeches, bending, hang a veil of boughs,
> And sweep against the roof ...
>
> Behind, the scene is wilder. Heath and furze
> Are everything that seems to grow and thrive
> Upon the uneven ground ...
>
> Our house stood quite alone, and those tall firs
> And beeches were not planted ...
>
> So wild it was when first we settled here.

There is an idea running through this poem into Max Gate. Hardy, like his grandfather, was building on an open, empty upland, looking past ancient landscapes

Max Gate and Conquer Barrow in the early 1880s.

south-west towards the invisible sea; he was planting those much abused trees – and stepping up socially, intellectually, creatively, into the century beyond.

When he was a grand old man of letters, Hardy said that if he had his life again, he would live it as an architect in a small country town.[12] It has been seen as a piece of typical Hardy perversity. Pugin, one of Hardy's early architectural sources,[13] had damned the whole course of apprenticeships like Hardy's: from paid pupillage to winning medals; from London exhibitions to becoming 'a common surveyor, a measurer of land, a valuer of dilapidations'.[14] That is a close approximation of many aspects of Hardy's career. And at the end of his life, as a world-famous author, he was, deliberately, owning it.

To an architectural writer, all this is gripping. Hardy is trailing his coat for us, luring us on. *Look* at Max Gate, it is not the house we expected, and that tells us something important. As in his writings, Hardy defied expectations, and placed himself socially and architecturally where he wanted to be – back in his homeland, but squarely in the modern, everyday suburban world, which would take the twentieth century by storm. Perhaps it sounds strange to see living in a suburban house as an act of intellectual defiance. But a century later, J.G. Ballard would be noted for it. Perhaps it sounds unlikely that, for an architectural writer, this squarely locates him in the most uncomfortably radical outpost of architectural thought. But Hardy *was* an uncomfortably radical thinker, and he *was* an architectural writer. If you look at Wessex from the point of view of modern experimental thought, that is just where you keep finding him.

*

Oddly, the previsionary and radical nature of Hardy's work has been studied in almost every field *except* architecture. In Literary Criticism, he is placed between the social realism of George Eliot and that quintessential 'modern', James Joyce. In music, his proximity to (and often collaboration with) the modern pastoral music movement – Vaughan Williams, Benjamin Britten, Gustav Holst and Edward Elgar – is also established, even though the wonderful Hardy settings and compositions themselves are little known.[15] More famous, intriguingly, is the idea that Hardy foresaw a cinematic vision. The link between architecture and cinema has been discussed for a century; yet no comparative study has ever been done of Hardy's anticipation of *modern* work in architecture itself.

If Max Gate was a deliberate architectural provocation, it was certainly not Hardy's only one. His novels are full of them, and so are the images he produced. Not just the written ones – the ones he makes you see so vividly that you can find them lodged in your mind decades later – but also Hardy's own pictures too. There are many of these, and they become more remarkable through his life: the architectural notebook he maintained into his eighties; the illustrations he directed; and the maps he deliberately introduced into his books. His startling *Wessex Poems* illustrations are sharply like experimental architectural drawings of a century later. So are the remarkable 'empty' long-lens landscape photographs by Hermann Lea, made working closely with Hardy. Even the various, little-known theatre design collaborations of his later life seem to be ahead of their time. None of this may suggest a coherent architectural position to those unfamiliar with the peculiar ground of architectural experiment. But those few should be nodding their heads.

A contemporary architectural writer, rereading Hardy's work, can find themselves unexpectedly stumbling onto native ground: into an assembly of vision, drawings, experiment, maps, argument, polemic and real buildings. A realm where pictures and text are naturally used and read together, where a whole meaningful world can be drawn, imagined and discussed. Where imagined places are intended to change the real world too.

So Max Gate becomes a detail – a key – to what any modern architectural critic should acknowledge to be Hardy's great work. Because Hardy built *Wessex* – a highly evolved, richly documented, fully mapped and vastly influential conceptual architectural project of ideas; and one which was a full century and several major architectural revolutions ahead of its time.

2

A KIND OF EDUCATION

The Practices of Architecture

The traditional view of Hardy's architectural work is as a career stepping-stone: that he acquired a few specialised skills – surveying, technical language – and moved on into a spectacularly realised literary career. But architecture – then as now – is an unusual, lateral form of education in itself, with far more dimensions (technical, theoretical, instinctive) than non-architects might imagine. Hardy's day job, naturally, included recording places in drawings and notes; analysing how they worked, how they once were, and how they could be altered; learning habits of description, criticism, invention and analysis.

The complex mixture of drawing and writing skills; practical knowledge; and detailed and aesthetic visual imagination needed to do all this is developed in education and practice, through trial and error. It links physical and spatial imagination, aesthetics, technological detailing and abstract thought, in projects both real *and* imaginary. It can explore art and philosophy while designing the guttering. The inventive relationship of many different things is fundamental to the working, changing practice of architecture. And it would be critical to the most ambitious work that Hardy would make.

*

Hardy was an architectural native. He was born into a family of builders, in the thatched cob house his master-mason grandfather had built. His father and brother continued the business. When his father extended their house, young Thomas probably helped 'puddle' the walls, treading the clay used to build them.[1] Hardy grew up knowing how things were made. But he was not primarily a builder. He was a visionary, clever child, who read and did well at school: his formidable mother's favorite. He carried an inherited telescope around with him and imagined the world in his own strange ways. In the *Life*, officially authored by his second wife,

Florence, he describes in startling detail the guilty moment of watching a man being hanged three miles away through this lens: 'he seemed alone on the heath with the hanged man.'[2] Architectural readers should take note. Hardy was, from childhood, someone to whom the wider, visionary fields of architecture came as easily as knowing how to build.

He was certainly good at surveys: the detailed, written and drawn observations of existing buildings. Working with his father on Woodsford Castle, the 16-year-old Hardy caught the eye of the local Dorchester architect, John Hicks. Hardy's redoubtable mother Jemima negotiated a cut-price deal – forty pounds up front – for Hicks to take him on as an articled assistant. That was the normal educational step, damned by Pugin: '... the youth is placed with some architect in town who has acquired a name, and who will allow him to waste a few years in daily attendance at his office for the consideration of some hundreds he receives from him.'[3]

Jemima Hardy evidently drove a hard bargain, but it must have been a very good survey and Hicks must have had a good eye. Woodsford retains a remarkable amount of authentic detail, even by our fastidious standards, both in the engravings of 1861 and today. The windows have not been regularised, and remarkably, both planting and thatch have been retained (it is the largest thatched roof in Dorset). The rough edges of a vanished wing have been kept, a former, built-over door and composite windows retained. It is hard to persuade builders to do that in any age, let alone at the height of wholesale restoration.

Hardy said Hicks was 'exceptionally well-educated for an ordinary country architect'.[4] While architectural education beyond the workplace was only available through clubs or societies in places like London, Hicks, with his cheerful young staff, studied Greek and Latin and went to lectures. Reading and debates were

Woodsford Castle: Hicks and the Hardys' restoration. Left: in 1861, J.H. Le Keux; right: detail of preserved ragged stonework and walled-up door.

actively encouraged. 'During the ensuing two or three years [Hardy] often gave more time to books than to drawing.'[5]

That suited Hardy's formidable ambitions. He rose every day at five to study and walked to work across the fields, composing Latin hexameters about his projects. He played in his father's band at night. He was still perhaps hoping to study at Cambridge. But the day-to-day work was educational too. Hardy saw 'rustic and borough doings in a juxtaposition unusually close'.[6] He had access into all kinds of people's houses and businesses. He had to consider their aesthetic aspirations, the peculiarities of their lifestyle, every inch of their houses, their sleeping arrangements and their drains. The work included writing too: specifications and short accounts of Hicks's restored buildings (something like press releases) which Claudius Beatty believes were those which appeared in the *Dorset County Chronicle*.[7]

When Hardy sought to move his career on, Hicks gave him a letter of introduction to architects in London. One, John Norton, let him use a desk in the office – by chance, in the week that Arthur Blomfield was asking around for a young Gothic draughtsman. Hardy had struck lucky. Blomfield was one of the leading architects of his day: a protagonist of the fashionable Gothic-Italianate Victoriana, and a 'Restorer'. He was well-connected, President of the Architectural Association, later to be knighted, and was running a lively, successful practice in the middle of the great Victorian building boom.[8] Office life sounds recognisably close to London practice today. And Hardy flung himself into it. He went to the second Great Exhibition, again and again. He would have seen paintings, products, materials, new inventions, stereoscopes – and possibly early moving images.[9] He would remain intrigued by all forms of art and picture-making, something crucial to all phases of his career. He wrote, drew, kept

Mass-produced stereoscopes from the second Great Exhibition;
Hardy was a frequent visitor.

notebooks. He won competitions: one for design, one for an essay. If Pugin was right about the format of architectural education, he was wrong about the level of critical engagement it could support.[10]

Hardy called his time with Blomfield 'his student years',[11] and this is not an analogy but a real architectural fact. He was a member of the nascent Architectural Association, set up in 1847 by a group of working pupils to develop a culture beyond the working demands of architectural practice.[12] It challenged and extended the paid pupillage system, developing its own patterns of mutual criticism, visits and lectures on a wide range of subjects.[13] As Beatty says, 'Hardy ... could hardly have been introduced to a more avant-garde association ... The members learnt from each other. Papers were read and discussed and in the design classes students criticised each other's work.'[14]

Hardy's asides should always be taken seriously – especially when they seem peculiar. Architecture wasn't *done* at university. That *was* an architectural education; those *were* student years, in a profession inventing itself as it went along.[15] The peer-to-peer criticism (which might sound makeshift) remains a crucial plank of architectural teaching and practice, a deliberate collaborative method of design and criticism, still active in the crits and projects of today. And the architectural habits Hardy was learning are not quite what non-architects might think. Architects were trying to reclaim their broader, cultural territory, the kinship with art, experiment and philosophy developed in the Renaissance[16] – in a period of extreme commercial pressure. 'Restoration' in Victorian England was *not* a quiet backwater, but one of the most controversial areas for the architectural profession. Hardy (like Ruskin and William Morris) would become an increasingly outspoken critic of those who stripped the rotting heritage of England and rebuilt it in fashionable modern Gothic, and he would publicly regret his own small part in it. But it was probably clearer to Hardy, as a working part of this fast-changing world, than it is to us now, that conservation was itself a *modern* phenomenon[17] – a direct corollary of modernity. Another paradox, which Hardy would make his own.

London was the world's biggest, most rapidly expanding city, in a period of phenomenal change. The pace of life, the limits of his world were morphing beyond recognition as Hardy says.[18] Housing, hospitals, schools, railways, bridges, drains, libraries, railway stations, sewers: most of the infrastructure and much of the architecture which still supports Britain was laid down with ruthless speed in the second half of the nineteenth century – exactly the period of Hardy's writing. And Hardy was an active part of this – not a bridge between worlds, but an agent of modernisation itself: building, talking, visiting, listening, reading, writing; a working participant in a culture immersed and busy in the reconstruction and reinvention of both old and new. And he would remain so. He

St Pancras, the 'great arch' by William Barlow, 1864; Hardy supervised the levelling of
St Pancras churchyard as enabling works for the new terminus.

would call himself 'half a Londoner', and spend part of every year in London. The
unthinkably modern was as much part of his world as the unimaginably old.

Hardy was also working in a profession where building was *not* the only form of
practice. Drawing, writing and publishing were all valid and influential activities;
new ways of representation were always being tested and discussed. This was the
end of one of the periods where, Adrian Forty says, writing and architecture were
unusually close. Pugin's *Contrasts* (1836); Ruskin's *Modern Painters* (1843–1860),
The Seven Lamps of Architecture (1849) and *The Stones of Venice* (1851–1853), for
instance, were popular, inventive manifestos, merging morals, ethics and comments
on vernacular architecture, organic forms, the education of workmen and absolute
aesthetic judgements; woods, trees, vernacular construction, perception, and the
nature of architectural understanding in the rural craftsman. They are laced with
remarkable drawings, comparisons, photography and diagrams. Ironically, Hardy
had entered a world where urban aesthetes were preaching about his home territory.

Books have always had a powerful status in architectural culture. They emerged
alongside the profession itself,[19] and were instrumental in publishing buildings
which could only be seen by improbably vast travel. (Hardy spent his essay prize in
1863 on two illustrated folio books of mediaeval architecture in France and Italy.[20])

21

But their flexible structure and their capacity to assemble pictures, plans, details, ideas and polemics, also allow ideas to be discussed which had not been (or could not be) built. They are often inventive in format – Ruskin was the first to use photography in a book – and varied in purpose. Blomfield's office moved into a building at the Adelphi, designed, illustrated and published by the Adam Brothers, who used their popular illustrated books to fund the development. (Hardy talks about drawing pencil caricatures on the marble fireplace.[21])

At the time of writing, Kenneth Clark claims, Ruskin was almost universally revered 'from Wordsworth to Proust there was hardly a distinguished man of letters who did not admire him'.[22] But that does not sound like the picture in Blomfield's office. (Blomfield's nephew Reginald, a later pupil, did a fine caricature of *Modern Painters*: Ruskin, trumpeting 'Turner Turner Turner' on the one hand and 'Self Self Self' on the other. Reginald was an outright critic.) In a letter to his sister Mary in 1862, Hardy, newly established, is having *Modern Painters* read to him:[23] that famous, popular, infuriating polemic on aesthetics and morals, rural architecture, and the education (or not) of the skilled working masses. Here is Ruskin:

> It may not be the least necessary that a peasant should know algebra, or Greek, or drawing. But it may, perhaps, be both possible and expedient that he should be able to arrange his thoughts clearly, to speak his own language intelligibly, to discern between right and wrong, to govern his passions, and to receive such pleasures of ear or sight as his life may render accessible to him. I would not have him taught the science of music; but most assuredly I would have him taught to sing. I would not teach him the science of drawing, but certainly I would teach him to see; without learning a single term of botany he should know accurately the habits and uses of every leaf and flower in his fields; and unencumbered by any theories of moral or political philosophy ...[24]

Hardy places reading *Modern Painters*, deliberately, in the *Life*.[25] He is telling us he knew this argument, having done exactly the opposite: he had left his music, his trade, his village band, his social caste; he was educating himself to become an ambitious, leading figure in all the fields on which Ruskin was preaching.

Interestingly, Beatty points to Garbett's *Treatise* on architecture of 1850, a far lesser known text, deeply and intelligently critical of Ruskin, as Hardy's favourite architectural source,[26] and suggests Hardy owned a copy before he left for London.[27] Though billed as a primer, the *Treatise* is spectacularly ambitious, quoting from Hogarth and Reynolds and filled with remarkable discussions of architecture's mix of pragmatism and perception, colour, acoustics, proportion and vision: light and shade; 'sun-light', 'cloud-light' and 'fog-light'. This remarkable, forgotten book challenges and builds on Ruskin. It exposes the nineteenth-century obsession with the 'vegetable world' (a phrase Hardy used); analyses real trees, explains why they are 'never exactly copied' in architecture, and evaluates the architectural forms derived from them. It is startlingly prescient in describing the imaginative tactics of architecture as a creative discipline, the 'tacit knowledge'[28] of architectural practice:

> The principles of Taste in Architecture, as in every other fine art, can never be all elicited: if they could, the art would cease to be a fine art, it would no longer afford a field for genius, which consists in the discovery and practice of principles previously unknown. These are the secrets of great artists, kept secret ... because artists, seldom much skilled in the use of verbal language, can rarely translate into that language, even the principles with which they are most imbued. Nay the most important of these are so refined as to rarely admit of statement in words.[29]

It offers a remarkable discussion of the peculiar time-lag in architecture's slow projective processes: how architects develop their skilled work partly by instinct, and come to understand it retrospectively, often years later – with its critical theory 'discovered' by others, perhaps decades later. That is remarkably close to recent design research thinking,[30] and just the pattern Hardy's own work would follow.

A first reading of these books, especially Garbett's, against Hardy can be startling. The changeable language, the shifts from theory to history or radiant description, the embedded quotations from a free range of sources, the polemic, the description of how things are made, the adoption of ideas from art are all especially familiar. Joshua Reynolds's quote on 'the peculiar colour and complexion of another man's mind',[31] for instance, has a particular echo in Hardy's work. So do these books' peculiar use of varied illustrations, often including diagrams (Hardy uses these in notebooks too), plans, engravings, pictures and photographs as a contributing part of the argument. Garbett has a fine, distinctly odd drawing of an elephant, a hand and a Doric column, demonstrating the expression of strength and load. (Hardy will use elephants architecturally, too.) The range of argument in Ruskin, and in Garbett particularly, is exactly the stuff of Hardy's novels.

John Batchelor credits Ruskin (in *The Stones of Venice*) with 'the daring proposition that we can read architecture as we read Shakespeare or Dante, and ... can find central political and social truths about the civilisation which created the buildings'.[32] But in architecture, that's *normal*: a familiar, well-established argument, always embodied in architecture's peculiar experimental books,[33] and the mix of argument, detail, drawings, diagrams, speculation and criticism carried between pictures and text.[34]

23

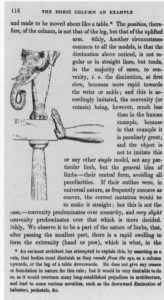

The curious world of architectural writings:
Reginald Blomfield's cartoon of Ruskin; Garbett's expression of loads.

Hardy's first named publication, published in *Chambers Magazine*, 'How I Built Myself a House', usually receives a general quote about arguments over the gradual loss of grand designs in designing your own home: 'Sophia, with all wifely tenacity, stuck to the pretty view long after I was beaten about the gravel subsoil ...'[35]

Interestingly, many aspects foreshadow the design of Max Gate (south-west-facing, trees to the north, views, convenience). Hardy, like the husband, tended to imagine rather small rooms. Sophia, the wife, more visually imaginative, shames her husband to go up the scaffolding: 'I am sure I should if I were a man ... the landscape must appear so lovely from that height.'[36] Hardy would often describe and project imaginative architectural visions through his female characters. But it is funnier, quirkier than that, covering the couple's arguments about the size of rooms, the curious, often-noted perception that when a new building is set out on site, it looks 'ridiculously and inconveniently small'. Or the early meeting with the architect: 'We were told the only possible size we could have the rooms, the only way we should be allowed to go upstairs, and the exact quantity of wine we might order at once, so as to fit the wine cellar he had in his head.'[37]

This was an engaging sketch of the design and construction of buildings, full of inside knowledge (architecture is made inside one's head, as Le Corbusier said in the 1930s[38]) – but written for the *public*, not a narrower architectural or critical elite.

Hardy was writing from the point of view of worker, designer, occupant – taking the opposite position to Ruskin, jokes and all. Like many writers and architects, he was both demolishing, and building from, the works of his immediate predecessors.

*

Hardy talks little of the buildings he worked on for Blomfield: it is clear he did not find that part of the life satisfying. He said the donkey-work of 'architectural drawing in which the actual designing had no great part was monotonous and mechanical'.[39] Beatty describes Hardy working in Oxford, on the new chapel for the Radcliffe Infirmary in 1864: 'His work at Oxford ... probably soured him ... Even as an assistant-architect of 24, a highly respectable post, Hardy remained an outsider in Oxford (like Jude Fawley in Christminster).'[40]

Hardy's time in Oxford is little known and intriguing, he may have made site visits by train (so it does not show as a place of residence in biographies). But this is just after the building of the contentious Oxford Museum.[41] In an office like Blomfield's, Hardy would certainly have known about this (and visited the building if he could); and the direct comparison with Ruskin's work does not go away.

Hardy certainly wanted to be an art-architecture critic – an integral part of the wider practices of architecture. There is even a category of writer-architect, dating from the early days of the profession: the 'Architectus Verborum'; the 'literary architect' of Hardy's day; the 'paper architect' of the 1970s and 1980s.[42] It is a position both influential and derided – sometimes at the same time. Hardy discusses this about Raphael Brandon, who he worked for briefly (his office was the source for Knight's in A Pair of Blue Eyes). Hardy empathised with Brandon, but did not want to be like him:

> It may have been ... partly because he was a 'literary architect' – a person always suspect in the profession in those days, Hardy used to say – that Brandon's practice had latterly declined, and he had drifted into a backwater, spending much time in strange projects and hopes ... Hardy was in something of a similar backwater himself.[43]

Literary architecture, strange projects and hopes: a very architectural way of seeing. Hardy says he wanted to be a poet, but 'he "(rather strangely)" thought that architecture and poetry – particularly architecture in London – would not work well together'.[44] Note those parentheses: 'rather strangely'; they are Hardy's own: he wanted them quoted. At the time he was talking *about*, the late 1860s, they recall Ruskin's career (the Newdigate Prize for Poetry; *The Poetry of Architecture* 1837–1838). But by the 1920s, when Hardy was *making* these comments, his own poetic status was assured. It was the link from his poetry back to his *architecture* which he was, at the end of his life, asserting.

*

Hardy started his architectural notebook in London. It is a curious document; not a typical working notebook. If he had carried it in his pocket and used it every day he would have filled it well before leaving Blomfield's. It spans about fifty years, including tracings from books, sketches, notes, working drawings for real buildings (and perhaps imaginary ones). It has early and late projects pasted into the same book and retrospective drawings of earlier work. He seems to have used it (like all his notebooks; and like his family's traditional music book), as a kind of palimpsest, an ongoing, living specialised index for himself (and others) to use: he always numbered notebook pages. The eminent historian John Summerson, said:

> Today, its monuments (the Victorian era) are begrimed and decayed, but through the young Hardy's sketches and memoranda we can feel the excitement of the new things – of 'early French' detailing, of Ruskinian naturalism in ornament and of the possibilities of construction in iron. This would be an instructive document if its author were un-named. That it is by Thomas Hardy gives it a startling aura. The sensibility to architectural forms and devices shown on some of these pages is a thing which, once acquired, can never be lost. Hardy had it and no study of him as a man, novelist and poet can be complete without recognition of this fact.[45]

Summerson was startled. Hardy was so very clearly operating, throughout his life, as a real *architect*, and indeed, that should shape the whole way we see him.

Beatty says the notebook might reasonably be called a microcosm of the Victorian age.[46] It works more like an architectural portfolio than a notebook: achieved by a fair bit of post-rationalisation. It shows cutting, pasting, numbering, drawing retrospectively, notes, copies, comparisons, experiments in ways of drawing, works pasted in, and some 'real' buildings especially towards the end. It is a suggestive, partly-constructed chronology of his 'real' architectural thinking, intended for future use. And as such, he is showing himself thinking and working as a *real* architect well into his eighties, especially in the projects at West Knighton, Stinsford, and perhaps Kingston Maurward, which seem to end the roughly chronological sequence. Other pages are filled in from the back. Clearly, in maintaining that book, Hardy feels as Beatty and Summerson do: however fragmentary his 'normal' practice, he never stopped working or thinking as an architect.

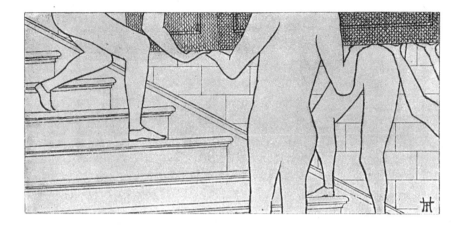

Wessex Poems, drawing for 'Heiress and Architect'. Poem dated 1867 from Blomfield's office.

But that small folio of everyday details is not the whole picture. When Hardy revisited this period of his life, in the *Wessex Poems* with their remarkable illustrations in the 1890s, he shows us an experimental side of his vision, too. There's a strikingly architectural drawing accompanying 'Heiress and Architect' (dated from Blomfield's office, Adelphi Terrace in 1867, dedicated to Blomfield).[47] It shows a narrative flattened elevation of people negotiating a coffin downstairs. ('How would you get a coffin downstairs?' used to be a standard 'crit' question, I was told, as a student myself in the 1980s). If Blomfield asked it, Hardy would have been easily able to answer. Or, perhaps, it was one of those quirks of thought that Hardy himself invented.

Of course, that experimental drawing is Hardy, reimagining that time with the benefit of hindsight; but that's an architectural method in itself. You imagine things, and then you draw them. Drawing is a way of thinking, projecting, testing ideas – and of analysing them later, too. If the drawing looks right, the project is working. Quite often, 'key' drawings are made after the project is built: to see yourself, and show others, how it works. It is the visual equivalent of his Prefaces, or his *Life*. Hardy may, or may not, have drawn something like this at the time, but later in life, this is how he remembered it. He is showing us the view through the mind of an architect thinking very experimentally.

It is also one of the strongest visual links between Hardy's work and the experimental architectural projects of a century later. Strange technical drawings of events are *exactly* what Bernard Tschumi would do in the 1970s and 1980s. Perhaps Hardy took his perverse brief from Ruskin in *The Seven Lamps*: 'It would be curious to see the result of this idea of the picturesque, in a painting of dead flowers and rotted fruit,'[48] for he does draw dead flowers in a vase, too. And as we will see, an architect's technical drawings re-used to describe life would become, a century later, a new architectural way of seeing the world.

*

Hardy stayed in London for five years. He had to supervise the exhumation and levelling of graves in the ancient St Pancras Churchyard, for the new railway line into St Pancras.[49] It was a grim and upsetting task which also generated a poem, 'The Levelled Churchyard', years later in 1882, when he was designing Max Gate: 'From zealous Churchmen's pick and plane / Deliver us O Lord! Amen!'[50]

He became ill. Joseph Bazalgette's formidable public infrastructure project of Victoria Embankment, integrating sewage, drainage, the underground railway and an esplanade, was being built outside Blomfield's office windows.[51] Architecturally, it was riveting, but the stench was terrible.[52] The conventional route to art criticism or practice was not working. Editors rejected his poems. He reworked and published them later,[53] but then had little inclination for 'pushing his way into influential sets which would help him start a practice of his own'.[54]

The juvenile professional bodies do not show up well here. The AA made it clear that his prize-winning design had few competitors; Hardy writes jovially to his sister Mary about 'speechifying' by lecturers; the Royal Institute of British Architects withheld (on a technicality) the £10 prize for his Silver Medal essay on

The 'Hardy Tree': rearranged gravestones from the levelling of
Old St Pancras churchyard; Hardy supervised this distressing job.

the use of terracotta tiles. The essay vanished (perhaps removed by Hardy)[55] and he did not speak there when invited later in life, but wrote a provocative essay, 'Memories of Church Restoration', for someone else to deliver instead.[56] He called the RIBA 'a body of which he had never lost sight'.[57] That would be ironic; he did a good black joke.

In the introduction to the *Architectural Notebook*, Claudius Beatty says: 'He felt frustrated. He had not been to university. He was not well-connected. If his potential as an architect is to be gauged from the Notebook alone it is evident that, while few draughtsmen could be more sensitive and precise, Hardy's fertile imagination was largely engaged elsewhere.'[58] And that, classically, is where Hardy's architectural career is supposed to die out.

But once you start looking at the *wider* practice of architecture – its ideas, speculative projects, theories, campaigns, polemics, experiments and books – it is clear that Hardy never gave up architecture. Its ideas, theories, details, subjects, and polemics are laced through his novels, poems and factual writing. They drive real conservation campaigns. They shape and give visionary and tactile force to his last great tragic novel *Jude the Obscure* – as well as forming a resonant and biting architectural criticism. The architectural arguments, content and ways of working, are everywhere.

*

Hardy began an odder, uncertain course. He left Blomfield in 1867, to return to Bockhampton and worked part-time with Hicks. Crickmay took over the practice after Hicks died. He kept his options open while writing his first novels, but these too were architectural. The unpublished and lost *The Poor Man and the Lady* was a 'sweeping dramatic satire' of class and church restoration: 'the views being obviously those of a young man with a passion for changing the world ... socialistic not to say revolutionary.' It described an architect's mistress and dancer 'taking in laundry' (the work done anonymously for other practices).[59] It was rejected, but with encouragement to try again.[60]

Architecture is always structurally *useful* in his novels, though just how far has been wildly underrated. That is the simplest version of its influence, in his work and his life. It cuts a cross-section through the changing boundaries of class: a profession where labourers and gentry work side by side, where their children might end up in the same job, with all the opportunities and embarrassment that might cause. All of these elements were now to come into play.

This was a turning point in Hardy's career and, like others, it happened on architectural ground. Crickmay offered Hardy some work making drawings

Boscastle/Castle Boterel, one of the photographs by Hermann Lea.

for the restoration of a small church, St Juliot, on the isolated north coast of Cornwall. His host the rector was ill, so Hardy was hosted by his sister-in-law, Emma Gifford. The date they met, 7 March 1870, would stay fixed on his desk calendar, through and beyond his marriage to Emma.

St Juliot is a nice restoration job. Despite its obvious Victorian work, it has a sense of space and detail; it feels old and loved. Hardy may, to his chagrin, have lost the mediaeval rood screen,[61] but you can see evidence of his care to save existing features elsewhere, in drawings and photos, fiction and fact. Hardy was proud to claim this work. Beyond the great outburst of guilt-haunted poems he wrote after Emma's death, he would add his own memorial, mentioning his drawings and supervision of works as an architect, and that she laid the first stone.

In the *Life*, Hardy labels 1867–1870 'Between Architecture and Literature'.[62] But this is one of those pairings which remain constant in Hardy's work, a necessary tension, as 'Between Town and Country' or titles of his collections of poems, say *Late Lyrics and Earlier*. In the full range of his amazing work, I would argue, between architecture and literature is where he stayed.

ARCHITECTURE IN THE EARLY NOVELS

Projective Visions

Usually, writers looking for architecture in Hardy's books quote obvious points.[1] Many of his characters are architects. Architecture forms a central part of many plots, notably the less famous books: A *Pair of Blue Eyes*, *Desperate Remedies* and *A Laodicean*. Sometimes he uses precise architectural language, in much-quoted fragments, such as this from *Tess of the d'Urbervilles*: 'The prospect from this summit was almost unlimited. In the valley beneath lay the city they had just left, its more prominent buildings showing as in an isometric drawing.'[2]

This seems to be an incidental architectural moment, a slight use of specialised language to describe a passing view. But for architects, there is nothing marginal about this. Drawings are of the first significance – for that is how architects actually work. Architects do not just go out on site and start directing builders. They survey and sketch, measure and imagine. They have to use all kinds of different, specific drawing types: to work things out themselves, to show clients what they are getting, to instruct builders what to do, to discuss ideas with other architects and critics. They select what to draw, and how to draw it. As the architectural historian Robin Evans says, drawings have, stealthily, gained a huge status in the way that architects work.[3]

Even that tiny fragment of *Tess* shows Hardy thinking and imagining, absolutely as an architect. He is projecting an architectural vision of the world – imagining a vision of a building as though it were a drawing. A specific type of drawing: an isometric is very different to a plan. It is a complex, high-code drawing (roughly 3D computer models before the fact), used to describe grand, detailed, highly resolved projects – implying that the building itself is of the highest status.

The use of specialised language is crucial too.[4] Hardy, unsettlingly, sometimes uses stonemasonry terms – ogive, cyma recta – to describe parts of his heroines' bodies (as well as, occasionally, buildings). But the average reader would not have known what cyma recta and ogive curves or isometric drawings looked like. Unless you *were* an architect, you would only learn what those words meant from reading the novels. Obscurely, Hardy was *teaching* his readers architectural language. And with it, fragment by fragment, architectural ways of seeing.

As minor points, these have been made before: the drawings, the language, to some extent the vision. What has not been recognised is what that *means* to an architect. If Hardy is using architectural language, drawings and visions, he is using the mainframe of architectural imagination: the fundamental, creative, projective scaffold of drawing, vision and description through which architects do their work.

*

This way of constructing things began at once. In an early scene in his first published novel *Desperate Remedies*, Cytherea Graye is looking out of the window at a dull concert, and can see the spire of a neighbouring church where her architect father is at work:

> Round the conical stonework rose a cage of scaffolding against the blue sky, and upon this stood five men – four in clothes as white as the new erection, close beneath their hands, the fifth in the ordinary dark suit of a gentleman ...

> The picture thus presented to a spectator in the Town Hall was curious and striking. It was an illuminated miniature, framed in by the dark margin of the window, the keen-edged shadiness of which emphasized by contrast the softness of the objects enclosed.

> The height of the spire was about one hundred and twenty feet, and the five men engaged thereon seemed entirely removed from the sphere and experiences of ordinary human beings. They appeared little larger than pigeons, and made their tiny movements with a soft, spirit-like silentness.[5]

As Cytherea watches, her father becomes visibly lost in reverie, steps backwards, loses his footing and falls, silently, out of frame. This is remarkable architectural content. First, Hardy is showing you an architect at work (*Martin Chuzzlewit* is less realistic); a building under scaffolding (rare in novels; everywhere in reality) – and an architect thinking, fatally, about something else. Then he is highly inventive in the form that constructed vision takes. He describes an illuminated miniature – a static image – and makes it *move*. As Cytherea faints, he pulls us into her blurred, psychological perception. 'Emotions will attach themselves to scenes ...

32

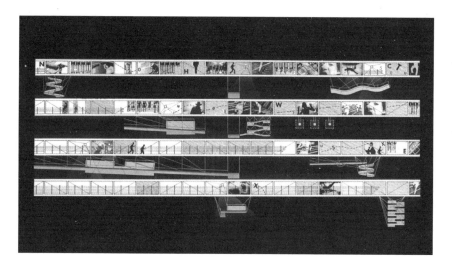

Narrative Section, Bernard Tschumi: Le Fresnoy 1991–1997.

as chemical waters will crystallize on twigs and wires. Ever after that time, any mental agony brought less vividly to Cytherea's mind the scene from the Town Hall windows than the sunlight streaming in shaft-like lines.'[6]

As Simon Gatrell says, the passage is as accomplished as anything he wrote: 'One of the startling things about Hardy was that he found his vision so quickly.'[7] The whole sequence feels like a scene from Hitchcock's *Vertigo*: strange crops, and a highly immersive psychological experience. He has hit on cinema's visual techniques – before cinema was invented.

The argument that Hardy predicted not just cinema but particular types of cinematic vision, well before the fact, appears from the 1920s onwards.[8] But it is hugely significant for architects, because so much has been written and argued about the intimate relationship of cinema and architecture.[9] The idea is, roughly, that cinema, offering a form of representation which mimicked the experience of a viewer moving through space, opened a new framework for how architects compose, and *everyone* perceives, architecture. It is usually linked with (capital-M) Modern and (small-p) post-modern architecture. Yet here we have an apparent anachronism: an architect, *predicting* that vision – *before* cinema, or Modern architecture as we know them, have even emerged.

Nor is it widely noted that Hardy's vision may have been an informed one. He had been repeatedly to the second Great Exhibition, where emerging photography and even film were on display. He would have seen the 3D stereoscopes being made; a team of 350 photographers was producing them, by a new rapid process, on site and for sale.[10] And almost certainly, as a person fascinated by use of lenses and vision, he would have seen early cinematic devices too. Writing of the evolution of early moving pictures, Stephen Herbert says:

> At least one of Desvignes' designs, which he called the Mimoscope, was shown at the 1862 International Exhibition in London (exhibit 2895), where it gained an Honourable Mention for 'ingenuity of construction'. The exhibition catalogue describes it as being able to 'exhibit drawings, models, single or stereoscopic photographs, so as to animate animal movements, or that of machinery, showing various other illusions.' One account even mentions insects being used, and notes that the device was 'furnished with pictures of exquisite artistic finish and beauty.' The inventor had overcome the problem noted by Horner, that the figures would appear thin and squashed up; 'In the exquisitely elaborate drawings prepared by Mr. Desvignes, this compression was allowed for, to the great enhancement of the effect.'[11]

Hardy had visited the Exhibition frequently,[12] he called his overtly architectural novels 'novels of ingenuity', and we will encounter squashed and artistically finished insects and photography in later novels. I am not merely suggesting that Hardy *had* probably seen moving pictures (the Zoetrope – the revolving drum of images seen through narrow slits – had been around for thirty years), but that he is able to *imagine* how they might be used, because, as an architect, he is trained precisely to assemble, visualise and develop – in a detailed, coherent imaginary form – constructions (in both senses) which do not yet exist.

Desperate Remedies is a bumpy novel, gripping but uneven, and there are many very different kinds of 'vision' in it. There are shimmering views: 'the wide expanse of landscape quivered up and down like the flame of a taper'.[13] There is the Gothic scene in which Manston plays the organ, in his part-restored, half-unpacked house during a thunderstorm,[14] and the fusion of architectural survey and painterly vision:

> an Elizabethan fragment, as much as could be contained under three gables and a cross roof behind ... the mullioned and transomed windows ... were mostly bricked up ... and the remaining portion fitted with cottage windows carelessly inserted.[15]

There is the uneasy landscape of Cytherea's engagement with its 'copper-coloured and lilac clouds' and 'swarm of wailing gnats'.[16] There is violent detail of Manston opening up a void in the brickwork with a crowbar[17] and the spatial metaphor of the 'labyrinth' in which Cytherea is trapped. These do not yet form a consistent vision, but the book is busy with art and inventive visualisations. And he

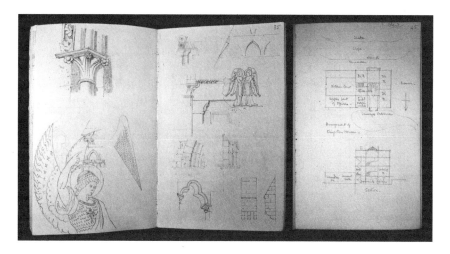

Hardy's architectural notebook: A miniature portfolio including tracings, arch moulds, plans and sections of part-real, part-imagined buildings and everyday details.

is *drawing* his settings, too. In his foreword to *The Architectural Notebook of Thomas Hardy*, Claudius Beatty contrasts the plan of 'Kingston House (nearly)' with its original: 'I contend that this drawing is Hardy's plan not of Kingston Maurward but of the mansion he was going to describe as Knapwater House in *Desperate Remedies* ...'[18] Hardy's drawings include other examples, such as a plan of St Juliot rectory, described in *A Pair of Blue Eyes*: an architect's drawings of buildings Hardy was *only* working on in fiction.

What is then interesting is that he does *not* exactly describe the things he draws. To an architect, those 'Knapwater' drawings (above right), conventional plans and sections, showing the back and front stairs which intimately link and physically segregate master from servant, suggest that Hardy was drawing the relationship of Miss Aldclyffe's maid's bedroom to the main parts of the house; and thinking how she would sneak into her maid's bedroom at night, and yet still hear the death rattle of her dying father.[19] Those drawings are for Hardy's own purposes: he is working out (or retrospectively showing[20]), how the architecture of his novels worked.

Desperate Remedies introduces a grand country house from the point of view of the servants. That is not surprising given Hardy's background – his builder father, his servant mother – but it previews a line of important architectural thinking. The term 'Served and Servant Space' was coined by Louis Kahn in the twentieth century as a key architectural idea of how buildings worked: their layout, hierarchy and functional circulation. It is strongly evident in the architecture of English country houses, where servants can almost magically appear in the main rooms from hidden service stairs. (Film fans may like to know that *Die Hard* was a popular architectural film in the 1990s for this very reason, with Bruce Willis working through the service cores of the buildings; a thriller exploring one of architecture's big ideas. Architects often find servicing sexy.) And Hardy was drawing it out, imagining an intimate personal, social relationship by drawing a building.

Hardy is always describing how things work, and not only how you might wall up a body or restore a ruined manor house. The fire at the inn, with its great eleven-page, three-day description of the tiny chain of mistakes, chances and events, and how they go wrong, is just what an architect has to consider. Hardy even puts his professional disclaimer in the mind of the passing railway worker: 'If those cottages had been his, he thought, he should not care to have a fire so near to them as that – and the wind rising. But the cottages not being his, he went on his way to the station.'[21] But the scenes in *Desperate Remedies* which received praise were the 'natural' ones; notably the cider-making scene. He was advised to write more of these rather than 'prostituting' his art by 'idle prying into the ways of wickedness'.[22] Another version of this scene, with the worker's arms stained by cider, apple pips and pomace would appear in *The Woodlanders*. Hardy would always listen to his critics, and by his second book, *Under The Greenwood Tree*, was opening, confidently, in what we hear as the clear voice of Wessex:

> To dwellers in a wood, almost every species of tree has its voice as well as its feature. At the passing of the breeze, the fir-trees sob and moan no less distinctly than they rock; the holly whistles as it battles with itself; the ash hisses amid its quivering; the beech rustles while its flat boughs rise and fall. And winter, which modifies the note of such trees as shed their leaves, does not destroy its individuality.[23]

It is worth remembering that Hardy's architectural sources are *filled* with descriptions of trees, their structure and aesthetics. In the mindset of Victorian architecture, trees were the Ur-text from which everything was drawn. Hardy is taking us, with a wood-dweller's working knowledge and an education in architectural practice and thinking, back to the source from which the architectural arguments of his age had developed: the woods themselves.

Under The Greenwood Tree was also subtitled 'A Rural Painting of the Dutch School': a deliberate, labelled experiment in visualisation – and right in the heartland of architectural debate. For architectural critics of Hardy's age, as well as ours, art and architecture are overlapping, intimately linked fields. *Modern Painters* is filled with discussion of architecture; *The Seven Lamps of Architecture* with art. Garbett quotes Reynolds; Ruskin references Turner (endlessly, as the younger Blomfield joked) – but the linking of the two fields may not be so obvious to non-architectural readers. Most importantly, Ruskin used the Dutch School as the epitome of 'Vulgarity', arguing its subjects were fundamentally inappropriate for artistic appreciation: 'No effort of fancy will enable me to lay hold of the temper of Teniers or Wouverans, any more than I can enter into the feelings of the lower animals ... All their life and work is the same kind of mystery to me as the mind of my dog when he rolls on carrion.'[24]

Hardy was, in direct and explicit opposition, 'painting' the vulgar as a thing of beauty, and had labelled it accordingly. That is a key architectural move this novel makes, the start of his reappraisal of rural vernacular, and though he preferred the original title 'The Mellstock Quire', he never questioned the subtitle.[25] Studying the vulgar; making written paintings: those ideas were working.

Of course, the major architectural content here is the substance of rural life: the exquisitely described, left-behind ancient village; its rituals and buildings, from chimney corner to church gallery, all vanishing. Hardy is writing about something close to his heart: the substance, the way of life it contained. 'A fairly true record of a vanishing life', Hardy put it in his 1912 Preface. And even in that first, soft-focus form, it had started something significant.

*

Yet despite hooking his key subject in his second novel, Hardy goes straight back to architecture. A Pair of Blue Eyes is another 'architectural' story, set in the thinly veiled Cornwall of his courtship, with a young architect seeking to marry 'above' him and a plotline anchored by 'Restoration'. Elfride walks around the parapet of the tower (Hardy has an eye for heights and danger). A church tower falls down (he tells us related stories of both Blomfield and Hicks).[26] Most powerfully, Elfride visits the crypt opened for the coffin of Lady Luxellian, squeezed into the same narrow space with her former fiancé, and her new one – and her precursor: she will be buried as Lady Luxellian too, in the same space. It is the vision type of the Wessex Poems: a narrative cross-section of black comic form.

Hardy draws the settings, too: not just that plan of the rectory, but extensive details and fragments of St Juliot, some for building purposes, some evidently retrospective. Most striking is a single photo, pre-restoration, surely taken by him or Emma, and a matching drawing of the vanished pew-ends: one of the clearest examples of Hardy copying or tracing from photographs, compounding modern and ancient techniques to capture a missing past.[27]

But as an architectural critic of the post-modern age, I am most strongly drawn to the most remarkable scene in A Pair of Blue Eyes: the cliffhanger. Elfride is walking on the cliffs, watching for the return of her fiancé. Her new admirer, Knight,

Bench Ends – St. Juliot Church – Cornwall.
1870.
J. Hardy. del.

St Juliot in 1870, before restoration; Hardy's drawing (overlaid)
is clearly traced from the photograph.

pontificates about updrafts on cliff-edges, and throws his hat up to demonstrate.
The wind catches it – and drops it on the shelving edge of the cliff. Knight, trying
to retrieve it, gets stuck on the damp, shaley slope. A lip of quartz – on which
he has gained foothold – breaks. He slips. What happens is extraordinarily visual.
Knight, hanging by his hands, finds himself eyeball to eyeball with a fossil,[28] and
the whole epoch between the fossil's life and his own flashes before his eyes: a stop-
frame animation of all known history; experience, knowledge and pure, visceral
fear compress time towards his own imminent death:

38

Time closed up like a fan before him. He saw himself at one extremity of the years, face to face with the beginning and all the intermediate years simultaneously. Fierce men clothed in the hides of beasts ... Behind them stood an earlier band ... Huge elephantine forms, the mastodon, the hippopotamus, the tapir, antelopes of monstrous size, the megatherium and the myledon – all, for the moment in juxtaposition. Further back and overlapped by these, were perched huge-billed birds. Still more shadowy were the sinister crocodilian outlines ... Folded behind were dragon forms and clouds of flying reptiles; still underneath were fishy beings of a lower development; and so on, till the lifetime scenes of the fossil confronting him were a present and modern condition of things.[29]

This is one of those moments that is familiar to any architect-critic. It feels radically architectural, and you have to trawl your mind for pictures or facts which might help you figure out why.

Obviously, there is Hardy's fascinated attention to detail, to the behaviour of damp shale, of rock types. You could learn how to improvise rope from this passage. It is philosophical, evolutionary (Ruskin talks about evolution, naturally) and comic (there's a 'wet dress' cliché coming, too). Though not 'typical' of Hardy, it was anthologised at the time – Florence, his second wife, first read Hardy in this fragment.[30] But it is also highly cinematic. An article in the *New Yorker* says:

The sequence is both laughably artificial and entirely convincing, a manipulation that may have been motivated by commercial demands but becomes an opportunity for existential exploration. It is by far the liveliest moment in the book. And it foretells the way cliffhangers have come to be used in ambitious contemporary television ... not merely as an engine for excitement but as a narrative challenge, a glimpse into the extremes of human experience.[31]

It may even be the *first* cliffhanger in a novel. Dickens had gathered crowds at the New York Docks asking 'is Little Nell dead?' – but this seems to be the first with a character left hanging on a cliff for the next instalment. The *Oxford English Dictionary* gives the definition of 'cliffhanger' from movies of the 1930s. It seems that this is a cinematic cliché which Hardy *invented*, before cinema itself existed. And this is a real piece of what would later be called 'event-architecture', well before the fact. We have already seen that Hardy's later drawings look startlingly close to the experimental drawings done by Bernard Tschumi from the 1980s on. But Tschumi's first provocative exhibition was *Advertisements for Architecture*, 1976–1977. Its key image, taken from a B-movie, was of a man falling from

To really appreciate architecture,
you may even need to commit
a murder.

Architecture is defined by the actions it witnesses
as much as by the enclosure of its walls. Murder
in the Street differs from Murder in the Cathedral
in the same way as love in the street differs from
the Street of Love. Radically.

Cliffhangers: Tschumi's *Advertisements for Architecture* (1979); and
Hardy's 'original' cliffhanger, James Abbot Pasquier (1872).

a window, labelled: 'To really appreciate architecture, you may even have to commit a murder.'

That was a provocation, with philosophical-architectural intent. Tschumi's drawings would draw from, and influence, the philosopher Jacques Derrida. When they collaborated on Tschumi's Parc de la Villette in Paris, Derrida wrote:

> An architectural writing interprets … events which are marked by photography
> or cinematography. Marked: provoked, determined or transcribed, captured,
> in any case always mobilised in a scenography of passage … from one place
> to another, from a place of writing to another … Therefore, we can no longer
> speak of a 'properly' architectural moment.[32]

Without going down the rabbit-hole of architecture and philosophy, it is clear that Tschumi's work and Hardy's have surprisingly strong architectural overlaps. Tschumi calls this 'event architecture'; architecture being something which constructs an event or possibility (buildings can do this, but so can other things).[33] This exactly overlaps with Hardy's own thinking. You can *see* it in the drawings as well as hear it in the writings.

Tschumi's drawings, again, explore this by looking into cinema of the past; mixing filmstrip storyboards with architectural plans and technical drawings to explore both place and activity. There are plans and sections of firework displays, or the Le Fresnoy film school conversion, in which a film storyboard generates the architectural *cross section*: drawing like a cinematographer shapes the form of the building and the way it works (p. 33). But Hardy, before filmmaking itself has begun, was already describing, projecting exactly the same idea, and by the *Wessex Poems* was actually drawing this way too.

In Étienne-Louis Boullée's 'Essay on Art' he says that 'recalling forcefully and vividly what has aroused their sensibilities belongs to [architects] alone'.[34]

*

Even in these early, imperfect novels, Hardy is using his architect's skills of projective imagination, assembling his information and using it to project his vision of the future – which is what architects have to do. He was predicting, even inventing, a way that people would see in the future. It has never been realised that what he was doing was so profoundly architectural, nor so startlingly experimental. Or that it would take even the most radical of twentieth-century architects a century to catch him up.

4

A NATURAL MAGIC

Far from the Madding Crowd

If you wanted to argue that Hardy became a great writer once he stopped being an architect and stepped into the 'realist' novel, you could not hope for better material than *Far from the Madding Crowd*. It is a wonderful book, and a successful one, made using what Hardy would call 'a more natural magic'. It was first published by the famous editor Leslie Stephen in the *Cornhill* magazine and is still made and remade into television series and films – all casually confirming its central role in Wessex. But it is more like an exception that has been mistaken for the rule. Its rich, enjoyable sense of rural life is not compromised or doomed; its love story (eventually) reaches a happy end. And it is not known for its architectural content: there are no architects or builders; little architectural language; no obvious theory. It is only with hindsight – his own as well as ours – that one can see that Hardy has not, altogether, left architecture alone.

What there are, from the start, are accomplished descriptions of landscapes, people, animals and buildings – and particularly, how they work together. Hardy's scenes convey information because they describe how people's relationships with places work and how much information we derive from them.

Hardy was on home ground here. He was writing at home, in Bockhampton. The main village, Weatherbury, is based on Puddletown, where his mother grew up and his cousins lived. The road to Casterbridge, in the novel, was also the main road to Dorchester. The church is based on those at Stinsford and Puddletown. Bathsheba's house he identifies, precisely: Waterston Manor, taking 'a witch's ride' nearer Weatherbury to its fictional location. His vivid characters are those directly doing farmwork itself, and they are shown in relation to a precise and charted land: its seasonal workings, its weather conditions, its management and economy, its detailed field-work and skills, and its celebrations. And accompanied by the music they (like Hardy) would have heard, sung and played.

When it was published (anonymously) some thought the book was by George Eliot.[1] Like *Middlemarch*, it has rich descriptions, resists the picturesque or patronising view of the country and is written in sympathy with, and understanding of, working people. Rural workers were often then described in clichés, which makes the odd, close-up vision of Gabriel Oak which opens the book intriguing. It seems to *be* a 'Hodge', a rural stereotype,[2] although it also contrasts with the intimate description of Dorothea Brooke with which Middlemarch opens.

But that magnified caricature is a feint: a strong idea, immediately demolished. We never see Gabriel this way again. Hardy moves the reader, following Gabriel, into a vast, philosophically imagined universe:

> To persons standing alone on a hill during a clear midnight such as this, the roll of the world eastward is almost a palpable movement. The sensation may be caused by the panoramic slide of the stars past earthly objects, which is perceptible in a few moments of stillness, or by the better outlook on space which a hill affords, or by the wind, or by the solitude; but whatever be its origin, the impression of riding along is vivid and abiding ... After such a nocturnal reconnoitre it is hard to get back to earth, and to believe that the consciousness of such majestic speeding is derived from a tiny human frame.[3]

For Hardy, indeed for any architect, imagination and pictures are tightly fused together. He is making his readers imagine the characters differently, by setting them, and immersing us, in vast and meaningful environments. The unexpected imaginative and visual frame of the book is now established: Hodge; universe; philosophic imagination.

Hardy's descriptions are some of the most astonishing and precise instructions for imagining places of any writer. They are so vivid that they may make you ignore the extreme modernity of their framing and conception – let alone the use of architectural structure, detail, vision and content, through which Hardy constructed them. They are meticulously staged, precisely described passages in which the reader seems to watch events develop in a forensically visualised place. They have just the highly considered balance of detail needed to give instruction to builders to build. But these are instructions to *imagine*.

Of course, you could say that (more or less) of any writer. But Hardy was using a full, ambitious and experimental range of specifically architectural skills to construct his work. Like all architectural information, Hardy's descriptions cover many things: what something looks like, what it is made of, how it works and why. *Far from the Madding Crowd* is an astonishing study of how human beings' environmental intelligence works, how we naturally read and display character.

43

Fanny Robin, illustrated by Helen Paterson Allingham
for *Far from the Madding Crowd* (1874).

Causation, social status, physical attraction, threat and danger: Hardy is showing the way people behave in their environment and how much can be learned from it. Hardy is describing a highly intelligent, as well as instinctive, relationship between human and land, learnt by experience and imagination – and making the reader do the same.

From now on, *Far from the Madding Crowd* is entirely structured on pictures of places. Meticulously detailed, spectacularly visualised scenes follow one after another, carrying the whole story within them. Bathsheba at Gabriel's hut, or riding through the trees; the death of the sheep; the hiring fair; the fire in the hayricks. These are not just 'settings', they are the structure and substance of everything in the book – plot, character, action. We *watch* the characters and the story in the places he makes us see.

This book is actually economic, packed with incident, almost melodramatic. But it *feels* slow, because of these great, long, meticulously written descriptions of people in vast land- and skyscapes. The writing slows the reader down, to the speed of an earlier era, to the person walking, or standing on a hill; to the immediate, conscious present. The ponderous architectural language helps with this, its meticulous inclusion of detail, perception, argument and skilfully constructed vision. You cannot skip through it. He makes us *work* our visual imagination.

An architectural substance is appearing too.

They sheared in the great barn ... which on ground-plan resembled a church with transepts. It not only emulated the form of the neighbouring church of the parish, but vied with it in antiquity ... The vast porches at the sides, lofty enough to admit a wagon laden to its highest with corn ... The dusky filmed chestnut roof, braced and tied in by huge collars, curves and diagonals, was far nobler in design, because more wealthy in material, than nine-tenths of those in our modern churches ...

One could say about this barn, what could hardly be said about the church or the castle, akin to it in age and style, that the purpose which had dictated its original erection was the same to which it was still applied ... The old barn embodied practices which had suffered no mutilation at the hands of time. Here at least the spirit of the ancient builders was at one with the spirit of the modern beholder.[4]

Note the casual architectural 'plan'. Hardy is both telling his readers about, and championing, an important form of vernacular heritage – which was not known or esteemed at all. Ruskin, effectively, had condemned it wholesale: 'we have built like frogs and mice since the thirteenth century (except only in our castles).'[5] Hardy is informing his readers otherwise. Great aisled barns like this would be built well, right up until the Reformation: Abbotsbury (a named model) is fourteenth century. This is a deliberate architectural statement. Hardy is both sharing his knowledge and challenging architectural perceptions. 'The untutored average man will not be able to see nature by trusting his instincts'[6] says Ruskin. Hardy, with his first proper rural hero, the skilled, intelligent Gabriel, says the opposite. Then, you can see the architectural construction of his scenes, even where there are no buildings involved. Here is Sergeant Troy, about to dazzle Bathsheba with his sword practice:

The pit was a saucer-shaped concave, naturally formed, with a top diameter of about thirty feet, and shallow enough to allow the sunshine to reach their heads. Standing in the centre, the sky overhead was met by a circular horizon of fern: this grew nearly to the bottom of the circle. The middle within the belt of verdure was floored with a thick flossy carpet of moss and grass intermingled, so yielding that the foot was half-buried within it.

'Now' said Troy, producing his sword, which, as he raised it into the sunlight, gleamed a sort of greeting, like a living thing ...

... He flourished ... and the next thing of which she was conscious was that the point and blade of the sword were darting with a gleam towards her left side, just above her hip; then of their re-appearance on her right side, emerging as it were between her ribs, having apparently passed through her body ... seeing the same sword, perfectly clean and free of blood, held vertically in Troy's hand.[7]

As an architect, this is an incredibly precise instruction. You could *draw* this scene, to scale, in plan and section: circular site, 30 feet across, saucer shaped. You can work out the height of the ferns; specify the mix of planting, the depth of moss, the angle of sunlight. He even implies a cross-section through, or 3D drawing around, Bathsheba's body. J.M. Barrie, author of *Peter Pan*, said of this seduction scene, 'Many writers say their Troys do it – Hardy *shows* it being done.'[8] You could build from his descriptions: many filmmakers do.

You could say this of any number of his scenes: the highly realised landscapes, or the ones that tell you how to thatch a haystack. The ones which use architectural terms or describe buildings – and the ones, like this, which do not. In the realm of 'event architecture', *all* of this *is* architecture. It is the inverse of Eliot, who works by generating an emotional sympathy with each interacting character, gradually working outwards so that we understand a whole working society (and, more incidentally, its setting). Hardy is making the reader *see* and start recognising the characters from the start, precisely by *watching* their behaviour in those highly-described environments.

Hardy clearly loved writing specifications: his architectural notebook is filled with them, copied and observed. He preserved two versions of his full Specification document for his Turnworth Church restoration and he drops them into letters[9]). He must have been fascinated by the curious relationship between a written description and a built substance; many architectural critics (naturally) are.

For Hardy, like any architect, pictures, written or drawn, and especially imagined environments, are central. It is that visual sequencing of meaningful places which makes Hardy cinematic; which made architects embrace cinema. While Eliot moves you through *Middlemarch* on a complex, empathetic web of her characters' varying emotions, Hardy is making you *see* the novel, in a story he has constructed, place by place.

Hardy is starting to build up his working and occupied environment, using all kinds of images and information.[10] He is specifying the whole working place which we imagine, and bringing in philosophy, sectional drawing and vernacular building types, yet he is doing it simply here – through *description*. This is *not* typical of recent architectural writing: valuing description is far more normal in literature than in architecture. Descriptive writing was, Adrian Forty says, more or less written off by modern architectural discourse as 'an improper role for criticism'.[11] In its place a type of critical theory (following Derrida, Foucault, Deleuze, Guattari) has become the dominant type of 'architectural' academic writing.

But descriptive writing was one of Hardy's most powerful tools. It was exactly the way he communicated complex visual, working and theoretical ideas to a general audience. And perhaps architecture's own under-rating of the direct power of description is why we have not realised just how much of an architect Hardy is.

For the greatest scenes that Hardy constructs are *not* necessarily those quoted for architectural reasons because they use technical language. They are the ones *everyone* quotes. They are the great descriptions of landscapes, fires, weather, animal husbandry and social events. They are just as architectural as any of those which use architectural terms. They are *like* architectural drawings – precise, framed, the viewpoint constructed, the technicalities clearly denoted: scale, detail, texture, material, size, effect, vision.

Take, for example, *Far from the Madding Crowd*'s great sheep-shearing supper scene. Bathsheba is alternating between her two suitors: the working Gabriel and the landowner Boldwood. We are told, precisely, how the long table is set outside the house. One end is: 'thrust over the sill of the wide parlour window and a foot or two into the room, Miss Everdene sat inside the window, facing down the table. She was thus at the head without mingling with the men.'[12]

The staging of the scene is described with remarkable intensity. Unlike Eliot (who would *tell* us what was happening inside her characters' imaginations), Hardy has us *watch* this intense social and emotional engagement.

Bathsheba keeps the bottom seat of the table empty; when Boldwood does not appear, she asks Gabriel to take it. Gabriel does so, but when Boldwood arrives, Bathsheba makes Gabriel move. After the meal, Bathsheba (inside), sings 'On the Banks of Allan Water' to those outside. Boldwood has vanished from the foot of the table, and appears inside, singing so softly 'as to abstain' from it being a duet, but forming 'a rich, unexplored shadow'. Gabriel, bidden by Bathsheba, stands outside the window to play the flute. Bathsheba bids her work-folk goodnight, and Boldwood closes the sash and shutters.

This is a remarkable scene – and one of those which seem intensely architectural to other architectural writers. It is both precise and odd, detailing how table and window, shutters and sash, link and divide workers and their 'betters', adjusting the tension between the three principals, inside and out. The whole emotional content – rivalry, support, authority, class, sexual frisson, gender, cultural expectations and wider social understanding – is told in the detailed stage directions around this fragment of space.

Architects using tables as ways to describe how people use space also turns up in late twentieth-century architectural thinking – almost always connected

Bathsheba at the sheep-shearing supper by Helen Paterson Allingham: a definitive Hardy illustration – which is also a picture of a song, 'On the Banks of Allan Water'.

with some kind of female management of space. The Eames Partnership's multimedia installation *Think* (1964) shows a hostess planning seating at her dinner party as an illustration of creative thinking; Sarah Wigglesworth's drawings of 'increasing disorder at a dinner table' shows how architectural drawings can make you see, exactly, what human life is going on. And Isabel Allen precisely charts Jane Austen's table choreography.[13]

Like them, Hardy is using everday description as intense architectural method. He shows the way human beings (and animals, for that matter) behave in different places, how the places shape, limit or enable behaviour; and what a massive amount can be learnt from it – by seeing it happen, as a series of highly crafted pictures, in our 'mind's eye'.

*

Naturally, Hardy was fussy about the illustrations which accompanied his work. He was not alone: Dickens worked closely with his artists, while Thackeray illustrated his own books. Unsurprisingly, as architect as well as author, Hardy was trying to establish a grip on the images he was creating. He gave his illustrators directions to the original, inconveniently inaccessible places; he sent them sketches. For any architect, pictures are working content. He must have been hell to work for.

The *Far from the Madding Crowd* illustrations were his favourite: he kept a selection on the wall in Max Gate. Helen Paterson had an easier job than some (she married and became Allingham halfway through the series; Hardy considered marrying her himself). This book *did* present images which only gently stretched the format and expectations of magazines: Fanny sleeping in the haystack; the charming vignettes of rural work which opened each section, or the well-known sheep-shearing supper picture, replicated in the lovely Schlesinger/ Roeg 1967 film adaptation. Like several other images generated by Hardy, it is also remarkable in being the picture of a *song*: 'On the Banks of Allan Water'. A reader of the day should be hearing it in their heads – and so anticipating the arrival of the faithless soldier.

The book also holds more obviously challenging images: the death of the sheep; Gabriel among the stars; the figures looming out of the fires; thatching a rick (of course with full detail on how it was done), in a storm, at night; Bathsheba opening the coffin; the flooding of Fanny's grave: compelling visions, seized on by filmmakers. John Schlesinger and Nicholas Roeg did such a good job that their image of sheep falling into the sea (it's a quarry in the book) replaces Hardy's in a surprising range of places. Hardy's written pictures were always remarkable, but in this book they become the working substance of the novel.

*

Far from the Madding Crowd is seen now as a remarkably detailed, accurate and extensive depiction of rural work and life. Hardy wisely sent Paterson sketches of working people's smocks, to make sure she got it right, for even by the first Great Exhibition of 1851, Londoners observed that farming people, arriving on excursion trains wearing smocks, were more alien to them than the usual foreigners.[14]

So it is telling that, at the time, it sparked off a big public debate about its accuracy. R.H. Hutton, in *The Spectator*, said 'Wessex' was 'Dorsetshire probably' and that the reader 'carries away new images, and as it were new experience, taken from the life of a region before almost unknown.'[15] But also: 'a more incredible picture than that of the group of farm-labourers as a whole which Mr Hardy has given us can hardly be conceived.'[16] The *Saturday Review* agreed: 'Under his hand Boetians become Athenians in acuteness, Germans in capacity for philosophic speculation and Parisians in polish.'[17] But, it added, the book was 'the nearest equivalent to actual experience which a great many of us are ever likely to boast of'.[18] Henry James attacked Hardy's style as 'verbose and redundant' (that was the pot calling the kettle black). 'The only things we believe in are the sheep and the dogs.'[19]

Vignettes, Helen Paterson Allingham; details of clothing and tools were provided by Hardy.

Like any architect, Hardy was attentive to his critics. He recognised he was writing for an audience whose forebears had left the countryside and had no idea what it was like.[20] *Far from the Madding Crowd* was reminding them (as it still reminds us), of customs and manners long past, to which we still respond. In the age of massive urbanisation Hardy was making a detailed, working description of something real, but already passing. And he was also starting to use it, in part, to contest the architectural ground – where urban critics were laying down the law about the morals, aesthetics and ethics of what working people do and what rural buildings were like.

Yet *Far from the Madding Crowd* is itself not that much more architectural than *Middlemarch*. You can certainly compare Hardy and Eliot's detailed, sympathetic creation of a part-remembered, peopled community, at work and leisure, in place and time – and especially, their deflation of the 'romantic' view of rural poverty. But, with hindsight, the Wessex that Hardy was laying out would become increasingly architectural, in a way that Loamshire would not.

Hardy had recognised that described places could form the central structure of his stories. He was recognising that descriptions could engage with peoples' natural imaginations, as well as suggest new and constructive ways of seeing the land that they came from. He was noticing how readers imagine those places in their own right. He was starting to engage directly with the professional debate on English vernacular architecture. In content and place, he was on his home territory. You could say, architecturally, he had picked his site. He was on his way.

DOUBT AND EXPERIMENT

'Oddities and Failures'

Far from the Madding Crowd (1874) and *The Return of the Native* (1878) are such accomplished books, and so definitive of what Wessex would become, that it is hard to remember their uneven critical reception, or the process of trial and error of which they were a part. Here is Claire Tomalin, describing a kind of 'general idea' (which is naturally challenged by many Hardy specialists[1]): 'It went like this: failure (*Ethelberta*); masterpiece (*The Return of the Native*); slight historical oddity (*The Trumpet Major*); failure (*A Laodicean*); interesting oddity (*Two on a Tower*); masterpiece (*The Mayor of Casterbridge*).'[2]

For the 'oddities and failures' are interesting, often startlingly so; Hardy academics relish revisiting them. The 'snags' which trip up your progress through Hardy's work never seem like mistakes. Re-reading the middle novels is gripping: a bumpy terrain of extremely rich discoveries which exposes the territory – the very architectural territory – that Hardy was laying out.

*

If Hardy had touched on the 'served-servant' working of architecture in *Desperate Remedies*, he expands it fully now. *The Hand of Ethelberta* (1876) is a sharp view of society laced through with intelligent, aspirant servants and workers, making their way upwards through a seismic shift in society.

Ethelberta is thought to track Hardy's own awkward, upwardly-mobile career. ('Hand', as in marriage and as a writer, was his mother's family name). The story of a butler's daughter turned society author, it plays with types of truth and deceit, and slyly hints at Hardy the housekeeper's son's own career. It has been called a satire of the 'truthfulness' that editors like Leslie Stephen demanded, showing how 'constructed' fiction is.[3] And if so, this is a provocatively *architectural* construction.

Wessex Poems, 'narrative section'.

Ethelberta exposes working details of society from the point of view of servants – and builders. We see the story from the area steps, the butler's pantry, the lodge, the servants' attics, the staircases where guests may be glimpsed. We are told how these places are *built*, notably, the acoustic differences between rural cottage construction and that of London houses of quality:

> Picotee, who had been accustomed to unceiled country cottages all her life, wherein the scamper of a mouse is heard distinctly from floor to floor, exclaimed, in a terrified whisper, at viewing all this, 'They'll hear you underneath, they'll hear you, and we shall all be ruined!'

> 'Not at all,' came from the cautious dancers. 'These are some of the best built houses in London – double floors, filled in with material that will deaden any row you like to make ...'[4]

In fact, we see all kinds of building in detailed constructional *section*: a key drawing for constructing buildings, but a very unusual storytelling position. (Later, Georges Perec's *Life: A User's Manual* (1978) or Wes Anderson's films would explore this too). Even Hardy's chapter titles contribute: 'The Dining Room of a Town House – The Butler's Pantry'. *Ethelberta* slices through the way this world is *made*, exposing the parts than only an architect or builder would know. Here are some peculiar tiles:

... upon the glazed tiles within the chimney-piece were the forms of owls, frogs, mice, bats, spiders in their webs, moles and other objects of aversion and darkness, shaped in black and burnt in after the approved fashion.

'My brothers Sol and Dan did most of the actual work', said Ethelberta, 'though I drew the outlines and designed the tiles round the fire. The flowers, mice and spiders are done very simply, you know, you only press a real flower, mouse or spider out flat under a piece of glass, and then copy it, adding a little more emaciation and angularity, at pleasure ...[5]

That is very close to the squashed and artistically-edited insects described in the Great Exhibition Mimoscope: it suggests experience. So does the description of fast-developing London:

Slush-ponds may be seen turning into basement kitchens, a broad causeway of shattered earthenware smothers plots of budding gooseberry bushes and vegetable trenches, foundations following so closely upon gardens that the householder may be expected to find cadaverous sprouts from overlooked potatoes rising through the chinks of his cellar floor ... Its first erections are often the milk-teeth of a suburb, and as the district rises in dignity, they are dislodged by those which are to endure.[6]

While Dickens's *Bleak House* (1852–1853) cuts a social section through London from richest to poorest, and where *Dombey and Son* (1846–1848) charts tidal changes in railway-time London, the uneven *Ethelberta* is an *architect's* detailed, working section through how Victorian life was built. Here is the description of the unpleasant Lord Mountclere's house:

It was a house in which Pugin would have torn his hair.[7] Those massive blocks of red-veined marble lining the hall ... were cunning imitations in paint and plaster by workmen brought from afar for the purpose, at a prodigious expense ... The dark green columns and pilasters ... were brick at the core. Nay, the external walls, apparently of massive and solid freestone, were only veneered with that material, being, like the pillars, of brick within ... a stone mask worn by a brick face ...

This had happened, Hardy explains, because the visiting King George had criticised the original:

'Brick, brick, brick' ... [Mountclere] sent frantically for the craftsmen recently dismissed, and so the green lawns became again the colour of a

Nine-Elms cement wharf. Thin freestone slabs were affixed to the whole series of fronts by copper cramps and dowels, each one of substance sufficient to have furnished a poor boy's pocket with pennies for a month, till not a speck of the original surface remained, and the edifice shone in all the grandeur of massive masonry that was not massive at all. But who remembered this save the builder and his crew? And as long as nobody knew the truth, pretence looked just as well.[8]

This also parodies Pugin's *Contrasts*, and Ruskin's 'Lamp of Truth', a forty-page tirade 'touching the false representation of material ... all such imitations are utterly base and inadmissable'[9] and '... wrong; it is as truly deserving of reprobation as any other moral delinquency; it is unworthy alike of architects and of nations, and it has been a sign, wherever it has widely and with toleration existed, of a singular debasement of the arts.'[10]

But it also describes in detail the recladding of Kingston Maurward house:[11] Hardy's grandfather was one of the builders. *Ethelberta* is clearly a builder's satire, aimed at the heart of architectural debate. Comedy hovers round many scenes on the tourist trail: the architectural tympanum briefly formed by Ethelberta and her three suitors on the hotel balconies for instance (you can see something like this in the photographs of the stage designs made for *The Dynasts* shown on p. 226). *Ethelberta*'s 'comedy' lies where famous modernist Mies van der Rohe says God does – in the (architectural) details. Here is Mountclere's spiral staircase:

Who, unacquainted with the secrets of geometrical construction, could imagine that, hanging so airily there, to all appearance supported on nothing, were twenty or more tons dead weight of stone, that would have made a prison for an elephant if so arranged? The art which produced this illusion was questionable, but its success was undoubted. 'How lovely!' said Ethelberta, as she looked at the fairy ascent. 'His staircase alone is worth my hand.'[12]

Spiral stairs like those are amazing pre-computer constructions; the steps, part cantilevered, also transfer weight, step by step, like a waterfall to the ground. They are a direct metaphor for Ethelberta's apparently unsupported rise to fame – and, by extension, Hardy's too. He is showing, in detail, that both fiction and architecture are carefully crafted constructions – elephants and all.

Ethelberta forms part of a group: the 'middle novels', which continually use, test and remake all kinds of visionary and technical architectural perceptions. It deals with experiential perception too. Here is the view from the top of Rouen cathedral (visited by the Hardys on honeymoon):

Ethelberta leaned and looked around and said 'How extraordinary this is. It is sky above, below, everywhere' ... Out of the plain white fog beneath a stone tooth seemed to be upheaving itself ... As the fog stratum collapsed, other summits manifested their presence ... the dome of St Madeline's caught a first ray from the peering sun ... its scaly surface glittered like a fish. Then the mist rolled off in earnest and revealed far beneath them a whole city ...[13]

Next came *The Return of the Native* (1878) which took astonishing leaps in the visualisation of Wessex. We will come back to the *Return* – a 'masterpiece', requiring a chapter in itself, but Hardy was trying out different types of book, revising one for volume publication, writing serial instalments for the next. They would have formed a working assembly of ideas and connections, sparking and differentiating themselves from each other.

The *Return* was closely followed by *The Trumpet Major* (1880), a sad romance. Luxurious in its intimate environment, harshly evolutionary in its wider sweep, it both simply suggests a folk history of Dorset – and lays the ground for *The Dynasts*, Hardy's later experimental verse drama. It draws from local history: written, spoken, and costumes researched in the British Museum. And it is richly visual, in landscape, costume and architecture, from the ruinous manor-house to the watermill where Anne Garland is copying one of her late father's landscape paintings:

The reserve, was however ... broken down by the appearance one morning ... of the point of a saw through the partition which divided Anne's room from the Loveday part of the house ... As the saw worked its way downwards under her astonished gaze, Anne jumped up from her drawing; and presently the temporary canvassing and papering which had sealed up the old door of communication was cut completely through. The door burst open, and Bob stood revealed on the other side, with the saw in his hand ...

She followed him along a dark passage, in the side of which he opened a little trap, when she saw a great slimy cavern, where the long arms of the mill wheel flung themselves slowly and distractedly round, and splashing water-drops caught the little light that strayed into the gloomy place, turning it into stars and flashes ... they went on to the inner part of the mill, where the air was warm and nutty, and pervaded by a fog of flour ...

They climbed yet further ... long rays like feelers stretched in from the sun through the little window, got nearly lost among cobwebs and timber,

marking the opposite wall with a glowing patch of gold ... she descended
to the open air, shook the flour from her like a bird, and went on into the
garden amid the September sunshine, whose rays lay level across the blue
haze ...[14]

This is a remarkably written, moving painting, filled with roaring sound,
damp, dust, details, sunlight and colour; the full range of the 'mind's eye'. This
representational reach is becoming *normal* to Hardy; he is bringing the whole
world of technical and aesthetic architectural abilities into play to generate a
visual, sensory experience for his readers.

And then, he goes straight back to architecture. *A Laodicean* (1881) is flawed,
awkward, sometimes hammy, dictated from Hardy's sickbed to Emma, who is
sometimes credited with its uneven final shape.[15] But it was centrally about
architecture: architect-hero, client-heroine; architect stooge and villain. The
plotline is driven by the rebuilding of an ancient castle with polemic debates on
professional ethics, conservation, the 'style wars', even contract management – and
a whole realm of architectural perceptions. It opens with the architect Somerset
using 'moulding' strips: pressing strips of lead to take the profile of an ancient church
door (there are several examples of such stencil-moulds in Hardy's notebook). An
archetypal craft moment – from which we immediately depart. Somerset (who is
lost) follows a telegraph wire – to find an ancient castle.

> There was a certain unexpectedness in the fact that the hoary memorial
> of a stolid antagonism to the interchange of ideas, the monument of hard
> distinctions in blood and race ... should be the goal of a machine which
> beyond everything may be said to symbolise cosmopolitan views and the
> intellectual and moral kinship of all mankind ... the little buzzing wire had
> a far finer significance to the student Somerset than the vast walls which
> neighboured it. But ... the modern mental fever and fret which consumes
> people before they can grow old was also signified by the wire ...[16]

Remarkably, *A Laodicean* is *not* a conventional architectural history, but a highly
charged exploration of what conservation means in the modern world. Paula, the
heroine, daughter of a railway engineer, inheritor of a castle, is startlingly modern.
She uses telegrams with the excitement and obsession of a social media addict,
'sending messages from morning till night'.[17] Somerset watches with disquiet, a
telegram conversation between Paula and her friend Charlotte: 'about himself,
under his very nose, in language unintelligible to him.'[18]

And she is interested in architecture. Havill, the 'uneducated' local architect,
says:

As regards that fine Saxon vaulting ... I should advise taking out some of the old stones and reinstating new ones exactly like them.

'But the new ones won't be Saxon' said Paula, 'And then in time to come, when I have passed away, and those stones have become stained like the rest, people will be deceived. I should prefer an honest patch to any such make-believe of Saxon relics ...'[19]

This is sometimes quoted as a modest example of Paula's good conservation thinking. However, this was *not* the standard good practice of his time, but an unusual stand within a contentious field of debate. Indeed, the whole book is structured on the juxtaposition of conservation with the shifting realities, communication, shape and speed of the early electrical age. It directly challenges the architectural thinking of Hardy's time. Ruskin condemns such interest: 'of mechanical ingenuity there is, I imagine, at least as much required to build a cathedral as to cut a tunnel'.[20] Paula asks: 'have you seen the tunnel my father made? The curves are said to be a triumph of Science.'[21] Somerset tells Paula, 'You represent ... the steamship and the railway, and the thoughts that shake mankind.'

That is another remarkable architectural prevision. Le Corbusier, arguably *the* Modern architect, became famous for comparing steamships with architecture in *Towards A New Architecture* (1921), an idea which pervades modern thinking. Somerset is also surprised by the beauty of the tunnel: 'When he had conscientiously admired the massive archivault and the majesty of its nude ungarnished walls, he looked up the slope ... mentally balancing science against art, the grandeur of this fine piece of construction against that of the castle and thinking whether Paula's father had not, after all, had the best of it.'[22]

Somerset goes into the tunnel, musing on that speck of light – and is nearly run down by a train, stepping into a recess to let it pass. Another great cinematic trope; another working detail; another way of jolting reader-viewer into visceral reaction. Another piece of event-architecture, before the fact.

Paula wants to convert a mediaeval courtyard in Greek Revival style: architectural heresy, especially when Gothic was all the rage. Somerset (though allegedly eschewing the style wars) objects – then, for romantic reasons, draws it up. His rival, Havill, stirs up an outcry in the press; Somerset redesigns according to his better original judgement. Here is his revised proposal – far more radical, in the age of Gothic 'Restoration', than it sounds now.

It was original; and it was fascinating. Its originality lay partly in the circumstance that Somerset had not attempted to adapt an old building to the wants of a new civilisation. He had placed his new erection beside it as a slightly attached structure, harmonising with the old; heightening and beautifying, rather than subduing it. His work formed a palace with a ruined castle annexed as a curiosity.[23]

We will be returning to Hardy's remarkable conservation thinking. But here, also remarkably, Hardy is describing the world from inside an architect's head. Hardy said in 1900 that *A Laodicean* had more facts of his life than any:[24] it is surely the intimate discussion of architectural ways of imagining which must be his own. Somerset shows Paula how to read traces of the building: '... pointed out where roofs had been and should be again, where gables had been pulled down, and where floors had vanished, showing her how to reconstruct their details from marks in the walls, much as a comparative anatomist reconstructs an antediluvian from fragmentary bones and teeth.'[25] Or: 'She pulled off her glove, and, her hand resting in the stone channel, her eyes became abstracted in the effort of realisation, the ideas derived from her hand passing into her face ... Somerset placed his own hand in the cavity ...'[26]

Besides its erotic charge, this is a remarkable account of architectural imagination, working between hand, eye and brain, instinct and knowledge, one person and another. Somerset challenges Havill on the 'Saxon' vaulting: 'not an arch nor a wall' of the castle can be older than 1100, he says. Paula, astounded, calls architecture 'An art which makes one independent of written history.'[27] Architecture, as shown here, is 'an alternative way of knowing' as John Schad says.[28] It is still rare to describe how architectural ideas are produced,[29] but we see *four* people at work on this building – Somerset, Paula, Havill and Dare. This book turns on unusual accounts of how people actually *do* design, how they make, see and interpret buildings.[30] Paula, leaning over Somerset as he draws, says: 'Ah, I begin to see your conception.' For Havill, secretly viewing his rival Somerset's drawings: 'the conception had more charm than it could have had to the most appreciative outsider; for when a mediocre and jealous mind that has been cudgelling itself over a problem capable of many solutions, lights on the solution of a rival, all possibilities in the field seem to merge in the one beheld.'[31]

But Havill does *not* simply copy; he is *inspired* by Somerset's work: he has 'possessed himself of Somerset's brains'; 'When contrasted with the tracing from Somerset's plan, Havill's design, which was not far advanced, revealed all its weaknesses to him ... the bands of Havill's imagination were loosened, he laid his own previous efforts aside, got fresh sheets of drawing paper and drew with vigour.'[32] There is a fascinating new body of research, by architects doing PhDs on their own 'tacit', hugely sophisticated, part instinctive, part learned, part technical working design practices[33] – but such analytic description is, even now very unusual. A *Laodicean* even gives an imaginative description of different building *contracts*:

> At his suggestion, Paula agreed to have the works executed as such operations were carried out in old times, before the advent of contractors. Each trade required in the building was to be represented by a master-tradesman ... who should stand responsible for his own section of labour, and for no other, Somerset himself as chief technicist working out his designs on the spot ... Notwithstanding its manifest advantages ... the plan added largely to the responsibilities of the architect, who, with his master-mason, master-carpenter, master-plumber, and what not, had scarcely a moment to call his own ...[34]

Hardy is not just showing how architects work, but how they must imagine how *other* things work: the understanding which comes from seeing a building, or another person's designs. Even things which are *not* entirely visible: age, electronic communication, the processes behind photography: things which change how the world works – and the way we see, imagine and understand it: 'the message sped through the loophole of Stancy Castle keep, over the trees, along the railway, under bridges, across three counties – from extreme antiquity of environment to sheer modernism – and finally landed itself on a table in Somerset's chambers in the midst of a cloud of fog.'[35] It is important that troublemaking Will Dare, an illegitimate (in both senses) architect's assistant, distorts photographs maliciously, warping the plot by making his subjects appear drunk or mad. This is a world of faked images and unreliable evidence.

The number of postmodern architectural obsessions which can be found in this imperfect, little-known novel is astonishing: social media, Photoshop, Derrida; Roland Barthes' 'complete madness of photography' (surely meant here in comparison to 'Restoration's fakery'); 'Phantasmagoria' and staged illusions (mentioned in Walter Benjamin's seminal Arcades Project essay); the Camera Obscura qualities of the castle; and the cinematic vision in the flickering, animated portraits in the fire at the end. John Schad points to all these texts,[36] which are absolutely central to post-modern, literary and working architectural thought. This is a whole new Hardy film waiting to be made.

In this lumpy novel, this can seem clumsy theatricality. But alongside Hardy's own explorations of architectural thinking, it is electrifying. All four architectural workers: Somerset, the thinker; Havill, the untrained local; Dare, the maverick chancer and manipulator of pictures; and Paula, the imaginative client (Hardy often projects constructive visions through female characters) can be seen as versions of Hardy's architectural self; all four classic architectural 'types'. Hardy

Hermann Lea: trick photography by Hardy's later photographic collaborator.

Dunster/de Stancy Castle, Hermann Lea, showing printer's
crop marks. A view across the railway line.

was lying in bed with his feet above his head, dictating his written description to Emma, perhaps often lying in darkness, like a projection machine himself. Shifting between new and old frames of vision, he can already see the architectural future.

A review of this book in *The Architect and Building News* after Hardy's death[37] calls it curious and outdated: but the boot is on the other foot. Representation, modernity, heritage, steamships, speed, distortion, plagiarism, authenticity: *A Laodicean*'s substance turns on ideas which were to obsess the critical architectural age of the coming century, and on the act of architectural imagination that we are still, even now, reconstructing.

*

Hardy's illness did not slow his output. Straight after *A Laodicean* came *Two on a Tower* (1882), an 'interesting oddity' with an allegorical tower-obsession, exploring space beyond normal vision. It opens with an oblique quote from Garbett: 'The vegetable world was a weird multitude of skeletons through whose ribs the sun shone freely.'[38] And in some ways, the architecture is the most interesting part of the book. The story turns on a tiny awkward space: the top of a memorial tower, in the middle of a wood, accessible across a ploughed field, set against infinite space. During the course of the novel a surprising amount happens to that tower. Here it is 'as found', in its original Freudian glory:

> It had been built in the Tuscan order of classic architecture and was really a tower, being hollow, with steps inside ... Below the level of their summits the masonry was lichen stained and mildewed, for the sun never pierced that moaning cloud of blue-black vegetation. Pads of moss grew in the joints of the stonework ... Above the trees ... the pillar rose into the sky a bright and cheerful thing, unimpeded, clean and flushed with sunlight.[39]

Hardy wrote to the Royal Observatory at Greenwich claiming to be designing an observatory, asking whether a hollow memorial column would be suitable for the purposes; mentioning that he had 'written astronomical passages which are quoted in both England and America' (presumably the passage already quoted in *Far from the Madding Crowd*). This is usually seen as a conceit, but it is a *normal* thought for an architect, and accurate too. Here is Hardy's design:

> The top of the column was quite changed. The tub-shaped space within the parapet, formerly open to the air and sun, was now arched over by a light dome made of lath-work covered with felt. But this dome was not fixed. At the line where its base descended to the parapet there were half a dozen iron

balls, precisely like cannon-shot, standing loosely in a groove, and on these the dome rested its whole weight. In the side of the dome was a slit, and towards it the end of the great telescope was fixed. This latter magnificent object, with its circles, axes and handles complete, was securely fixed to the middle of the floor ... the whole dome turned horizontally round, running on the balls with a rumble like that of nearing thunder.[40]

It is unusual for architects to think of buildings being demolished (Cedric Price was a notable exception, arguing architects had a duty to work out how their buildings be taken down as well as built). But Hardy does something similar here: '... she experienced the unutterable melancholy of seeing two carpenters dismantle the dome of its felt covering, detach its ribs, and clear away the enclosure at the top till everything stood as it had before ...'[41] Indeed, Viviette cannot bear to see the hut where she had met her young husband taken down: 'She had the junction of the timbers marked with figures, the boards numbered, and the different sets of screws tied up in independent papers for identification ...'[42] Both accepting (and trying to ignore) the phallic metaphors, this book insists on the *impermanence* of human constructions. In many ways, the architectural construction and demolition of *Two on a Tower* is more satisfactorily resolved than the novel itself.

*

At this stage, you might say: the more architectural the novel, the more uneven and flawed it will be. The architectural workings of Hardy's Wessex – content, detail, technology, visual framing, professional debate, powerful, polemic argument, and constantly inventive method – are exposed in these 'middling' novels. Hardy did not leave any of these things behind as he moved into the later phases of his work. He just became more accomplished in making the workings disappear.

Yet Hardy keeps coming back to architecture. There's something about this obsessive return which suggests architecture is more than a scaffolding for constructing his novels. It suggests a way of thinking, an instinct, an irritant, something bugging him. He is trying many architectural experiments, but the popular ones clearly do not entirely satisfy him. The overall shape is not right. In practice, as architect or critic, you have to notice your instincts. If something looks or feels wrong, it probably is wrong. If you keep coming back to something that does not work, it signals a need to step back and rethink the shape of your project. And that is just what Hardy would do.

6

UNSAFE PICTURES

The Return of the Native

Egdon Heath, by Hermann Lea. A definitive empty landscape.

Speaking as an architectural critic, *The Return of the Native* (1878) seems consciously architectural, in a way that *Far from the Madding Crowd* (1874) does not. That is despite the complete lack of architects, the scarcity of buildings, the relative paucity of technical description. The big architectural thing that Hardy is seeing and constructing is the place itself.

The *Return* is a particularly intense and conscious experiment in describing landscape itself. The place is the working substance of the story, its main character. It opens:

A Saturday afternoon in November was approaching the time of twilight, and the vast tract of unenclosed wild known as Egdon Heath embrowned itself moment by moment. Overhead the hollow stretch of whitish cloud shutting out the sky was as a tent which had the whole heath for its floor.

The heaven being spread with the pallid screen, the earth with the darkest vegetation, their meeting line at the horizon was clearly marked. In such contrast the heath wore the appearance of an instalment of night which had taken up its place before its astronomical hour was come: darkness had to a great extent arrived hereon, while day stood distinct in the sky. Looking upwards, a furze-cutter would have been inclined to finish work; looking down, he would have decided to finish his faggot and go home.[1]

This begins a whole *chapter* describing a view: the land itself. It is not until the next chapter, 'Character Appears on the Scene, Hand in Hand with Trouble', that people turn up. That opening chapter is empty of people – except for that hypothetical furze-cutter, and the imagined viewer's perception.

The time seems near, if it has not actually arrived, when the mournful sublimity of a moor, a sea or a mountain, will be all of nature that is absolutely in keeping with the more thinking among mankind ... to the commonest tourist, spots like Iceland may become what the vineyards and myrtle-gardens of South Europe are to him now; and Heidelberg and Baden will be passed unheeded as he hastens from the Alps to the sand-dunes ...[2]

Hardy is predicting a future way of seeing, a shift in understanding place and beauty – and he is remarkably accurate. He could *see* the rural world through the aesthetic frame of the future, and it has come into sharp focus; the mainframe for his work. By Chapter 2, with figures crossing the heath, that view contains the whole plot in embryo.

This will become one of Hardy' defining techniques. Most of his great novels: the *Mayor*, *The Woodlanders*, *Tess*, start with a version of this establishing scene: a great, fixed view of isolated figures crossing an otherwise 'empty' landscape. This is more than a 'setting'. This novel is *about* the landscape, and our relationship to it.

The *Return* was Hardy's most intimate home territory, a detailed, part-fictionalised account of the surprisingly remote heathland east of Bockhampton. He was writing at Sturminster Newton, where he and Emma had their 'two-year idyll' in the pretty, modern semi-detached Riverside Villas. He was near his parents, but not too near; and facing west, as he liked to do.

In the book, Clym has given up a successful career as a jeweller in Paris to found a local school. His infatuation with Eustacia is partly through seeing her as part of

Egdon's pagan wildness: preposterously, he hopes she will become a teacher. But it is the heath, with its 'friendly face', which is his real love story.

A darkening vision runs through the book. When failing sight halts his studies, Clym gladly takes up furze-cutting: that is, gorse – a harsh job and a huge slide down the social ladder, which outrages both the restless, passionate Eustacia and Clym's redoubtable mother (a portrait of Jemima herself). Eustacia loathes the heath, and longs for the relatively bright lights of Budmouth/Weymouth.

The plot is entirely driven by people's relationships with Egdon. Clym's love for it; Eustacia's hatred, and Clym's cousin Tamsin's sunny, pragmatic engagement with it. The heath, roughly speaking, kills Clym's wife and mother: Mrs Yeobright, lost and exhausted in a heatwave, accidentally denied entry to her son's cottage by Eustacia, is finished off by an adder bite; Eustacia drowns – suicide or accident – in wild flight across unknown country on a stormy night.

Weather and landscape, indivisible and ruthless: Hardy shows that we romanticise landscapes at our peril. Tamsin escapes unscathed from far worse conditions than those which kill the other women:

> To her there were not, as to Eustacia, demons in the air, and malice in every bush and bough. The drops which lashed her face were not scorpions, but prosy rain; Egdon in the mass was no monster whatever, but impersonal open ground. Her fears of the place were rational, her dislikes of its worst moods

Clym and Eustacia's cottage, Alderworth, Hermann Lea.

reasonable. At this time it was in her view a windy wet place, in which a person might experience much discomfort, lose the path without care, and possibly catch cold.[3]

Wrap up well, take water, or die. Don't walk in the dark if you don't know the way. And here is an unproven folk remedy for snakebite. Hardy's tales are always informative. And just *look* how far from Ruskin's smiling, flower-strewn tapestries. There could hardly be a stronger polemic *against* the cult of the picturesque than *The Return of the Native*. It is highly realised, vividly informed, full of passion – but pretty it is not. Clym's loving return makes him a damaging catalyst, fixing the heath as Eustacia's prison and nemesis: her tragic medium. Hardy was already getting letters, often from young women teachers, asking him where they should settle. If this did not warn them off, there was more to come.

The criticisms of Hardy's rustics, which had flared up over *Far from the Madding Crowd*, went into overdrive now. 'The language of his peasants may be Elizabethan, but it can hardly be Victorian.'[4] Note that hesitant clause, the critic (or editor) wasn't sure. Hardy was taking the criticisms of *Far from the Madding Crowd* head on.

And he was working on that representational experiment. Critics preferred simpler, 'natural' descriptions: he would work at making his writing 'natural' while ratcheting up the experiment, too. Gradually, he would hone down his inventive framing and juxtaposition – his paintings that moved – into a vision that worked so well that people could (if they chose) forget the technical invention through which it was made.

David Lodge's 'Thomas Hardy and Cinematographic Form' (1974) takes the *Return* as the great example of how 'Realist' novels anticipated cinema. He points out Hardy's insistence on vision, on making you *see* things, rather than *telling* you things. Here is a character: 'One would have said that he had been, in his day, a naval officer of some sort or other'. There's nothing to stop Hardy 'telling us this is Captain Vye, retired' says Lodge. That feels right: as an architect: you have to *show* your audience what you are imagining.

Lodge argued that this book predicted not just films, but a sophisticated type of films: the Westerns of John Ford. 'The methods he uses can be readily analysed in cinematic terms: long shot, close-up, wide-angle, telephoto, zoom, etc. ... It is the artistry with which he controls the reader's perspective on the relationship between character and environment, through shifts of focus and angle, that makes him a powerful and original novelist.'[5]

And the pictures, says Lodge, charge up the vision beyond its plot. The redness of the Reddleman (moving dot or startling red face) adds resonant strangeness to a stolid character. Eustacia's allure is heightened by her view against the brooding

Arthur Hopkins's illustrations for *The Return of the Native*,
1878: to be read against the map.

landscape. Diggory and Wildeve, gambling by the light of glow-worms, have little effect on the story, but it remains an indelible image in its own right.

So illustrations were crucial. Hardy wanted Helen Paterson to do them, and was sometimes critical of Arthur Hopkins's images,[6] although many are extremely powerful. Hardy had fairly stratospheric expectations, as well as providing challenging visual content to work from. Gatrell says: 'Hardy perhaps saw that the very conventionality of the illustrations might help to render publishable a text that pushed persistently against the limits of the then acceptable ... Eustacia in boys' clothes, though pleasant enough to the imagination, would perhaps be unsafe as a picture.'[7]

If that was the problem, it was an important one. Hardy was making us imagine unsafe pictures. Sexy ones, like the voluptuous Eustacia in boys' clothes. Strange ones, that depended on saturated or peculiar colour. Empty ones – filled with nothing but landscape and sky, before the taste for empty landscape has arrived. Sharp juxtapositions, when magazine publication used one plate per issue. Wide landscape views, when most publications were portrait. Ones you cannot see at all, like the heath in profound darkness. Hardy's novels have the force of cinema partly because of their capacity for immersive, visual shock, to make you imagine something you have never seen before: the shocking view through the telescope. They burn into the retina of your imagination.

67

Egdon Heath in spectacularly bad weather, Hermann Lea.

*

If Hardy felt the serial illustrations did not quite do the job he needed, he had an entirely architectural response: he added a map. It appeared in the book form of the *Native*; the first of his maps. This was carefully and (of course) disingenuously argued in with his publishers Smith, Elder:

> I enclose for your inspection a Sketch of the supposed scene in which the "Return of the Native" is laid – copied from the one I used in writing the story – & my suggestion is that we place an engraving of it as frontispiece to the first volume ... I am of the opinion that it would be a desirable novelty, likely to increase a reader's interest. I may add that a critic once remarked to me that nothing could give such reality to a tale as a map of this sort: & I myself have often felt the same thing ... In the drawing for the book it would be desirable to shade the hills more fully than I have done in the sketch.[8]

This was not quite the first time a map had been published in a novel, or been used to imagine one. Daniel Defoe's *Robinson Crusoe* included one, in 1719. The Brontë children had been drawing Angria and Glasstown in their parsonage from childhood; Hardy's publisher George Smith had been friend as well as publisher of Charlotte. But it was certainly a novelty. Probably the first map pinning a novel to a real place, and a hugely successful move. (Other famous fictional worlds such as Narnia and Middle Earth followed suit). Even *drawing* a map suggests an author seeing the world of the novels in a different way: not as just a setting, but as something with an independent, geographical, three-dimensional reality of its own.

Calling this a 'sketch map' is misleading too: it is a finished and intricate drawing, of a particular type; a bird's eye or aerial view – a classic architectural format for presenting complicated ideas to a non-professional audience. But 'sketch' in Hardy's usages, suggests something else; it suggests it is his: the author's, not the illustrator's.

If you compare it with an Ordnance Survey map of the area,[9] you can see how Hardy is using the frame of the book to capture that landscape. The aerial view foreshortens it: he has turned the conventional map orientation (North at the top) around to capture a view of the landscape, through the book, without having to turn the book on its side. Without the reader knowing how to read maps.

Victorian novel-readers were used to reading serial fiction with at least one illustration per episode. Thackeray drew his own and included several in each instalment; Dickens wanted illustrators to add details he had had to cut from the text. Maps were also a 'hot medium' in the mid-nineteenth century, intimately linked to building of the railways, construction of the cities, and the complete

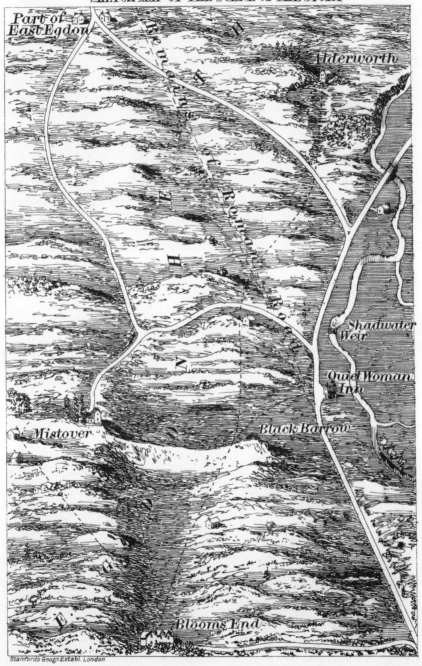

Stanfords Geogr. Establ. London

Hardy's 'sketch' map of Egdon, *The Return of the Native*.

re-structuring of the countryside that entailed. But what Hardy was doing was especially coherent in architectural terms.

Plans or maps are almost essential in architectural books.[10] They help you imagine where you are meant to be. Hardy was starting to help his readers assemble the imagined world of his novels – maps, pictures, texts – for themselves. He was using normal architectural techniques to help his readers read his novels as he does, as a coherent place. Adding a map to the illustrations makes our imagination of Egdon stronger than that generated by the story alone; something we can imagine independently of the story; something existing more substantially because it can be seen through different media. It will get stronger still with the later Hermann Lea photographs of Egdon. Hardy is starting to show his readers how they, like any architect reading drawings, can construct a place in their heads.

*

The *Return* was not much admired at the time. Its challenging and predictive philosophical-narrative gambit felt more like Tolstoy or Flaubert than Eliot. It was considered too 'French'; Eustacia was compared to Emma Bovary, which was not intended as a compliment.[11] (*The Trumpet Major*, hard on its heels, seems to be consciously referencing *War and Peace*, 1869, pinned against the vast canvas of the Napoleonic wars.) But in hindsight, the *Return* is acknowledged to be a 'masterpiece'. And it lays down his ground.

If *Far from the Madding Crowd* was where Wessex was named, then *Return* – where it starts to be mapped – is a change in method. Hardy is starting to draw together a wider set of information,[12] so that attentive readers can assemble this world as he does. Hardy sketched a little drawing from a painting in an exhibition, also in 1878, the year of the novel's publication, which has the book's odd qualities: the bleak, empty lansdscape, people outside an inn, a road vanishing into the distance.[13] Something has come into focus. Hardy knows what his headline image *looks* like: an ancient road, disappearing across a vast, empty landscape. A harsh, hypnotic view watched for a long time. A curated vision: widescreen, detailed, bleak, empty. A journey (as Patrick O'Brian would say[14]) whose ends are out of sight.

Wessex, or Dorset has not just become *a* character in the novel, but *the* character running through all the subsequent novels. He says this directly of Egdon. But it continues through the *Mayor*, *The Woodlanders* and *Tess*; through poems and plays. This *place*, partly real, partly invented, was what he was creating.

TYPES OF CONSTRUCTION

Ways of Seeing

The end of the 1870s is well into the period when Hardy is supposed to have left architecture. Claudius Beatty says: 'He continued to behave, in public at least, as if architecture didn't exist.'[1] But he adds, 'after an interval of eight or nine years, he continues, in an advisory capacity at least, to make use of his professional skills for the rest of his life'.

Yet even that 'interval' is full of remarkable architectural work of all kinds. Hardy is drawing, mapping and writing. He is using all kinds of technical and aesthetic knowledge to construct his stories. He is engaging with the age's major architectural debates in published work. He is packing the novels with architectural content, techniques, structures, language and ways of seeing. He is *using* architectural ways of working, to write. He has published a map, so that readers can begin assembling his imagined-real place, as he does. He is predicting cinematic vision so clearly that we have observed he could well have seen moving pictures himself. He is always experimenting with pictures, written and drawn. He is assembling them, in his books, in a way more familiar to architects than novelists. And now he has a distinct, coherent vision of what his work looks like.

And he is continuing to work as a practical architect: small, occasional, 'everyday' pieces of work, apparently: but sometimes very interesting ones. From an insider's point of view, Hardy never gave up architecture.

*

Most directly, there are the buildings on which Hardy worked. Even now, using Beatty's lifelong forensic work, this is a difficult picture to uncover. Hardy worked in fragments – first by accident, later consciously and as part of a coherent idea. Beatty concentrates on identifying the sources or locations of each drawing and remains the key source for tracking them down. This book (more normally for architectural criticism) takes a more interpretative approach. For sifting his mass of drawings – this uncertain world of possible buildings and projects; interpreting things seen, imagined, designed, changed, and only sometimes built – is a *typical* job for a critic, albeit in unusually aggravated form.

When the late, wonderful, challenging architect Cedric Price asked me to write about a new project, he would leave me in his attic workplace, with a mass of unexplained information: maps, notes, diagrams and peculiar drawings. Two hours later, he would return and ask 'what do you think?' Somewhere in the middle of writing this book, I realised Hardy was doing the same kind of thing.

So I will start, in the same way, with the drawings. Until the 1880s, almost everything Hardy built was for other architects, and he had little control of it.[2] He was doing drawings which we know (from the *Life*) he saw as hack-work; he was clearing graves which we know (from 'The Levelled Churchyard', *Jude* and the *Life*) he regarded as desecration; and he was trying to save heritage which we know (from Beatty, 'Memories of Church Restoration' and the *Life*) he often failed to do. He was working in elaborate contemporary styles, in the middle of a style war, which we know (from *A Laodicean* and 'Memories of Church Restoration') he thought was irrelevant. But he did not write this work off.

From his great purge of papers, which Florence continued after his death, a range of direct architectural work had been saved. Some drawings are exquisite, some are scrappy and peculiar. Some are detailed roughs, some are clearly for presentation, and there are several for laying out drains. There is the architectural notebook, that carefully assembled mini-portfolio of sketches, copies, notes and designs, which he continued into his eighties – and a big quarter-scale, carefully coloured drawing of the lavatory at Max Gate: the biggest design drawing of all. Some were jobs Hardy designed in his own right, some were for other architects. Some were built, others not, and there is no immediate way of seeing which is which.

The shape of this inchoate, far-from-perfect mass of saved architectural drawings is interesting. Hardy is showing he could draw, competently and with skill, in the manner required by his profession – but elevations of new buildings are the most mechanical parts of his work. His sections are much better; his surveys of *existing* buildings are lovely. His rough working drawings – plans and sections – are often more engaging than the 'finished' ones: you can see Hardy working everything out, in intense detail.

Some finished drawings are extremely revealing: the lovely drawings of his Piddletrenthide school extension (perhaps coloured to show to the children) or the complete church design, which Beatty uncovered (and which looks like a competition entry). It is an accomplished, sparse Arts & Crafts style, with unusual random modern stained-glass windows, but most remarkable is that immersive, wonderful section drawing. To see it as close, as Hardy would have drawn it, is like

73

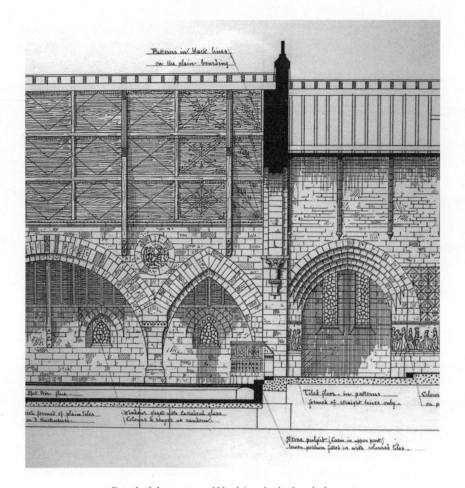

Detail of the section of Hardy's unbuilt church design.

actually being in the building: an astonishing level of skill (if too time-consuming to use often). The coloured pew-end series in the manner of Owen Jones's *The Grammar of Ornament* (from which Hardy copied many of his drawings[3]) suggests a detailed catalogue from which to work. The regal lavatory drawings are expressive and accurate: grand, personal indoor plumbing as the 'throne' of Max Gate. And the drawings of the Greenhill houses in Weymouth, a richly detailed conventional terrace in Victorian Gothic coloured brick look like a textbook exercise in formal style.

But beware of thinking that accomplished styles or exquisite, finished drawings define Hardy's architecture: the opposite is often true. Hardy moved away from elevations, first to 'inside out' Arts & Crafts type thinking, and on to a kind of accretive patching in which his later designs were not drawn in complete elevation at all. He was *not* leaving us a finished vision in those drawings, but a sample of the range of ways in which he was visualising and constructing the world.

The Notebook, though stiff with decorative details, is intercut with notes on housemaids' sinks or details of a 'French' drain, acoustic floor-packing (as in *Ethelberta*), or everyday, lightweight, functional roof construction details, both drawn and written. Later, there are detailed, rougher measured studies of projects he was actually building. He is showing himself to be working, thinking, designing as a hands-on, capable architect: alongside, and through, everything else.

I am also considering the remarkable things he is *not* drawing. Signs of sketching ideas for buildings are scarce or conventional. He is often copying, tracing or scaling up. He does not seem able to draw in isometric (however lovingly he describes that aristocratic architectural drawing). He does not seem to draw in *perspective* at all: there is no sign of the vanishing points or 'setting out' lines used to construct them, although several drawings use grids to help with the simple 'scaling-up' of flat images.

Many of the drawings are miniscule; some in strange focus. I am constantly wondering about his eyesight and his lifelong use of lenses. Remarkably, he seems to be tracing *photographs*, reproducing their framing, focus and photographic distortion. There are small, detailed, complex images, stopping in a neat rectangular frame, in the middle of a large piece of paper (Stinsford House); there are ones where the distance is more in focus than the foreground (Melbury Osmund); and a neat, finished drawing of the pew-ends of St Juliot before restoration, which can be neatly fitted over the photograph itself.

There are few original photographs left in the archive (the one of St Juliot was saved by the vicar), but this is not a coincidence. Camera lenses construct the view in one way; perspectives, drawings and human perception in others. They would not naturally produce the same views. Other drawing devices might, however: notably the nineteenth century camera lucida, described and illustrated in Martin Kemp's *The Science of Art*.[4] The Fox Talbot and Basil Hall drawings which Kemp shows in his book are very like Hardy's otherwise peculiar, scrappy drawings, dated 1861 and 1862, when he first moved to London and started visiting the Great Exhibition. This device used a little mirror lens, focusing a picture onto a flat desk, working a little like an overhead projector. A further peculiarity is that the user is looking through the lens while drawing, rather than looking directly at the paper, making it much harder to do. I am struck by the way that groups of trees, or even blocks of landscape are drawn as a single, solid outline block, sometimes in frenetic detail, rather than drawn tree by tree, or hill by hill, as untrained humans tend to do. Some of the finished-looking views from windows also suggest some similar process with detailed outline and infill; others perhaps are taken from photographs. From

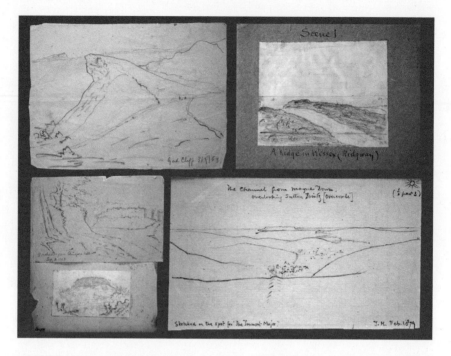

Hardy's experiments in drawing include tracings, scaling-up and these curious outline drawings suggesting the use of 'camera lucida' projection methods.

a visual point alone, I would suggest that Hardy was, from his arrival in London, exploring image projection as one of his many working tools for capturing and developing his view of the world.

He uses old techniques as well as new. All the tracings, overlays, arch-mould stencils, copies and experiments in the Notebook, the lenses, photographs, home-made carbon paper (where lead would be rubbed on the back of paper and the original re-drawn, so that the image was 'transferred' onto a fresh page below), are in this realm. From his obsessive drawings of tombstones and memorials – a move backward into the 'traits' or tracing used by mediaeval craftsmen (he does masses of full-size gravestone drawings) – to the photographic cut-out of his family's exquisite traditional music book in Hermann Lea's book and the stage set work late in life, Hardy is working in the familiar realm of architecture's continual reinvention of itself through drawing and representation, through precedent and invention.

There is plenty of internal evidence within the novels suggesting an experimental fascination and familiarity with lenses, photography, and phantasmogria. No-one reading *Ethelberta* or *A Laodicean* should be surprised by this. But it takes some familiarity with 'normal' architectural drawing techniques to recognise peculiarities in these drawings – and hence in this form of his drawings we see a new way of understanding how Hardy saw and represented the world.[5]

Hardy's drawings are a key part of his intense, broader interest in perception, which extends to the way an architect imagines the *invisible* qualities of architecture: – which can be designed, built, touched, experienced – but not exactly drawn or photographed. Acoustic space; age value; social experience; the craftsman's understanding of worked stone. (Even those *Dorset County Chronicle* local news articles mention the experience of the congregation.)

All forms of representation are limited, selective, partial. Hardy's architectural vision is certainly not contained in any one particular type of drawing, and the whole range of representation and drawing was, I would argue, by now part of the processes he was using to generate his work. Even if, at this point, it was largely emerging in written and fictional form.

*

Largely written and fictional – but not entirely. The star of his early built work is all but invisible, and very interesting indeed. The lovely church of St Mary Turnworth is a restoration job Hardy started for Hicks and finished for Crickmay on his return to Dorset in the late 1860s. Cautious historians limit his 'certain' involvement to its richly decorative columns, but Beatty has him fully in charge.[6] The drawings and specifications confirm this; and the church itself shows just how much architectural thinking Hardy was doing.

Turnworth is in a lovely part of Dorset, central and remote, below its central shelf of hills. It grew (like other good projects) from an excellent client relationship. Hardy became friends with the vicar, Thomas Perkins, campaigned with him on conservation matters, and often cycled the 17 miles to read the lesson in the church he had restored.[7]

Turnworth is a bigger project than cautious emphasis on those capitals suggests. It is fully and beautifully drawn, in plan, section and elevation, with a rich composite font, and a very full written specification. The fact that today it seems essentially an *old* church is evidence of extreme care – an unconventional 'restoration' – and not that little was done.

You enter through a beautiful, unlevelled churchyard (care was taken to retain graves and floor levels) into an old interior, where those capitals catch the eye. The helpful Dorset Churches website says: 'The capitals represent various kinds of foliage inhabited by song birds (including a very striking owl) and sand lizards, and were carved by Boulton and Son of Cheltenham in some kind of oolitic limestone (probably Corsham Down stone) and have been picked out by Pevsner in early French

Turnworth with its stonemasons' owl.

gothic style.'[8] Hardy had worked with those masons on Rampisham church for Hicks.[9] He would have known they were good.

Photographs and drawings can flatten the magical qualities of those capitals: the soft stone blackberries tempting you to pick them, the creatures flourishing everywhere. Hardy must have verbally discussed the carvings with the masons – the prominent owl; the sand lizards in the foliage – for they are not in the drawings. Hardy was following Ruskin's direction about allowing skilled masons their creative liberty, which was the opposite of what Ruskin, himself, did.

These are *extremely* close to the capitals used in the Oxford Museum, and the hidden sand lizards surely reference Oxford's exquisite snake amongst the leaves. And that is where, in one of the most startling and comic *volte-faces* of the Arts & Crafts, Ruskin and colleagues turned their wonderful stonemasons off site, precisely for adding inappropriate, 'caricature' creatures – famously *owls*.

We will come back to the story (it is closely connected with *Jude*), but this building precedes that novel by a good decade. Hardy was in Oxford, for Blomfield, not long after the Museum opened. He had surely seen the building or known the story. Hardy and the Boultons must have decided to give one of Ruskin's exorcised owls sanctuary – as permanent a piece of built architectural commentary as could be imagined.

Hardy's beautiful 'spec' also draws attention to a less-noticed part of the design: the 'Children's Seats'; shown in plan and section, and described and drawn with particular care. It might sound like nothing, but in converting the area under the tower into a stepped seating area for children, with views straight up the aisle, Hardy is making a creative variant of those Georgian church galleries which he loved and which the Victorians largely eradicated. It would have made the church work like a theatre in the round, re-establishing the west-end (which Hardy describes, in the *Mayor* as joyously chaotic). It would have had its own special acoustic, noisy singing part-swallowed in the space of the tower above. The tower floor has (sadly) been levelled since, but some of the miniature pews are still there: unregarded, everyday fragments of Hardy design.

Turnworth is a wonderful piece of social and acoustic, free-thinking, life-affirming architecture. Along with the sand lizards and eradicated owl, Hardy is warmly inviting some childish chaos into the elderly life of the building. It is an architecture which joins, rather than takes over, the ongoing fabric of the church. And yet those polemic columns are playing a game, drawing the viewer back to the forests and the quarries – and architectural arguments – from which this building came. And, in that tiny detail of arcane knowledge, condensing the most biting architectural polemic of all.

*

Close similarities of text, drawings, forms or details are no coincidence in architectural criticism. We have seen Hardy's Wessex Poem drawings looking like Bernard Tschumi's experiments, before hitting Derrida through academic routes (and Derrida says Tschumi's *is* the radical vision of architecture). But we came to this through working architectural criticism: *looking* at Hardy's own work, not by following other people's texts.

Hardy himself is not looking like a high theorist either. He is not dumbing down, and he is weaving theory, construction, philosophy and high art into his books. But the methods or forms he is using are the instinctive, technical, working, everyday, skilled, often unspoken ones, both human and architectural: describing what it is like to be in a landscape, how you actually do design, build or imagine buildings – and how you use drawings and language, pictures and books to do it.

The architectural writers who feel closest to Hardy are not wholly or principally theorists either: they are *practitioners*, working architects who write too. Outside conventional academia, they have a freer, constructive hand in the form their books take. They can assemble a mix of ingredients so that readers might 'see' their conception, and they use them to test and discuss their own emerging work, rather than to illustrate, or advertise for, built work.

Here is the famous Brutalist architect Alison Smithson, in the text accompanying *Patio and Pavilion*, the remarkable, 'as found' installation that the Smithsons made as part of the Independent Group's seminal 1956 *This Is Tomorrow* exhibition of challenging post-war work: 'I work with memory, and it allows me to make connections to the past, interpolations of the present and gives foresight – a most valuable facility for an architect – as a possible future.'[10]

Both the Smithsons[11] and Venturi and Scott Brown, interestingly, explore the idea of the 'view from the road' as crucial to architecture. In *Learning From Las Vegas*, a hugely-influential book of 1972, Robert Venturi, Denise Scott Brown and Steven Izenour surveyed the 'ugly and ordinary' architectural environment of casinos, tarmac and neon, using the drawing conventions used to map classical Rome to learn architectural lessons from 'non-architectural' places. It opens: 'Learning from the existing landscape is a way of being revolutionary for an architect. Not the obvious way, which is to tear down Paris, and begin again, as Le Corbusier suggested in the 1920s, but another, more tolerant way: that is, to question how we look at things.'[12]

That is exactly what Hardy did himself and it leads to the most counter-intuitive comparison of all. Le Corbusier and Hardy could hardly be more different in intention: Le Corbusier advocating the most extreme mechanised future; Hardy, before the fact, considering the losses that vision was already starting to entail. They are on opposite sides – but in the same game.

Le Corbusier was always experimenting with media. As Beatriz Colomina shows,[13] he thought in advertising slogans and mixed media, and he was pivotal in establishing the idea that architecture and cinema are inextricably linked. His own buildings define a new kind of cinematic vision: the 'architectural promenade'. The films of them run in empty, voyeuristic sequence, seeing just traces of occupation: a fish, a hat, a pair of glasses. Colomina says:

> We are following somebody, the traces of his existence presented to us in the form of a series of photographs of the interior. The look into these photographs is a forbidden look. The look of a detective. A voyeuristic look. … 'where did the gentleman go?'[14]

Even by *The Return of the Native*, Hardy's predictive vision has reached this point: the empty landscape, the shadowy figure of the viewer, the traces of occupation, the view through the lens. The vision of abstracted or alienated modernity itself.

Le Corbusier's seminal books, too, were a working part of his design method.[15] He explicitly linked typographical art to the art of building[16] and the 'singular appearance' of his books was noted by Elie Fauré in 1935[17] as being composed of 'polyglot' imagery 'pell-mell, photographs of animals, buildings, everyday objects, clippings from newspapers and sales catalogues, cartoons, old-master paintings, scientific diagrams and so on' (he even bound his copy of *Don Quixote* in the shaggy skin of his pet dog).[18] And we have already seen Hardy considering architecture against steamships: perhaps Le Corbusier's most famous visual provocation of all.

Of course, Le Corbusier was working in a modern idiom, using actual film. But Hardy was using photographs and lenses experimentally too, and cinema, though often given a solid-looking birth-date (1880, 1895 etc.), comes from a history of image projection stretching back thousands of years, with a wealth of experiments staged and published throughout the nineteenth century. The fascinating 1843 book *On Natural Magic*,[19] incidentally, suggests a rather different interpretation of a phrase Hardy himself used.

In the 1870s, Hardy is certainly seeing past his age into the age of mechanical reproduction, of sophisticated, popular cinema, of photographic unreliability and social media. He is already seeing a rural world in which information is transmitted by mass media, whether telegraphs, photographs or realist novels. He is sequencing images as though films already exist. He is acting as architects and their critics have to: constructing a vision of the future and imagining how it would work.

*

The problem with the view of Hardy's architectural thinking until now is that people seem to be trying to see it as *normal*; as conventional, even traditional architectural practice (if such a thing exists). But even the everyday workings of architectural practice – the mix of technical and aesthetic knowledge, guesswork, theory, drawing and reading of drawings, collective discussion, and the reframing of ideas in response to critics' feedback (core skills which architects and their critics use all the time) – are so 'tacit', such an acquired and internalised set of motor skills (rather like learning to drive) that the profession barely, if ever, describes them. We are only tentatively now, in research terms, learning to describe the processes Hardy was already, remarkably exploring: how an architect – *any* architect – actually does design in practice.[20] And Hardy was certainly ahead of us.

Hardy is critical of uninformed analogies with architecture elsewhere. Of an ill-informed critic of *The Dynasts*, he would say: 'he had better have left architecture alone'. But Hardy *was* an architect, and he did *not* leave architecture alone. In all his work he was using its visionary tools, its written polemic, its working details, its actual construction, its immersive experience, and its assembly of information. That is, roughly, the full package of an architects' working design thinking.

And though his way of building is completely different, he is doing *exactly* what the most radical architects of a century later would do: taking architecture's own, practical and imaginative tactics, and inventively, creatively, cinematically, applying them to find a new way of seeing the wider world. In literature, it is well-known that Hardy was highly experimental. The same, I would argue, is true of his architecture.

PART 2

REALISATION

Overleaf: *Wessex Poems*, showing the 'Great September Comet',
Wimborne Minster is visible on the skyline.

8

THE INVENTION OF WESSEX

A Reconstruction

In the early 1880s, Hardy did something profoundly architectural, something that architects do so naturally that they do not even explain it. He started putting things together, looking at the work he had already done and post-rationalising it; seeing which things had worked and which had failed, and finding connections between them.

He was recognising a peculiar quality to his own work: a forensic presentation of a vanishing rural past through a modern, experimental frame which was playing a role in the real world too.

For Wessex, as soon as it was named, had taken on a life of its own. He had noticed that his novels were making up an imaginary world which went beyond the books themselves: a big, popular imaginary world, already being discussed outside the novels. He started seeing that world, drawing and publishing it, as a single thing: a coherent, imaginary entity. He started developing Wessex as though it were an architectural project.

An 'architectural project' is a very particular thing – the heart of architectural practice, teaching and thought. In architecture schools, it is the core of the curriculum. Design tutors might start by setting exercises of various types: drawings, models or other work, which may be speculative, pragmatic, realistic, modest, fantastical, strategic, experimental, conventional, or any combination of the above.[1] At some point, the student learns to find patterns and connections within their own work; they begin to link fragments, ideas and drawings, their understanding of the site and 'programme' of uses together, and to give it its own coherence. They can start to see it as coherent – as an imaginary building, strategy or fictional narrative – and develop it, in detail, in those terms. At that point, tutors and critics would say: 'you've got a project.'

That is not just a conceit: it teaches how architects actually do their designing. They *have* to use drawings, models, texts and other things to construct and test imaginary buildings to see what seems to work. They then share these projects with builders or colleagues, clients, critics or legislators – using drawings, books, instructions and pictures – so that others can discuss, criticise, or build them. They have to develop their imaginary worlds in coherent detail; and they typically use their major projects to change the world, not only by building, but by publication, by starting a debate. And that is just what Hardy started doing with Wessex.

*

By 1882, the Hardys had moved from London to a modern suburban house, Lanherne[2] in Wimborne, a North Dorset market town with a beautiful Minster church. Hardy was 42 years old, and becoming famous. He was still working on those 'experiment' novels: A *Laodicean* was in proofs, and *Two on a Tower* was written in Wimborne. His last great novels *The Mayor of Casterbridge* (1886), *The Woodlanders* (1887), *Tess of the d'Urbervilles* (1891) and *Jude the Obscure* (1896) were just in the future. And with them would come a big shift in his work.[3]

He was laying the ground for the evolution of Wessex from a setting for his novels into something more ambitious and unusual. Hardy was not going to simplify, but to *re*-integrate the visual experiment, the ingenuity, the awkward architectural characteristics of the middle novels into the 'natural magic' of his emerging work (a more technical phrase than we thought). And at the same time, expand its whole scope. In the general introduction to his novels, Hardy says:

> It was in the chapters of *Far from the Madding Crowd* ... that I first ventured to adopt the word 'Wessex' from the pages of early English history, and give it a fictitious significance as the existing name of a district once included in that extinct kingdom ...

> Since then the appellation which I had thought to reserve to the horizons and landscapes of a partly-real, partly-dream country, has become more and more popular as a practical provincial definition; and the dream-country has, by degrees, solidified into a utilitarian region which people can go to, take a house in, and write to the papers from. But I ask all good and idealistic readers to forget this, and to refuse steadfastly to believe there are any inhabitants of a Victorian Wessex outside these volumes in which their lives and conversations are detailed.[4]

That disingenuous lawyer's trick – asking you to ignore an idea he has just planted – is typical Hardy.[5] He is asking us to believe in the reality of his novels – while pointing out (in parentheses), that it is imaginary.

The attacks by that first wave of critics had started a public defence of Wessex's accuracy. It began with an anonymous review by another literary man from a poor Dorset background, Charles Kegan Paul, later a well-known publisher. The article was called 'The Wessex Labourer'[6] (1876), but it was about the *real* population of Dorset. The real and fictional realms were fused together, from the moment Wessex was named.

Hardy's time in Wimborne was a fruitful one. People came, by train from London, to his normal, modern house. Others began to contact him as an expert in real, local matters. He joined the Dorsetshire Field Archaeology Society; he was sought out by the Society for the Protection of Ancient Buildings. He was persuaded – apparently reluctantly – to write his first factual essay. Perversely, Hardy's career and fame as a novelist was giving him influence in the real world. (Dickens discovered that same side-effect of fame.) 'The Dorsetshire Labourer' (1883) was Hardy's response to the debate about 'real' rural life.[7] It is long, ponderous but interesting,[8] describing the uprooting of rural workers through shifting hiring patterns, the end of 'life-hold' leases from land which their families had worked for centuries, and the great loss of local knowledge and human community which followed.

From 'The Dorsetshire Labourer' on, the reader would be able to thread facts from Hardy's essays straight in to the environment they would 'know' (already or soon) from the novels. An old man at the hiring fair is described, like the man hired by Farfrae in *The Mayor of Casterbridge* (1886); the eldest daughter of the family moving house at Lady-day cradles the family mirror on top of the wagon, like Bathsheba in *Far from the Madding Crowd* (1874); the ruthless clearing of the cottages as life-hold leases fall due expands on the stories in *Desperate Remedies* (1871), *The Mayor of Casterbridge* (1886), *The Woodlanders* (1887), *Tess* (1891), and many others. *The Woodlanders* described the disappearance of this age when the country-dweller:

> ... must know all about those invisible ones of the days gone by, whose feet have traversed the fields which look so grey from his windows; recall whose creaking plough has turned these sods from time to time; whose hands planted the trees that form a crest to the opposite hill ...[9]

The rural labourer, about to be given the vote, was of fresh interest to the magazine-reading middle class and Hardy was putting the realities of Wessex firmly on record; teasing his readers; correcting their assumptions. He talks of one wily cottage woman, saying:

> 'I always kip a white apron behind the door to slip on when gentlefolk knock, for if so be they see a white apron, they think ye be clane' an honest woman

said one day whose bedroom floors could have been scraped with as much advantage as a pigeon loft ...[10]

Meanwhile another, whose 'natural thrift' included maintaining her cottage beautifully was considered 'a frightful example of slovenliness' because the gentry mistook her clean and practical burnt umber coloured clothes and furnishing for dirt.[11] (The 'burnt umber' is specific; perhaps Jemima Hardy is implicated.) The cunning white aprons appear in Casterbridge too, wrapped around the seller of furmity (a kind of porridge), spiked with contraband rum 'extending an air of respectability around her as far as it went'; and on the women hanging around doorways at the sleazy end of Casterbridge. Hardy (like Kegan Paul) was pointing out how easily urbanites could be fooled by a knowing rural population.

Hardy was so selective about writing factual articles that it is worth noting the territory he covered. There were articles on Dorset, on social history and archaeological discoveries, on traditional construction and materials – all detailed, practical, social and imaginative. Many deal with abstract ideas about imagination, notably 'The Profitable Reading of Fiction' (1888), an amazing piece of writing. Often the physical and conceptual are tied together, as in Hardy's beautiful essay on the Portland stone used to build London itself, memorably describing the tide beating against the stone of St Paul's Cathedral.[12] The writings are pungent, detailed, sometimes ponderous, sharply visualised, intensely informative, and each with their own solidly expressed argument. And taken together, they describe the outline of Wessex itself: a social, physical, material, human, environmental, historical entity – taking a coherent, experimental form in the modern world. They are typically read as 'simple' facts (as Hardy intended) – and their carefully curated extensions to the construction and structure of Wessex, in fact and fiction, therefore, are often overlooked. For the *published* factual writings almost all tie directly into the novels. When those 'Romano-British' graves (actually Palaeolithic) were found during the building of Max Gate, Hardy gave a paper to the Dorset Natural History and Antiquarian Field Club[13] but those bodies, more famously, turned up in fictional Casterbridge:

Casterbridge announced old Rome in every street, alley, and precinct. It looked Roman, bespoke the art of Rome, concealed dead men of Rome. It was impossible to dig more than a foot or two deep about the town fields and gardens without coming upon some tall soldier ... He was mostly found lying on his side, in a[n] oval scoop in the chalk, like a chicken in its shell; his knees drawn up to his chest ...[14]

This constant cross-referencing between fiction and fact was not because he was short of material: far from it. The notebooks – especially the one started now,

'Facts from Newspapers, Histories, Biographies & other Chronicles (mainly local sources)' – are stuffed with anecdotes, few of which turn up in his fiction. Note that title. The notebook gives *all* kinds of written and spoken information equivalent status as 'facts': a strong, polemical point.

The control of histories, now, is seen as something determined by the powerful, since 'facts' (effectively things which have been repeatedly asserted and published) depend on the status of those asserting them and their access to forms of media. 'Is not the quasi-scientific system of writing history mere charlatanism?', said Hardy.[15] His notebook's title runs through the whole range of academic 'reliability' from word of mouth to written history. He gives them all equivalent status – and he writes them himself. I am not suggesting he was making them up, but that he was suggesting that this is how, more or less, *everything* gets made up. History 'legitimising arguments', as Forty says.[16]

The name Wessex is important too. It described the Saxon kingdom, united by King Alfred, against the Danes. This was the beginning of England, of written English in law and the *Anglo Saxon Chronicles*. Wessex had already been re-adopted by the Dorset dialect poet, teacher and preacher William Barnes, but Hardy too is continuing something already in place: language, law, lore, history, England, English writing, poetry and place. The name alone triggers a sense of continuity, as an early commentator would write.[17]

Hardy began to use this name more deliberately. He re-edited his earlier novels, so that the fictional places were consistent. All the villages and towns, such as Swanage (Knollsea), Bournemouth (Sandbourne), and even Dorchester (Casterbridge), which had their own names, or other pseudonyms, in earlier novels – were changed for *The Mayor of Casterbridge* and used from then on. The earlier novels were revised to match, whenever the opportunity arose, so that Hardy's imagined Wessex became increasingly coherent, between and beyond the novels – and more obviously connected to the real countryside. Unlike many famous, later fictional worlds (for example, Narnia and Middle Earth), Wessex gained its identity the moment it seemed, debatably, to be *real*. This was becoming a deliberate, fictional surrogate for the *actual* older Dorset; his parents' and grandparents' world, which Hardy could see his own world erasing and which those early critics no longer recognised. It was a fully coherent, working, imaginary world, extracted from a real place and memories of the past.

It is worth stressing the *oddness* of Hardy's Wessex. Unlike other famous settings (George Eliot's Loamshire and Trollope's Barsetshire, for example), Hardy drew Wessex; he mapped it, and gave it a detailed coherence outside and between the novels. It made little difference to the stories themselves, but he continued doing it throughout his life, long after the last novel was written. And its sense of purpose was deliberate. In his 'real' account of the Max Gate excavations, Hardy says:

> It would be a worthy attempt to rehabilitate, on paper, the living Durnovaria
> of fourteen or fifteen hundred years ago – as it actually appeared to the eyes
> of the then Dorchester men and women, under the rays of the same morning
> and evening sun which rises and sets over it now ...[18]

By 1890, when this was published, that was *exactly* what Hardy had been doing (although for a later period of history), for at least eight years. From the 1880s on, the factual and fictional Wessex cannot be prised apart.

*

To anyone used to architecture's experimental books, this feels familiar. It is not so much related to the imaginary visual designed places, often Utopian or idealistic as it is to architecture's analytical, critical books: *AS in DS*, or *Learning From Las Vegas*. The closest comparison may even be another, hugely influential 1970s project. In 1978 a Dutch journalist screenwriter-turned-architect (he had also recently left the AA), published a strange book, drawn from his time in the architectural research Deconstructivist hotbed of New York. *Delirious New York* is a speculative research project recovering the history of Manhattan and Coney Island's remarkable ad hoc development; of its fabric of skyscrapers and amusement parks which were all – at the time – considered beneath 'architectural' notice.[19]

Rem Koolhaas recovered masses of original drawings and photographs, reconstructing and redrawing this lost past. He developed the argument that Coney Island – with its theme park incubators for real premature babies and dwarf firefighters – became a subliminal testing ground of urban experience, which had subconsciously shaped the congested, thrilling dramatic form taken by New York itself. Like Venturi and Scott Brown, he was reading architectural meaning out of a found, and overlooked and important place.

Subtitled *A Retroactive Manifesto for Manhattan*, this was not a work of theory. It was a piece of speculative architectural interpretative work, by a youngish architect, using design methods as a form of speculative research: reading pictures, texts, drawings and places; using the freedoms that books can offer architects; and ending with surrealist paintings (which had actually been made first) by himself and his partners in the Office for Metropolitan Architecture.

Koolhaas was partly exploring the *methods* of experimental architectural projects, creating his own 'project' of assembled evidence. Drawings, photographs, plans, maps and other accounts of buildings were arranged, reconfigured, assembled and re-read to find an imaginative strategic and building pattern in the remarkable form of New York. Koolhaas describes this as Salvador Dali's 'Paranoid-Critical method';

it is also very like the way TV detectives assemble pictures on the wall to work out patterns of behaviour. It is the blueprint of architecture's 'projects' and 'crits'; of versions of 'research by practice'; the method used to generate this book; and the technique Hardy himself, in 1882, describes himself using. He says:

> As in looking at a carpet, by following one colour a certain pattern is suggested, by following another colour, another, so in life the seer should watch that pattern among general things which his idiosyncrasy moves him to observe, and describe that alone. This is, quite accurately, a going to Nature; yet the result is no mere photography, but purely the product of the writer's own mind.[20]

Delirious New York is a disturbingly predictive book, with its focus on firefighting, disaster, collapse and on New York's Twin Towers, then just newly completed. It foresaw a new love of congested urbanism which would fuel our own times. Projects like this, looking into the past or present through new ways of seeing, *are* predictive. As Alison Smithson suggested, that is what they are for.[21] Koolhaas would go on to become a famous architect on any terms,[22] but this book was how he became known.

Like Koolhaas, Hardy was slowly assembling his experimental, coherent, imaginary and polemic project, using the speculative freedoms books can give architects. He too was taking issue with his peers; assembling drawings, images, maps and photographs from which to construct his argument, to imagine the past, and, unexpectedly, to foresee the future.

*

The sense of being on the edge of things is sometimes called a key condition for inventive design practice[23] and it was fuelling Hardy now: 'Woke before it was light. Felt that I had not enough staying power to hold my own in the world.'[24] But his critical charge came from not fitting in.

> I find that a certain defect in my nature hinders me from working abreast with others of the same trade. Architecture was distasteful to me as soon as it became a shoulder to shoulder struggle – literature is likewise – & my only way of keeping up a zest for it is by not mixing with other workers of the same craft.[25]

The time at Wimborne seems to have been a creative period of Hardy's life[26] and, significantly, one when Hardy would have been doing a lot of drawing – a

Architecture reframed: the cinematic upview, *Wessex Poems*.

key way of thinking, for architects. He was designing Max Gate; he was visiting buildings for the SPAB; and he must have been developing those other drawing types too.

Two of the most beautiful of all the *Wessex Poems* illustrations describe this particular time. The 'Great September Comet' of 1882, one of the brightest ever seen, was visible until February 1883. Hardy describes in *Two on a Tower* how it grows in vision, from 'the as-yet minute tadpole of fire' which Swithin watches (like Hardy?) from his bedroom window,[27] to 'the nucleus of the fiery plume that now filled so large a space of the sky as to completely dominate it'.[28] It was a turning point for Swithin St Cleeve; perhaps Hardy, too.

Only two photographs of the comet are known to exist,[29] but this too could be a traced photograph, perhaps a tracing from window glass; even a camera lucida, set up in a window (the rear top windows of Lanherne would face towards the Minster). It is lovely, a pre-cinematographic widescreen crop; and obsessive: look at the detail with which he inked in the night sky (the cropped skyline of Wimborne seen just at the bottom of the picture). It looks (as comets do) like a picture of time and space itself; the very vision of frozen time which, as John Berger says in *Ways of Seeing*, 'changed the way men saw'.[30]

And the other star of the *Wessex Poems* too: the beautiful Hitchcock-like crop which seems to describe the spires of the Minster. Think of *Desperate Remedies* and *Vertigo*, the vision of fainting, falling; the view up at the towers and into the sky. (The tower Hitchcock showed was actually *built* to reproduce the *fake* one constructed for the film.) And again, that drawing may have been traced or set out by camera lucida, for its outline suggests Wimborne, but its arcading and detail do not. Perhaps if it is the Minster, Hardy made the outline, like those other curious outlines, and filled the detail in later for the *Wessex Poems*.

If so, this is a telephoto view. But there *was* such a thing as a 'graphic telescope'; a long-lens version of the camera lucida. And Hardy would go on to develop, with Hermann Lea, a remarkable long-lens camera. In fact, he was in correspondence with the Royal Observatory at Greenwich, at exactly this time, obtaining details of how to construct the observatory in *Two on a Tower*, describing its arrival and installation.

However he made them, for an architect these pictures are incontrovertible evidence of Hardy's experimental thinking. If the one with the coffin being carried downstairs shows Hardy stretching technical vision, to see the architectural workings of life and death in the 1860s, his pictures relating to this time show us an experimentally framed and captured architect's drawing of vision itself. The ambition, the representational reach of Wessex is changing its shape and appearance. Hardy is imagining in new ways: you can *see* it.

*

Back in 1882, Hardy sat up late discussing ideas. One visitor was his old friend Henry Moule, now a co-member of the Dorset Natural History and Antiquarian Field Club, about to become the first director of the Dorset County Museum. Emma suggested they produce a history of Dorset using Moule's words and Hardy's illustrations. Hardy said it would not sell.[31] Moule did go on to do this in his *Dorchester Antiquities* book of 1901 – which was indeed of minority interest. But Emma, too, was by no means wide of the mark. Hardy's living, popular, vastly influential history of Dorset was, effectively, well under way.

9

THE CHARACTER OF
THE STREETS

The Mayor of Casterbridge

What Hardy did then is well described. Michael Millgate says it was:

> ... part of a preconceived intention on Hardy's part to establish the fictional Casterbridge as a densely and concretely realised image of a busy market town, and to base that image firmly upon whatever research, imagination and personal memory could recover of the second quarter of the nineteenth century ... intimately related to its role as the social, economic and geographical centre of an entire Wessex world, hitherto evolved in a somewhat piecemeal fashion, now for the first time perceived and projected as distinct, integrated and autonomous.[1]

This was the heart of Hardy's project. Like the *Return*, the *Mayor's* medium was a very full, very complete description of a place (in this case, a town) fully constructed and imagined. But it was not esoteric; it was done principally by description, was anything but empty – and was immediately accessible. Work-folk gather outside the window of the King's Arms to discuss the local dignitaries; groups of ladies or schoolchildren squeeze into cross-passages through the houses to avoid bulls on market days; planks are laid across the stream at Mixen Lane to bring in illicit goods; grimy stains have been made by generations of customers in the pubs. The town of his youth in the 1840s and 1850s – as reconstructed by Hardy – comes vividly to life in astonishing, detailed form.

*

In June 1883, the Hardys moved briefly into Dorchester, the town where Hardy had first worked as an architect. He was actively collecting that local 'factual' material. He had always drawn on family stories and experiences, but this was more concerted.

He talked to old inhabitants, visited places, read the *Dorset County Chronicle*, used the newly opened library of the Field Club.[2] And there was the place itself. One of their first visitors, Edmund Gosse, described the town:

> ... extremely bright and pretty; there are two barracks just outside it, one cavalry, one infantry, so that the narrow streets are full of colour and animation, & being a country town, the farmers and labourers were crowding in to their Saturday night's shopping, so it looked in the dusk like a bright foreign town ... Hardy & I continued to walk in & out of the town, and round the old walls ... avenued with chestnuts, until 10.30, by the light of the moon.[3]

The Hardys had rented Colliton House, a large, rambling, half-forgotten house, now in a backwater, but once the middle of town (an impressive Roman villa was later uncovered nearby). This is where a few lucky readers were to visit Hardy 'in the nice house';[4] in a richly present past. Colliton House turns up as High-Place Hall, the temporary home of Lucetta and Elizabeth-Jane; the busy market place, the hirings, new machinery and wrangles between hay-wagons of the past were all vividly imagined from those quiet windows.

It has its own architectural commentary too:

Colliton House/High-Place Hall,
Hermann Lea.

It had in the first place, the characteristics of a country mansion – birds' nests in its chimneys, damp nooks where fungi grew and irregularities of surface direct from Nature's trowel. At night the forms of passengers were patterned by the lamps in black shadows on the pale walls ... the architecture deserved admiration, or at least study, on its own account. It was Palladian, and like most architecture erected since the Gothic age was a compilation rather than a design. But it's reasonableness made it impressive. It was not rich, but rich enough. A timely consciousness of the ultimate vanity of human architecture, no less than of other things, had prevented artistic superfluity.[5]

Hardy could not help thinking architecturally at this time. Max Gate was on site; and as we will see, so was the Dorset County Museum of which he is called a 'founder'; and he was busy for the Society for the Protection of Ancient Buildings too. He was actively thinking about the built substance and intelligence of the vanishing past: how it worked and changed what people could do. Walking to site at Max Gate took him right past St Peter's Church (which he had worked on for Hicks), as well as the emerging Museum building and Hicks's old office. One way or another, architecture was all around him. He was immersed in it. He was right on site.

*

Here is part of the *Mayor*'s famous opening:

> What was really peculiar, however, in this couple's progress ... was the perfect silence they preserved. They walked side by side in such a way as to suggest afar off the low, easy, confidential chat of people full of reciprocity; but on closer view it could be discerned that the man was reading, or pretending to read, a ballad sheet which he kept before his eyes with some difficulty ... the woman enjoyed no society whatever from his presence. Virtually she walked the highway alone, save for the child she bore.[6]

This is definitive Hardy: we *watch* these imagined people, in this imagined place, for a long time. And by seeing them, we understand the tense relationship between them. We absorb the concentrate of the story through watching the highly crafted pictures that Hardy makes for us (and tells us how to interpret) in our heads.

But picking out 'classic' Hardy scenes can give a misleading, over-resolved view, shifting attention away from the extreme *variety* of his work. The *Mayor* is vastly different from *A Laodicean*, *Two on a Tower* or the *Return* – not only in tone or in sentence structure, but in ways of making us see; and in architectural characteristics and content.

This 'typical' description belies an extraordinary range of descriptive writing which is personal to *The Mayor of Casterbridge*; there is nothing quite like it anywhere else in Hardy's work, just as the descriptions and sentence structures of *The Woodlanders* remain deeply personal to that novel. Each book has a base fabric of its own: its distinct colour, flavour, sound, word-pattern, rhythm and scale. And in the *Mayor*, an extraordinary body of different types of description start flooding through the book from the moment we reach the town with Elizabeth-Jane and her mother.

> 'What an old-fashioned place it seems to be!' said Elizabeth-Jane while her silent mother mused on other things than topography. 'It is all huddled together; and it is shut in by a square wall of trees, like a plot of garden in a box-edging.'

The Dorchester town map of 1772 suggesting the 'Box of Dominoes'.

If Elizabeth-Jane and her mother had come straight from Weydon Priors (Weyhill, in Hampshire) they should have walked down Stinsford Hill – but Dorchester would not seem square from there. Instead, Hardy makes them arrive randomly via the higher ground of Max Gate itself – just as he had described the 'worthy enterprise' of re-imagining Durnovaria:

> Standing for instance on the elevated ground near where the South-western station is at present ... we may ask what kind of object did Dorchester then form when viewed in the summer landscape from such a point, where stood the large buildings, where the small, how did the roofs group themselves, what were the gardens like, if any, what social character had the streets ...?[7]

The *Mayor* does just this:

> Its squareness was, indeed, the characteristic which most struck the eye in this antiquated borough, the borough of Casterbridge – at that time, recent as it was, untouched by the faintest sprinkle of modernism. It was compact as a box of dominoes. It had no suburbs – in the ordinary sense. Country and town met at a mathematical line.[8]

Wessex Poems illustrations can be arranged to form
storyboards for many parts of Hardy's novels.

You can *see* that box of dominoes quite clearly in the Town Map of 1772.[9] The spots on the garden-plots are trees, but they give exactly that domino effect to the closely packed plots of land. 'To birds of the more soaring kind, Casterbridge must have appeared on this fine evening as a mosaic-work of subdued reds, browns, greys, and crystals, held together by a rectangular frame of deep green ...'[10] The normal viewer, Hardy says, coming down to earth, would just see the enclosing trees. But then he refocuses again to a Ruskinian *architectural* vision:

> The mass became gradually dissected by the vision into towers, gables, chimneys and casements, the highest glazings shining bleared and bloodshot with the coppery fire they caught from the belt of sunlit cloud in the west.[11]

This is very close to Ruskin's imaginary travellers[12] who: 'from the long-hoped-for turn in the dusty perspective of the causeway, saw, for the first time, the towers of some famed city, faint in the rays of sunset',[13] or the glowing pinnacles of Venice. But Hardy's sunset visions are *better* than Ruskin's: more forensic, more abstract *and* more socially engaged. And they would reach a far wider audience. In *The Mayor of Casterbridge*, Hardy reached a whole new level of evocative description, using new tactics as well as old, architectural as well as popular.

That wonderful opening description of the town keeps changing, becoming more varied, more sensory and immersive. He *tells* us that the town ramparts were replanted as promenades, but he *describes* how the women move on though the dark tunnel of trees as 'they passed down a midnight between two gloamings'.

He moves us on, describing the town, snug and comfortable, its lamps starting to glimmer, a brass band heard in the distance; then he gives a quick, rich survey of the houses, architecture and furnishings alike:

> ... timber houses with overhanging storeys, whose small-paned lattices were screened by dimity curtains on a drawing-string, and under whose barge-boards cobwebs waved in the breeze. There were houses of brick-nogging, which

derived their chief support from those adjoining, there were slate roofs patched with tiles and tile roof patched with slate, with occasionally a roof of thatch.[14]

'Most of these old houses have now been pulled down', he adds in the 1912 footnotes. Then comes a list of items on sale in the shops:

Scythes, reap-hooks, sheep-shears, bill-hooks, spades, mattocks, and hoes at the ironmongers; bee-hives, butter-firkins, churns, milking stools and pails, hay-rakes, field flagons, and seed-lips at the cooper's; cart-ropes and plough-harness at the saddler's; carts, wheel-barrows, and mill gear at the wheelwright's and machinist's; horse-embrocations at the chemist's; at the glovers and leather-cutters, hedging gloves, thatcher's knee-caps, ploughmen's leggings, villager's pattens and clogs.[15]

This is one of his specifications: a written, precise list of the things we need to imagine to recreate the richness of the town. He walks us on through the darkening, illuminated streets, past the church with mortar joints 'nibbled out by time and weather' housing 'little tufts of stone crop and grass almost half way up' the tower (this could be old All Saints, or St Peters). The bell starts ringing: the eight o'clock 'curfew'; time to close the shops. The clatter of shutters mixes with other bells: from the gaol, the almshouses, a row of 'case clocks' in the clockmakers, and the stammering chimes of the Sicilian Mariners' Hymn ('long since silenced' by 1912), so that the clocks 'of the advanced school were well on their way to the next hour before the business of the old one was satisfactorily wound up'.[16] And finally, to the King's Arms where the town band 'was now shaking the windows', and a group of idlers discussing the terrible quality of the bread, sold by the corn factor Mayor, heading the grand dinner inside. The window, they say, is left uncovered 'that we may get jist a sense o't out here'. The whole sequence – five pages of delicious reading – gives us a *mass* of information – as real travellers absorb it, using all our human, animal environmental senses to understand the place in the 'mind's eye'.

Casterbridge is so well described, so sensory, and so easy to read, that it feels *less* architectural than the odder novels. But look how he constructs it – how he sets out plan, history, overview, vision, urban fabric, building materials, detailed descriptions of the houses, layouts and fittings, gardens, plants, archaeology and the whole urban plan – one of the few architectural texts on Hardy is about it.[17] And yet it is overtly human; by no means specialised. You can get into Casterbridge by sheer osmosis.

Hardy is working as architectural tutors have been observed to do using body language to describe familiar and famous buildings,[18] or as Garbett suggests, 'teaching' his audience about architecture.[19] He is describing things he *knows* the audience will be able to imagine, and slipping all kinds of architectural knowledge into it. Like Egdon Heath – perhaps even more so – the *place* is arguably the main character: Casterbridge is the most living, vibrant, cheerful thing in the novel. That intense social character is unique to this book; its strong, human quality of rubbing shoulders with the inhabitants of the town. We keep seeing things from natural human viewpoints, usually Elizabeth-Jane's. We squeeze onto the steps with her to watch the Mayor and councillors at dinner through the bow window. We peep round the settles in the Three Mariners with her to hear Farfrae charm the pub-goers. We open the hinged window casement and lean out into the September morning – that stretch of the arm feels like ours too.

> When Elizabeth-Jane opened the hinged casement next morning the mellow air brought in the feel of autumn almost as distinctly as if she had been in the remotest hamlet. Casterbridge was the complement of the rural life around; not its urban opposite. Bees and butterflies in the cornfields at the top of the town, who desired to get to the meads at the bottom, took no circuitous course, but flew straight down the High Street without any apparent consciousness that they were traversing strange latitudes ...[20]

This is unusual for Hardy. It is that great jostling crowd of people, buildings and the sensory pleasures that gives the *Mayor* its sense of cheerful life and continuity despite the self-destructiveness of its main figure. We are *not* in the vast landscapes of *The Return* or of *Tess*, and the book has a warm, intelligent humanity, an empathy, which (one often forgets) is deep in the fabric of Wessex. This is Hardy's easiest, most fluid writing. You scarcely see Casterbridge; you absorb it through every sensory mode possible: people, townscape, landscape, detail, architecture, modes of life, agriculture, jobs, weather, money, views, clothes, furniture, insects, scents, tools, prophecies, dust, pubs, clocks, songs; the peculiar misery of a washed-out fairground; the excitement of market-days. To speak personally, the more I re-read Hardy, the more I realised that my whole idea of rural England was structured, illustrated and animated by thousands of tiny fragments like these of Hardy's novels.

I do not think I am alone, or that this is an accident. *The Mayor of Casterbridge* was clearly, successfully, aimed at a mass family audience. It had only a few, and minor, of the painful or shocking episodes of the later novels. It is enjoyable, but also vastly informative. As Millgate says, it shows *exactly* how the countryside and its towns had once worked together: the relationship of different working people, the effects of weather and harvest, of festivals and market-days, of good and bad business, affecting a whole working society.[21]

Bringing the town of the past to life is *exactly* what Hardy described in that paper to the Dorset Natural History and Antiquarian Field Club; the 'worthy enterprise' of imagining the town 'as it actually appeared to the eyes of the then Dorchester men and women'.[22] It was his *intention* to make us imagine the town of the past, and he would underline that in 1888, in 'The Profitable Reading of Fiction'. He intended his readers to 'know' this other place and time.

And despite the ambitious and polemic ideas behind it, this is the *opposite* of what the architectural profession tends to do. Casterbridge is the easiest to read of his novels: shorter sentences; immersive, immediate descriptions. But the profession (of his age and ours), has tended to downgrade descriptive writing, as the architectural historian Adrian Forty says,[23] and to build up specialised or theoretical texts instead – precisely to form its professional barriers.[24]

Hardy – though he could lay theory and complexity on with a trowel – is using empowering, descriptive writing here. He is recalling a sense of buildings based on our simplest, oldest environmental senses. He is operating at a level which architecture has abandoned to its own great loss: where description connects with the sensory, where imagined places offer another, older way of knowing about the world and the people we share it with.

*

Casterbridge is, in fact, surely one of the great descriptions of a town in fiction or in history. He was not (apparently) theorising about it. But he was using all kinds of architectural tools to describe it; not least the coherent, detailed sense of how it actually worked. It was the heart of his rich, everyday working model of the past. He remained deeply engaged with its existence in reality, down to becoming, like Henchard, a magistrate himself, and arguing for the reinstatement of original street-names (citing the disappointment of American tourists at the arbitrary new naming of old places). When he was given the Freedom of the Town in 1910, he replied that he had, 'through the medium of the printing press', made very free with it already.[25]

And in doing so, he gave the town a working sense of its own identity, which has survived the ring roads and the demolitions. The green walks survived the 1960s – while other market towns carved one-way systems, as did the lavish display of goods from the ironmongers or the cheery traditional cafe under Hicks's old office, which claims 'even Hardy would have been pleased'. It is hard to know if it will survive the Prince of Wales's large, surreal new urban appendage of Poundbury, but I am sure Hardy would have been fascinated. The older town was often-photographed too. Draper and Fowles's wonderful book shows photographs (some by Lea) of many of the things Hardy described which have since vanished: the cattle in the street, the barns by the church and by the Dorset County Museum itself. Dorchester's identity has been, demonstrably, strengthened – because it is also Casterbridge; as 'someone' told Hardy, 'a place more Dorchester than Dorchester itself'.[26] A world-famous, partly real, partly imaginary place. And one which was part of a new phase of deliberate, professional, 'real' architectural work as well.

THE WESSEX CAMPAIGN

Conservation and Fiction

In the short timeline of its history, The Society for Protection of Ancient Buildings' website notes: '1927: Thomas Hardy, novelist and architect, dies. He had been a very committed SPAB caseworker and worked particularly hard protecting churches in the West Country.'[1] The date is wrong,[2] but that headline status tells us something about Hardy's influence on the English conservation movement. A level of influence which remains almost entirely unrecognised – and which keeps operating to this day.

Back in Wimborne in 1881, Charles Kegan Paul had introduced him to SPAB as: 'a man who would be thoroughly in sympathy with our society.'[3] He suggested that Hardy might keep an eye on the restoration of Wimborne Minster, a few minutes' walk from Lanherne. Kegan Paul, who wrote 'The Wessex Labourer' and helped Hardy complete *A Laodicean*, always seems active in the 'real' and 'architectural' potential of Wessex; and Hardy's various collaborations are worth watching.

Hardy replied: 'with the greatest pleasure – for I am entirely in sympathy with its movements. I ought however to add that my influence here is nil – I am only a temporary resident ...'[4] That is important: Hardy is immediately considering the matter of influence. SPAB had no official status: by this date (Christopher Miele says) it had only had an arguable effect in a handful of cases and 'even in these I am not convinced that the Society won on a level playing field'.[5] The Town and Country Planning Act would not exist until 1947. SPAB could only seek, in polite and 'gentlemanly' fashion, to *persuade* clients, vicars or 'benefactors' driving these damaging, well-meaning projects, to change their minds.

Hardy invited the Secretary to tea at his 'cottage'[6] on the way to the Minster. He got on well with the architect in charge, Walter Fletcher: they were both members of the new Dorset Natural History and Antiquarian Field Club. Fletcher wrote thanking SPAB for the 'deputation's useful hints' (that sounds like Hardy). He accepted the 'list of recommendations as to the best way of preventing any further failure' (a potential bombshell), 'in a very friendly spirit, and accepted and carried out the Society's scheme, with the happy result that up to the present time, there has been no sign of any further damage'.[7] It was a modest, little-celebrated and significant start.

Because of the huge success of the conservation movement in Britain, it is hard to remember what a mountainous job SPAB faced. One of their first major campaigns was to protect St Mark's Basilica in Venice from demolition. Making sure Stonehenge survived was a later campaign (in which Hardy would play a part). Kegan Paul's own book *Memories* (1899), shows a fragment of the incredible state of the problem. Describing his own childhood in Writhlington, Somerset in the 1830s and 1840s, he says:

> In the chancel were the monuments to the Goldfinch family ... in the vaults below were their coffins mouldering to decay. On the walls was an ominous green slime ... a ray of light struck from the windows through the said holes to the bulging coffins and showed us their nauseous state ...[8]

This would change with astonishing speed. A century later conservation was embedded in British culture, with 'one of the furthest-reaching legal systems of architectural conservation to be found anywhere in the world'.[9] Heritage had become 'commonplace', says Michael Hunter. And he notes a curious, unexplained boom in conservation consciousness around the 1890s[10] just as Hardy's work became really famous.

And perhaps Hardy's role in this has been severely underrated. He is not mentioned in the usual conservation histories; after all, he was 'just' a novelist. The detailed study of his conservation work was done by Beatty (a scholar of Modern Languages) and the wealth of things he found out have not been much analysed by architectural writers. And especially not by *modern* architectural writers, who might see conservation itself as a contested, debatable, fast-changing construct;[11] and who might consider whether Wessex was also the greatest, most influential and forward-looking conservation campaign of them all.

For in 1881, SPAB had gained an astute, informed and critical supporter. Hardy was truly well-informed, technically skilled, modest, disingenuous and very shrewd, and he could turn out a detailed specification on the spot. He was already a well-known novelist, with a very ambitious, creative attitude to his work – and direct access to the public, through a diffuse and powerful medium.

*

You could hardly get more powerful PR for the early conservation movement than Casterbridge. It is exquisitely described everywhere: dusty, detailed and alive. The shape of the town; the promenades of trees around it; the shop fronts jutting onto the pavements used as livestock pens on market days; the cross-passages leading into the scented gardens; the items on sale in the streets; the dust; the petty crime; the shifting seasons; the haymaking; the lamplight and furniture; the rooms, the streets, the yards and the barns; the clothes; the wagons in the street; the bells and clocks; the songs and music from pubs and churches. This is the substance of the utterly convincing sense of being in a busy, human, real working town.

To *us*, Hardy's fantastic evocation of the past seems normal. But in *Hardy's* day, this empathetic position was radical. The vernacular was only applauded in certain forms. Ruskin actually *condemns* English vernacular: the 'formalised deformities' of the market towns of Kent;[12] the way of building 'like frogs or mice'.[13] The sense of a vanished past; working through sympathetic feeling for continued, human use of objects and places; the value of the stories attached to them and embedded in conservation legislation have all since become really fundamental to English culture. And that, I am suggesting, is just what Hardy set out to do.

SPAB were normally dealing with the high-end, high-art side of restoration. Hardy's correspondence with SPAB almost entirely describes *churches* rotting, falling down, overtaken by ivy, with enthusiastic patrons, vicars and architects straining at the leash to modernise them, and Hardy and SPAB chivvying, coaxing, and suggesting better, lesser works: to patch, repoint, strap up, drain – and leave a lot of things alone.

Hardy was a real expert on church restoration, and would keep on doing it himself: West Knighton (1893–1894) is his definitive job. He had even worked on St Peter, the main church in Dorchester, for Hicks (the plan drawing is his). But in *The Mayor*, churches scarcely get a look-in: we barely even see the three weddings in the book. SPAB was *already* working on saving the churches. What *Hardy* was prioritising, through his now factually-extended fiction, was the *vernacular*, right down to cottages of a type almost written out of history.

So we see Henchard's rich, wonderful but unfashionable house with its fabulous, scented garden, its cross-passage, its rich furnishings and its working yards behind; Lucetta's neglected but engaging High-Place Hall, but also all kinds of lesser houses, too, down to the very poorest, like the place where Henchard is finally given shelter by Abel Whittle:

> ... they approached what was of humble dwelling surely the humblest. The walls, built of kneaded clay originally faced with a trowel, had been worn by years of rain-washings to a lumpy, crumbling surface, channelled and sunken

from its plane, its gray rents held together here and there by a leafy strap of ivy which could scarcely find substance enough for the purpose. The rafters were sunken, and the thatch of the roof in ragged holes ...[14]

Buildings like these would be cleared as slums until well into the 1960s and 1970s, but would now be recognised as part of the precious substance of built human history. If Wessex was deliberately revising the myths Hardy's urban readers believed about rural people, he was now, increasingly, doing it about the buildings, the towns, the way the whole environment worked, and what it was like.

And we are *still* startlingly ignorant. Tomalin calls the Hardy's house at Higher Bockhampton a 'cottage', as many of us tend to: it is pretty and thatched; and the implication is that Hardy was trying to advance his family's status by calling it a house.[15]

But Hardy was right. In *The Truth About Cottages*, and drawing on Victorian surveys, John Woodforde shows that what we now see as 'cottages' were enviable dwellings for the rural middle classes.[16] True cottages were one or two-roomed hovels, built of scavenged materials, with mud floors, no chimneys, excrement (at best thrown out of doors), rooms shared by one or more families and their animals. 'At least three-quarters of all rural labourers' cottages were slums', says Woodforde, and they have not survived at all.[17] Literature had already joined in the 'joke' of calling modest country dwellings a 'cottage'. The architectural historian Nikolaus Pevsner alludes to Jane Austen's description of the Dashwoods' house in *Sense and Sensibility* (1811) as 'a cottage ... was defective, for the building was regular, the roof was tiled';[18] the younger Musgroves in *Persuasion* (1816) live in a farmhouse that had been 'elevated into a cottage'. Hardy played this game too – but on the other side: calling both Max Gate and Lanherne a 'cottage for writing in'.

But in his *novels*, Hardy is utterly serious. The descriptions of the homes of the actual working poor, down to the elusive thatched hurdle shelters (which we will see in *The Woodlanders*), deliberately charted a reality which had been edited out of middle-class fiction and history. And it passed them on – in the newly authenticated, newly coherent Wessex – to a growing, popular and increasingly interested audience.

*

Even more remarkably, Hardy loves *pubs*. He was an abstemious man (although he liked cider), but pubs play key roles in all his later novels, especially *The Mayor of Casterbridge*, where they denote and facilitate the social climb and slide of his key characters. It seems so natural now – the pub as the heart of English rural life – that it is hard to imagine how provocative this was. Pubs were then a contentious area of shifting legislation and public attitudes, seen more like drug dens than the valued social places we imagine today. The Garden City movement (dating from 1898, but already latent in Arts & Crafts and reforming groups) would plan and build towns and suburbs deliberately *without* pubs, precisely to establish a healthy environment for working people.

But in *The Mayor*, all the major social events take place in pubs. The peak of Henchard's career and the beginning of his decline at the King's Arms Inn; the arrival of Farfrae and the chorus of town characters in the cheerful Three Mariners; the exposure of Lucetta and Henchard's love letters, the return of the long-lost Newson and planning the skimmity ride at the rough end of town, Peter's Finger. Hardy is making a clear but radical point: except for the cheerful, non-aligned singing in the west end of churches, the centre of social life is not there. It is in the pubs. All three pubs receive excellent, generous treatment, especially the lower class ones. Two appear under their own names,[19] the highest Wessex status of all. (The third name comes from Lytchett Matravers, nearer the coast: it derives from the story of St Peter the fisherman and a gold ring: the implication being that this is a den of thieves[20]).

The King's Arms is the grandest (and the only one with a remaining original in Dorchester – a staple of any Hardy town trail), but we only see it from *outside*, rubbing shoulders with the watchers on the (vanished) steps opposite. Yet, we get pages and pages of *wonderful* descriptions of the Three Mariners – a pub already demolished when Hardy wrote the book:

> This ancient house of accommodation for man and beast, now, unfortunately, pulled down, was built of mellow sandstone, with mullioned windows of the same material, markedly out of perpendicular from the settlement of the foundations. The bay window projecting into the street ... was closed with shutters, in each of which appeared a heart-shaped aperture ...[21]

We are shown the pub (and its 'worthy' occupants, seen through the shutters) in loving detail. The flat-as-a-shadow, cracked, faded, revered, pub sign; the four-centred entrance arch (ogive) to the narrow access passage where pedestrians and horses 'rubbed shoulders indiscriminately' suffering damaged toes in search of the good ale and good stabling. We are told how its landlord and landlady aim 'to compensate for the antique awkwardness, crookedness and obscurity of the passages, floors and windows', with 'dazzling' quantities of clean linen; about the brewing equipment; and that the 'intrusive beams and rafters, partitions, passages, staircases, disused ovens, settles and four-posters, left comparatively small quarters for human beings'.[22]

The Three Mariners. Left: Robert Barnes' illustration (and a
Robert Burns song); right, Hardy's retrospective sketch.

The black 'settles', in the bar, behind which Elizabeth-Jane hides to hear Farfrae
charm the locals with his Robert Burns songs are exquisitely drawn by Robert Barnes
(he and Hardy must have enjoyed the pun). Social architecture *and* a well-known
song: Hardy has devised a lyrical multimedia experience – somewhere between
Dutch 'vulgar' pictures and the singing of Irish emigrants in *Brooklyn* (2015). Hardy
drew the Three Mariners too, for publication, and in Casterbridge we keep coming
back to it – as we would in person, if only we could. As Beatty says (of another
pub), Hardy is immortalising a vanished piece of the fabric of the world, in potent
fictional form.

There is almost as much information about Peter's Finger in Mixen Lane,[23] a
pub so dubious most of his readers would never have dreamed of going near it. Its
neat, sanded, unused front door; its grimy, rubbed alleyway entrance into which
passers-by apparently disappeared; its rumbling skittle alley; its settles tied up to the
ceiling to stop them falling over when things got rowdy, its plank bridges brought
out to help smugglers bring illicit drink across the river; its women hanging around
in doorways with those suspicious white aprons.

Constables pursuing the perpetrators of the skimmity ride are confounded:
'In the settles of the large room, guyed to the ceiling by cords as usual for
stability, an ordinary group sat drinking and smoking with statuesque quiet
demeanour.' The landlady is caught putting a tambourine in the oven:
'"Ah," she said, apologetically, "that's what we keep here to use when there's
a little quiet dancing. You see damp weather spoils it, so I put it there to keep
it dry."'[24]

Mixen Lane/Fordington, Hermann Lea. The original framing
emphasises the murky environment.

Hardy makes us *love* those pubs, see them as ours, mourn and fume for their loss. This was certainly not the mainstream view – far from it. Just *imagine* the fastidious Ruskin in Peter's Finger.

This might have irked some ascetic colleagues in the anti-scrape movement. But since he did not label it conservation, or talk about architectural styles, or include any architects in the text, perhaps they did not notice.

Yet Casterbridge sits squarely in the middle of vernacular conservation thinking (as noted above, one of the rare discussions of Hardy in architectural books is about it[25]). Hardy's 1912 prefaces and footnotes would bitterly mention the destruction of much of the Dorchester vernacular since it was written, and in 1910 (receiving the Freedom of the Town), he would criticise Ferrey (not by name) for demolishing old All Saints because 'its buttresses projected too far into the pavement ... a milder-mannered man never scuttled a sacred edifice'.[26] In moving to Dorchester, writing about it, campaigning, Hardy had taken his own conservation campaign to heart and was working on it, consciously, in fact and fiction.

*

If it seems unlikely that Hardy's interplay of fictional and factual writing adds up to a deliberate conservation campaign, it is worth re-reading Beatty's work in detail, for its remarkable content, scrupulous discussion, and strong flavour of Hardy's way of working. While SPAB 'huff and puff', as Beatty shows,[27] Hardy talks people round. He flatters, he persuades, he plays down his own role. He does not lose his temper; he is disingenuous, and extremely resourceful.

In the Stratton case of 1889, Hardy alerts SPAB to 'rumours' of a restoration – asking for his and Henry Moule's names be kept out of it, as people might 'resent outside interference'. Nonetheless, he is telling them the head of the DCM and a famous novelist are strongly against it. This is delicate, behind-the-scenes work. Crickmay, the architect, tells SPAB that the tower is dangerous. Moule nudges SPAB to ask Hardy to send over a sketch. Hardy (who must have helped set this up) does so, showing the best feature – the stair with its linen-fold panelling – but asks for the sketch back. Crickmay, of course, might know the hand.

Hardy is always keeping just out of sight, but subtly shifting the balance. For all his pessimism, he has the architect's essentially optimistic search for an inventive solution. He backs Crickmay about structural and damp problems, advising SPAB that Crickmay is not unsympathetic. He proposes do-able modifications which would help: leaving the windows as found instead of re-spacing them regularly; putting in a proper damp-proof course instead of raising the floor and roof. He proposes doing *less* – a rare and underrated architectural ability; and a very important conservation one.

And he writes a brilliant draft letter for SPAB to send to the lead patron, Mrs Ashley, as the 'most influential member of the committee, and probably the most appreciative of the past history ...' He gives her a mass of interesting information, explains the significance of the old chancel arch with its two hagioscopes or 'squints', and offers beautifully quotable phrases: 'Irregularity is the genius of Gothic architecture.' He references G.E. Street's restoration at Bere Regis,[28] a nice *famous* architect's name to drop, however critical he would later be of Street. He stacks up ammunition to help her change her mind.

SPAB were less astute. They cut the best bits of the letter – and probably sent it only when Hardy (cannily) asked them to forward a copy to the Archbishop.[29] Hardy got an appreciation of the church published, by William Barnes' son Miles – another clergyman and 'Wessex' name. Then the Ecclesiastical Commissioners, fired up by the idea of a fresh restoration, weighed in – and the whole argument started over again.

Almost incredibly, the battle to keep the chancel wall was won – in theory. For the wider arch is there now. Beatty (naively), says 'quite simply, when work on unblocking it began, the old chancel arch was found to be too weak to stand unsupported'.[30] That sounds suspicious. Precious bits of well-studied, awkward heritage, do have a habit of proving unexpectedly 'unsound' when no-one is around.

Beatty's book is also rich in evidence suggesting Hardy was deliberately using his fiction as part of the campaign. The White Horse Inn, in Maiden Newton, another failed campaign of the late 1890s, has Hardy's fingerprints (perhaps literally) all over it. It was Hardy's old boss Crickmay who quietly notified SPAB that one of their clients, Weymouth brewers Devenish, were planning to knock down the fine Elizabethan building. Crickmay were *architects* for the project, so informing against their paying client was what Beatty calls 'public spirited' – in the extreme. I'm wondering what excellent impulse – or whose – prompted this extraordinarily disinterested action.

Hardy and Emma seem to have cycled straight over. Perhaps Hardy left Emma painting her watercolour outside (SPAB says 'even from a commercial point of view the front was most valuable'[31]) as a demonstration, while Hardy carefully examined the inn and talked to the irritated landlord. Hardy is carefully sympathetic. He scrupulously charts the problems to SPAB – 'roof, floors &c., are so bad that something must be done soon to keep the building together', the terrible condition of the upper rooms; 'the insurance of thatch is enormous'. He also gave the landlady a copy of his *Wessex Tales*, which mentions it as a fine Elizabethan building.

Hardy, Crickmay and SPAB all seem to propose workable compromises, all possibly coming from Hardy himself. Hardy (and SPAB, presumably quoting him) think the solution would be to keep the rooms at the front; sacrifice partition walls which are not original 'for instance, a fine, four-centred stone fireplace, that formerly warmed a large room, is now shut up in a small one'. He tries and fails

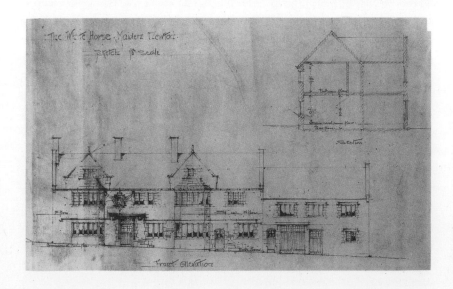

The White Horse, Maiden Newton. Unbuilt alternative scheme by Crickmay.

The White Horse, Maiden Newton. A blurred, 'action' photograph of
demolition showing the stripping of 5 feet of dusty thatch.

to talk the landlord out of his dogged requirement for high-ceilinged rooms, but
got him to say *exactly* how high he would regard as acceptable (1' 3" to the lower
rooms; 2' 6" to the front wall). These measurements appear on the alternative
scheme, purportedly by Crickmay, for a better rebuilding of the whole thing (a
device much used by our own latterday conservation campaigners[32]). Crickmay
would not have been paid for that work and the drawing style looks, at least
possibly, familiar: look at the little section, and the oddly hybrid handwriting.
The drawing, in fact, follows SPAB's/Hardy's brief: it is quite possibly his.

But the brewers weren't interested. The whole thing was pulled down, and
replaced.[33] There is a photographic account – a blurred action photograph of the
five feet of thick, dusty thatch being stripped and thrown down, and a carefully
saved shot of the distinctly poor modern replacement, now flats. SPAB's report
regretfully said: 'It might be thought that even from a commercial point of view,
the owners would have decided to retain the building, as there are many who spend
their holidays in travelling about to see buildings such as this ...'[34]

Beatty says this led to a specific course of action in Hardy's fiction. The building
had first appeared (anonymously) in the 1874 story 'Destiny and a Blue Cloak', then
in 1884 as The Pack Horse in 'Interlopers at the Knap'. By 1896 it has the high
Wessex status of its own name. In 1912 revisions it is 'the fine old Elizabethan Inn
at Chalk-Newton'; a footnote adds, 'It is now pulled down, and its site is occupied

by a modern one in red brick' – 'as if he wanted to make quite certain that it should never be forgotten', says Beatty.[35] This sounds just like what Hardy did with The Three Mariners in *The Mayor of Casterbridge*. He was disseminating a warm, human, loving polemic for everyday, unfashionable buildings which most middle-class people would have avoided. He was doing this in fact *and* fiction: deliberately informing, impassioning and charming his vast readership; staking out a new, informed vision of the built past – and silently shifting the context for those working to save it.

So directly alongside his work on SPAB's own campaigns, Hardy is projecting an informed, extreme idea of conservation, through his novels, to his now considerable audience. He is using loving descriptions, technical and social background, footnoting lost buildings. He is extending the factual basis behind his novels, and keeps doing so, building his status as a reliable source.

Of course, Hardy was not working alone. He was part of a local movement as well as a national one. Dorchester was the first town where local protest got a railway diverted to save the earthworks of Maumbury Ring in 1846[36] – Hardy was six years old. But now they had Hardy, ever more famous, extremely shrewd and highly committed, working behind the scenes, right at their heart and with an expanding and diversifying readership. Just as Hardy established Wessex as a coherent, part-real entity, he was making its concerted, coherent argument for an intelligent, sympathetic understanding of the ancient human fabric of the past, expounded and published, in fact and fiction, both above and below the line. And he never stopped.

Media effects are notoriously difficult to prove in any conditions, let alone those based on the influence of a fictional environment. But there is plenty of suggestive evidence to support this idea: the whole of the SPAB correspondence; Beatty saying 'SPAB was working overtime in Dorset';[37] Hardy having Paula Power hold her castle 'in trust for the nation' fifteen years before the National Trust was set up;[38] and conservation historian Michael Hunter's unanswered question: 'What prompted this peak of preservationist activity around 1900?',[39] just as the popularity and outreach of Hardy's novels grew. It is impossible to *prove* his effect in the remarkable growth of conservation consciousness in this country during and after his lifetime – but it is surely what he set out to do. We will come back to this argument, because many key examples happen later in Hardy's life.

But if Wessex was a deliberate campaign on public opinion (and I believe it was) it was extraordinarily disingenuous, well ahead of its time, and with an outreach – through over a century of continuous publication and presence on school reading lists, through films, television adaptations and regional tourism – of which any conceptual architect or conservation campaigner would be in awe. A campaign that is still going on today, any time anyone reads *The Mayor of Casterbridge* or *The Woodlanders*.

11

MAX GATE

A New Building

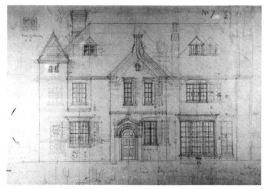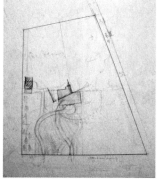

Max Gate: original elevation, showing rethinking of form and window position; and one of the site plans: the view of Maiden Castle is noted, bottom left.

Alongside this new level of literary construction and active conservation work, Hardy was doing what architects are supposed to want to do: building his own house. A chance for architectural self-expression, mastery of your trade, imagining and arranging how you want to live. But a daunting prospect for someone whose remarkable imaginative world was so well known – and who had never built a whole new building before.

By now we should be expecting (from fictional Myrtle Villa and the rented homes), a cheerful, modern and convenient suburban house. We know he does not care much about the style and is intensely interested in all kinds of working detail (plain and decorative), construction, plumbing and drains. We know he loves abstract qualities of place, trees, and bleak, empty views. And – in his own way – that is just what he would deliver.

But he also has problems. He does not draw readily in three dimensions; he has little experience at designing buildings from scratch; he is lacking the normal, cheerful groups of peers who naturally criticise and suggest improvements to work on the drawing boards. The builders are his father and brother: a mixed blessing. (Thomas Senior is reported as saying, 'never again'[1] – a common reaction to family building projects.) And there was his relationship with Emma, which at this stage was full of problems but still cumulatively positive. But building works are at least as likely to incubate marital problems as solve them. The famous 'anti' architect, Cedric Price, once told a client: 'you don't need an architect; you need a divorce.' The Hardys, like anyone embarking on building works, were pushing their limits.

*

Hardy never had a full architectural 'crit' on Max Gate. The eminent architectural writer Albert Richardson's view, as recounted to Claudius Beatty, was: 'Hardy showed his good taste in designing Max Gate. It was traditional and austere – like houses in Jane Austen.'[2] Blomfield, too, called it a very nice house.[3] But a true crit is composed of different, competing, not always polite voices. And it's never too late to start.

Like any critic, I am comparing *built* Max Gate with the *drawings* (and any other information available) to imagine what Hardy intended, whether he succeeded, what comparisons it suggests, how he might have done it better, and how far its ideas extend. It is meant as a constructive, rather than condemnatory process and is rarely described (although Garbett's book and A *Laodicean* both partly do so). But it is part of the everyday architectural practice described throughout this book. This is the capacity to assemble an imagined place reading pictures; making instinctive, perhaps illogical comparisons; using a well-exercised architectural imagination, to consider, develop, test and debate how that place works, in your own mind, and in collective discussion with others.

Drawings are crucial to this 'crit' process – even for a built project. They show peers and critics what the architect was thinking; what methods they used to work things out; what they took care over; what they struggled with; what they kept coming back to; what they ignored. They show which things turned out as expected, and which did not. They help you see both problems and hidden successes. They can make you notice things you might not (by rational means alone) have thought important. They show what got left out. Often, a critic will mention 'missing' drawings: those which architects *needed* to do, but had not done. And the drawings of Max Gate do all these things.

As Hardy had said, back in 'How I Built Myself a House', it is not easy to find the ideal site. But Mack's Gate, eventually purchased from the Duchy of Cornwall, on high ground just outside Dorchester, met many of his criteria. It offered healthy subsoil; uplands; a south-westerly orientation; convenient proximity to a bustling, cheerful town – and yet privacy and vast open views. Although he immediately hit major archaeological finds ('skellingtons', which would have stopped work today), they too, were fascinating for Hardy. A new house, on a very old site.

There were (at least) two site plans, with the house facing slightly different ways. He would start planting *before* building: good practice, but unusual, even now. On one, more finished plan, he specifies *which* trees are to be planted in the northern shelter belt screening the house from wind and the railway cutting. On the other site plan (probably earlier), he marked the view of Maiden Castle – presumably to keep it visible. Apparently it is in winter: the trees he planted in that area must be deciduous.

The vast sweep of horizon between him and the sea would have been bare, bleak: the type he unfashionably preferred. He obviously liked working in corner windows, and from one window of his first study, where he wrote *The Woodlanders*, he could see Rainbarrow and Egdon Heath. From another, he was looking straight at Conquer Barrow; from the third, he could see the needle of the Hardy Monument (the Hardy of Nelson, who he claimed as a distant relative) on the seaward horizon – that must have tickled his fancy. And right to the far side, Maiden Castle was just visible, fringed by the new trees.

He was clearly thinking of such views in *The Mayor* while designing these. Susan and Elizabeth-Jane come in from this direction, where they see the 'box of dominoes' and 'mathematical line' of pre-Victorian Casterbridge – now lost behind suburbs and railway. Here is the view from their first cottage in Casterbridge (another west-facer), by the Roman walls:

> The evening sun seemed to shine more yellowly there than anywhere else that autumn – stretching its rays, as the hours grew later, under the lowest sycamore boughs, and steeping the ground floor of the dwelling, with its green shutters, in a substratum of radiances ... Beneath these sycamores on the town walls could be seen ... the tumuli and earth forts of the distant uplands; making it altogether a pleasant spot, with the usual touch of melancholy that a past-marked prospect brings.[4]

Max Gate also sits on a line between isolation and society. It is near the town and railway: handy for trips to London, fascinating for watching Portland stone make the same journey. It is on a Roman road, and an Iron Age site, with wide views all round; a gateway to Wessex, as site, name and purpose suggest.

But gradually, famously, those views closed down. Hardy specified thick mixed planting and refused to allow any trees to be cut. The trees mattered to him: *The*

Woodlanders was the first book written here; those trees probably grew into the idea of the house itself. Seclusion and shelter stood against the view which could partly emerge through the seasons. And, of course, Hardy *could* see the long views, in his intense, powerful mind's eye. But that was a problem. The house was not just for Hardy, it was for Emma, for their staff, and later Florence, who, empowered by his death, had the trees cut back. If Hardy 'owned' those views, he was not thinking, or not thinking *enough*, about the house as something used, imaginatively as well as practically, by people other than himself.

Hardy should have drawn the views fully, to test how his vision would work. He might have planted more deciduous trees, or smaller ones. Armed with the drawings, his successors (Florence, Kate Hardy, and the National Trust) might have been better able to preserve Hardy's private vision; Conquer Barrow bought for the nation; the ring road not just run in a cutting (at the instigation of Bill and Vera Jesty, later tenants), but re-routed or re-thought altogether.[5] Max Gate would have ended up a more lovely house; the frenzy for ring-roads which loop round all Dorset towns might have been reconsidered; Stinsford suffered less from these; and Hardy's marriages might have found themselves in better places too.

But literary architecture *is* more solitary and introspective than the built type, and architects, as well as writers, often create introspective houses. (Peter Zumthor's lovely house and studio comes to mind: his wife commissioned her own separate hut, high up the mountain above the studio[6]). There is an interesting, nightmarish account of the interminable and emotionally destructive process of building a new house in the compelling short story 'Fellow Townsmen', written in 1880, before Max Gate was on site. Perhaps like the *Return*, as a cautionary tale to himself.

> Barnet got into a way of spending many of his leisure hours on the site of the new building ... trying the temper of the mortar by punching the joints with a stick, looking at the grain of a floorboard and meditating where it grew, or picturing under what circumstances the last fire would be kindled in the now-sootless chimneys.[7]

Hardy specifically said he did not want to 'ruin himself with architecture by building a great house as other literary men had done'.[8] Architecturally, that implicates Pugin, who built his own first house, St Marie's Grange (another first project, done when already famous), then redesigned it, and later sold it, losing a great deal of money.[9] He then built *another* house in Margate: plainer – except for having its own truncated church and gallery attached. Hardy might well have seen St Marie's

Grange (1835) outside Salisbury. It was also criticised for its exteriors at the time;[10] the original published 'sketch' was by Benjamin Ferrey, already mentioned, and of course, it is in Wessex. St Marie's second phase actually *looks* rather like Max Gate: the tower, the half-hipped roof, the varied and irregular windows.

Another, more famous model might be the Red House (1858–1860), by Philip Webb for (and with) William Morris, which also has an open hall with a neo-Gothic, backlit stair. Now seen as one of the greatest works of the Arts & Crafts movement, it too was criticised (at the time) for its irregular exterior; it too cost a lot of money; and despite its fame now, Morris also later moved out.[11]

Max Gate was simpler. The original plan (the early 1880s house, before the extensions) has a central door, a parlour on each side, and a kitchen at the back – with a traditional central hall, just like a miniature country house. Three bedrooms in a row above it (bedroom, dressing room, study) – three attics above that. (I am consciously paraphrasing E.M. Forster's *Howards End*, one of the most loving descriptions of a house in English Literature. Forster too would become a friend and regular visitor.)

In Hardy's Architectural Notebook, there are several pages showing comparative plans of houses Hardy knew or had worked on '(almost)'. Beatty suggests these may have been places he was going to *describe*; but they are drawn at the same size, all together, which suggests comparative design thinking – houses he was considering as models for Max Gate. (Imagining even fictional houses would certainly have helped stock his natural architect's image-bank of spatial ideas.) All look fairly normative (they are not famous); he must have been thinking how their layout worked. But on the *next* page are the 'Kingston' drawings which Beatty says he used

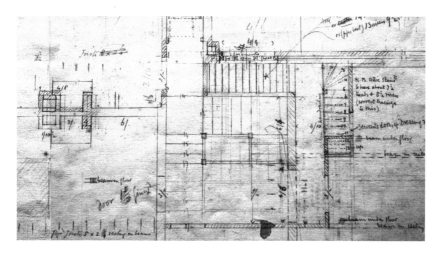

Max Gate: detail of Hardy's plan showing double staircase and service core.

Max Gate: the complex double stair from the hall,
and the steep, top-lit servants' stair hidden behind it.

for Knapwater in *Desperate Remedies*, with its grand central top-lit hall and two staircases. And *the* major architectural element in Max Gate is its hall and stairs. That is an absolutely key feature of the Arts & Crafts' modern reclamation of the English typologies of farmhouse and castle.

For a house of its size, Max Gate's hall is very elaborate. It is as big as the two main front rooms, with an open, top-lit, three-flight staircase rising to the first floor. But hidden behind the stair – in the depth of the two-layer window – is the servant stair, enclosed, narrower, leading in two steep flights into the pretty attics – without touching the first floor at all. So the hidden 'servant' stair wraps round the main 'served' stair, top-lit by its high-level window, forming an elaborate double 'clerestory' to the hall itself.

Staircases are complicated to design, and Hardy has *worked* on this. It is elaborate, complicated, and begging to be drawn in exploded axonometric (more 1970–1980s design tools; a sort of measured diagram) to show how its compact, interlocking circulation works. This is the heart of Max Gate, architecturally: a kind of comic staging of served and servant workings of the house – intimate, interlocking, separate – which is very good indeed. It is the architectural *parti*: the big idea. And about four-fifths of it works brilliantly. But it is too tight and crowded. Emma, reasonably, complained of falling over the servants. Hardy, at this stage, prioritised technical detail over sheer space: he would not make his main rooms big enough until the extensions.

But problematic or not, the 'served–servant' relationship – the *Desperate Remedies* and *Hand of Ethelberta* idea – was the heart of this project, and all the richest bits of Max Gate's architecture come straight from it. It shows us the problems the Hardys were facing in their own marriage in architectural form, and the way Hardy tried to solve (and sometimes contributed to) them through architecture. The problem was all about servants.

*

So let's talk about the clients. Emma was middle-class and impoverished, while Hardy's redoubtable mother Jemima had been a servant – and proud of it. Emma is typically ascribed poor household management skills. (I am vaguely reminded of Dickens's Betsy Trotwood ticking off David Copperfield for marrying a spoilt, sweet child and expecting her to manage a household on a small budget.) Raised by a ruthlessly good manager and cook, Hardy must have had impossible standards.

You can hear this mismatch echoing through the Hardys' world, from the young architect Stephen's housekeeper mother, in *A Pair of Blue Eyes*, roundly abusing the middle-class Elfride's uselessness, to Emma's dislike of *The Hand of Ethelberta* ('too many servants'). Quite late in life Emma was rephrasing Elfride's argument: that a man, rising in the world, with servant parents, should move to a different part of the country. But here we are, in Dorset, three miles from Bockhampton, with brother Henry and Thomas Senior building the house. That problem was not going away.

There were many tales of the Hardys' domestic chaos: cooks leaving; parlourmaids promoted to cook overnight ('with entirely predictable consequences', says Millgate[12]); cats and dogs on the dining room table at meals (again recalling Dora Copperfield). But the pet mayhem, at least, extended to Florence's day, with the aggressive and beloved 'Famous Dog Wessex'. Hardy must have enjoyed the chaos, on some level. But the architecture of the original house cannot have helped. The first kitchen was *tiny*. For three servants, and a cook coming in daily, this was ridiculously cramped: four busy people crammed into a small room or squeezing up the narrow stairs; cats or dogs ruling the roost downstairs. You can see why a servant might leave.

Hardy was far more immersed in how it was made. Some of the best drawings are of the chimney flues and drains, as well as that regal lavatory. Hardy invented what would now be called a grey-water system, with a tank where relatively clean water was stored for re-use on the garden. His countryman's sensible husbandry produced a kind of green plumbing which is still unusual today. The brick choice was (with hindsight) good. Raw red in his time, it has aged to a mottled grey-red – almost the colour of the Mayor's house in Dorchester. It has cavity wall construction, too; a very early example of something just starting to be used, but not common until the 1920s or 1930s; Hardy draws how to make the cavity wall ties in the notebook: his home-made versions (the notebook specifies dipping in tar) have since been replaced.

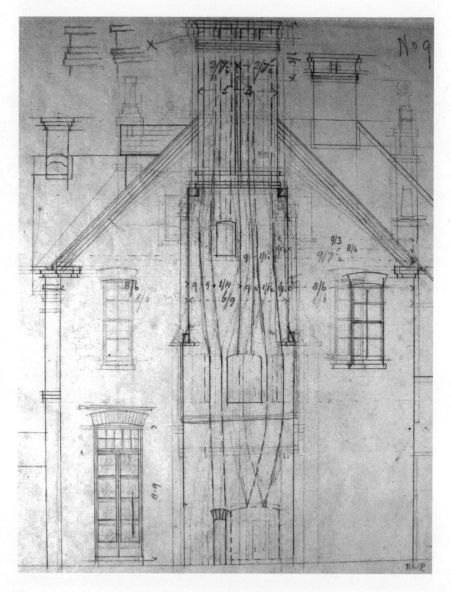

Max Gate: sectional elevation showing flue details.

Such care extends to the obsessive detailing throughout the house. The lovely window shutters – vertical sliding sash, in the dining room, running on counterweights and sliding below the cill. Almost every window is different, he must have detailed every bit of wood. He brought tiles back from a *bicycling* trip in Holland. That level of rich, but normal detailing is everywhere: outhouses, outside servants' lavatory, stables. (It is a shame there was never a horse; Emma's eccentric independence and love of animals always brought them together; her enthusiastic embrace of cycling certainly improved their lives.) This is an Everyman's version of the now-slightly unfashionable obsessional architecture that you find in Norman Shaw's Cragside or in Leighton House – important buildings of their age. It also has something of the Straw Bale house by Wigglesworth Till, a long, slow, self-build experiment, in which the façade is arguably incidental. A house made with a huge amount of skill and love – from the inside out.

Hardy was working in the midst of a shift in thinking about the exterior of buildings from the formally expressed façades of his youth. The Arts & Crafts movement was developing the 'vernacular' idea that buildings should be designed from the inside out, the resulting shape being irregular or ad hoc in the way in which old buildings often are. This was Hardy's view too: every room with windows placed for the best views and lighting, rather than to make a pattern on the outside;[13] and with lots of corner windows and dual aspects.

But 'inside-out' design was still an awkward new idea, and the working tools Hardy had at his disposal were the classic skills of the technician (as described by Pugin). Elevations are important drawings, but they are not ideal for *designing* the outside of a medium-sized, irregularly shaped, detached house on high ground. To see what that building would *look* like, outside, you would need to model, sketch, or draw in three dimensions, which, in my estimation, Hardy was more or less unable to do. Ironically, Max Gate's elevation is one of his nicer drawings *because* you can see the windows being rubbed out and re-drawn – classic inside-out thinking. It gives the drawing the patina of age which the house itself, later, achieved. Hardy's most revealing drawings are often rough, overdrawn or awkward ones. They are the ones which describe how he was working – and kept working – on this house.

There is no doubt the front is Max Gate's worst point. The composition is wrong: the turret and the hip are jammed together, where they might gracefully be at different ends; the eaves should drop down further. The scale is odd: the turret is too small to be useful; too big to be a quirk. The windows – though large – seem on the mean side in the scale of this building (broader cills and surrounds would have helped.) And of course, it is that front view which gets repeatedly photographed, discussed as though it *were* the architecture. That is a common architectural problem, one leading (in our age) to the rise of 'iconic' development: buildings designed for the publicity shots or the computer render – whatever the rest of the building is like.[14] It is a natural architectural preoccupation, but a perverse one too.

Given Hardy's skill in composing, framing and analysing *written* images, it can seem strange that he should fail in what seems such a banal way. But both the Red House and St Marie's Grange were criticised, when built (and still), for their exteriors. And however preposterously advanced his use of *experimental* visions was, as a writer and as an experimental thinker, Hardy probably did not in the early 1880s recognise how usefully *architectural* – how architecturally *useful* – such drawings and writings might be, in actually designing a building and its setting.

So Hardy is trying out something difficult, without any peers to help him. But those exteriors were not entirely accidental; he had drawn and redrawn them. The elephant in the room is that tower: what on earth was Hardy doing? Where were the plain neutral villas? Well, he was doing a milder, cheaper version of what Pugin was doing, perhaps even quoting him, and Pugin was taking flack for it too.

Max Gate is far more interesting in its relationship to the Arts & Crafts writers' houses – the ones he was surely referencing – than has been noticed. There is an interesting article in the *Architectural Review* in 1945, by the artist John Piper, who painted Pugin's house, and has many connections with Wessex; he lived and died in Fawley and is famous for his abstract stained glass work (which Hardy also tries in his unbuilt church, see p. 74). Piper says of St Marie's Grange: 'It is like a medley of suburban Gothic of the seventies and eighties, and there are plenty of villas outside London, Derby, Nottingham, Wolverhampton and Birmingham that bear strong resemblances to it and were built half a century later. It is of course in a sense the grandfather of all of them.'[15]

Both Hardy and Pugin's houses are different to the Red House, which, despite its accretive shape, is a highly finished, refined composition: a 'jewel box' was Morris's idea.[16] Pugin's two Granges and Hardy's Max Gate are not. Instead, they are trying out a kind of post-modern, eclectic thinking which would still cause ructions a century later. And you can see they meant it. The Ferrey drawing of St Marie's Grange (Pugin's first version) is all tower; something like a border tower house. He then substantially remodelled it; adding many more windows, which rather blows the idea. Finally, he would do a simpler, plainer second house – except he would stick a church on it too.

'Grange' suggests village; a tiny community. Pugin, like Hardy, had an idea in his mind. They are both trying, however imperfectly, and with more theoretical

Pugin's houses. Left: St Marie's Grange, Salisbury, original (drawing by Benjamin Ferrey); centre: as altered by Pugin; and right: The Grange, Margate, with its own church.

than practical experience, to make, and to architecturally express, an aggregate architecture: something built over time. And both of them would keep working at it.

*

So was Max Gate great architecture? Well, no, not quite: not bad for a first attempt; much more interesting than it looks at first. There is too much intricacy of the ordinary details, for our age's taste at least; too little emphasis on the *parti*: the big, coherent ideas (the interlocking family and servant space; those all-important views). Most obviously, it is let down by its exterior – which perhaps, Hardy should even have drawn *less*: allowing it to turn into whatever funny lumpen shape it wanted, as buildings do, over time. But that *is* what he would go on to do. You can see what Hardy knew he had got wrong, because he changed it, just a few years later.

And Max Gate had generated something else, too. As Hardy wrote *The Mayor*, or the 'Dorsetshire Labourer', campaigned for SPAB, saw the museum on site and planted the trees, he was walking back and forwards through town, his imagination filled with working building designs, a working, inventive everyday way of seeing which drew from and fed into his novels, essays and conservation campaigns. His sense of himself as a working designer *had* to be conscious. He would keep revising Max Gate. He would never stop working or thinking as an architect.

HOW THAT BOOK RUSTLES

The Woodlanders

The environment of *The Woodlanders* is as different from Casterbridge as a few long miles, a single ridge of hills and a new book could possibly make it. There is broad daylight in Casterbridge, and working moonlight, music and company, conversations, lists of buildings, implements and architecture. There is life, and plenty of it; the continuous, warm life of a still-bustling town. *The Woodlanders* is its opposite: an alternating step in Hardy's great journey forward; as different as can be. Again, like *The Mayor*, *The Return* and *Ethelberta*, it starts on an old road: already superceded, the 'forsaken coach-road from Bristol to the South coast, running suddenly through woodlands and apple country'.[1]

We do see fragments of orchards, but, like the bewildered hairdresser Percomb at the start of the book, we spend most of the story lost in deep, obscured woodland. There is a soft, pervasive hairdressing metaphor here: Percomb (pun intended) has come in search of the local girl Marty South's lustrous hair, to make a hair-piece for Mrs Charmond, the beautiful, ageing, often-absent owner of the big house. But (Hardy quotes *The Rape of the Lock*), Percomb's small piece of damage starts the blight and demise of an entire local ecosystem.

Little Hintock, the all-but invisible centre of this tale, is also described as:

... gardens and orchards sunk in a concave, and, as it were, snipped out of the woodland. From this self-contained place rose in stealthy silence tall stems of smoke, which the eye of imagination could trace downward to their root on quiet hearthstones, festooned overhead with hams and flitches.[2]

Planting, cutting, lopping, felling, and pruning are inevitably the daily work, going on as far as the eye can see through the trees. This cutting and grafting is even a part of the wonderful, exquisite, sentence structure native to this book: metaphor and content, carried on, changed and developed. It is so native as to be unnoticeable as metaphors. (It is *inconceivable* that Marty's hair could be anything other than chestnut.) Hardy could do simple details now, and make them work; with a sense of skill, where tiny phrases have vast resonance, or little hooks latch the end of one chapter to the beginning of the next. This is how a chapter opens: 'The news was true. The life – the one fragile life that had been used as a measuring-tape of time by law, was in danger of being frayed away. It was the last of a group of lives which had served this purpose.'[3]

But all this forestry is also in the high architectural ground of the time. Here is Ruskin, with an embroidered view of woodlands:

... earth becomes the companion of man – his friend and teacher! The characters which enable him to live on it safely, and work with it easily ... a carpet to make it soft for him; then, a coloured fantasy of embroidery, then tall spreading of foliage to shade him from sunheat ... still if human life be cast among trees at all, the love bourne to them is a sure test of its purity.[4]

What Hardy gives us is *far* better:

... they went noiselessly over mats of starry moss, rustled through interspersed tracts of leaves, skirted trunks with spreading roots whose mossed rinds made them look like hands wearing green gloves; elbowed old elms and ashes with great forks in which stood pools of water that overflowed on rainy days and ran down their stems in green cascades. On older trees still than these huge lobes of fungi grew like lungs ...[5]

This is not a romantic or theoretical view: we are informed, immersed, hypnotised, and sometimes shocked by what we find. 'Trees, trees, undergrowth, English Trees! How that book rustles with them!' said E.M. Forster in 1939.[6] More than fifty years after publication, and writing from Devi, he found *The Woodlanders* (1887) still alive, as we do today. It is one of Hardy's most sensual books.

Yet *The Woodlanders* is, deliberately, *not* a survival. The story mirrors and occludes *Under the Greenwood Tree* (1872), with Grace Melbury, undecided between the irresolute educated outsider Fitzpiers and her rough, uneducated, deeply skilled childhood sweetheart Giles. *The Woodlanders* is a tiny, critical point in the long, slow death of a landscape – a small patch of a local blight in a society and environment, just beginning to run downhill into extinction. We are watching an environmental struggle in progress – and through using a particular way of *seeing*. We see *glimpses* of the story, through those woods: too many to list. 'Except at midday, the sun was not seen complete by the Hintock people, but rather in the form of numerous little stars, staring through the leaves.'[7] Giles tracks Grace and her father first by glimpses of Grace's white clothes through the woods; then by sound alone: 'on the line of their course every wood pigeon rose from its perch with a continued clash ...'[8]

Grace learns of Fitzpiers in darkness, watching a light changing colour, through the twigs.[9] Hidden spectators, hear, rather than see, the girls' midsummer rituals. Melbury locates his adulterous son-in-law by the glimmer of his white horse tethered in the trees. Even Giles – often seen in clear view: holding his apple trees for sale on the market or rising up the hill to cheer Grace's heart 'like autumn's very brother' – moves into obscurity. As Grace breaks their engagement, Giles retreats, up a tree, out of sight, into fog, and as he dies his abstemious death – retires into a tiny thatched hurdle deep in the woods – he becomes so indistinguishable from the wood and its creatures that Grace cannot find him. And where there are great set piece Hardy pictures, we follow them to the extremities of sight. Here is the scene where Grace watches her faithless husband (who is riding her own white horse, Darling, her gift from the faithful Giles) heading, unmistakably, towards his mistress and out of sight:

> ... he was a silent spectacle to her. Soon he rose out of the valley and skirted a high plateau of the chalk-formation on his right ... He kept along the edge of this high, uninclosed country, and the sky behind him being deep violet she could still see the white Darling in relief upon it – a mere speck now – a Wouverans eccentricity reduced to microscopic dimensions. Upon this high ground he gradually disappeared.[10]

Hardy is still directly challenging Ruskin's rejection of the 'vulgar'; still exploring Garbett's sun-light, cloud-light, fog-light; the 'mind's eye' which reaches beyond the visual.[11] We hear the drip of mist, the 'scrape of snails creeping up the window glass',[12] and we sense the shadowy summers and perversely brighter winters well known to those who have lived in old, broad-leaved woodlands.

But it is also a remarkable cast forward. This is like wildlife photography, in its most extraordinary, long-lens form: David Attenborough's *The Hunt* (2016), for example. Grace, seen by Giles and Fitzpiers through her lighted and uncurtained window, in her reckless 'six-candle illumination' to dress to visit Mrs Charmond, the midsummer rituals, even Fitzpiers (and the two white horses one of which he mistakes for the other), are observed from a distance as though seeing wildlife in the forest. This long-lens voyeurism adds to the passive sense of the novel: to Grace, Giles and Marty's acceptance of their fate, and to the sense of seeing this world *through* something: a telescope; a lens; Hardy's glasses, someone else's distanced vision. *The Woodlanders* is like watching a great, sensory, Darwinian wildlife documentary charting the demise of a whole ecosystem, and the human life within it, from a distance.

*

In the middle of the book, there is a luminous, startling moment of complete architectural vision in the beautiful town beyond the woods, Sherton Abbas/ Sherborne: 'the churches, the abbey, and other mediaeval buildings on this clear bright morning having the linear distinctness of architectural drawings, as if the original dream and vision of the conceiving master-mason were for a brief hour flashed down through the centuries to an unappreciative age.'[13]

Beatty picks up the links to *A Laodicean*, telling us that the master-mason is Vilars de Honecor, known for his remarkable, stylised, animated thirteenth sketchbook (more characters than plans).[14] (The architectural writer Albert Richardson, Beatty says, cried 'Wilars de Honecor!' when shown the Wessex Poems coffin drawing).[15] Hardy keeps re-setting his imagination and ours against the high ground of architects' projective vision. Yet luminous, as this is, this is a fleeting moment. *The Woodlanders* takes Wessex back to the woods and its deeper environmental argument.

There are everyday houses, too, in this thicket. Here is Marty's:

... rather large for a cottage, and the door, which opened immediately into the living room, stood ajar, so that a riband of light fell through the opening into the dark atmosphere beyond. Every now and then a moth, decrepit from the late season, would flit for a moment across the outcoming rays and disappear into the night.[16]

The houses are an important part of this great environmental documentary. Marty is making spars – wooden thatching pegs – skillfully, painfully, by hand (her father is too ill to do it); by firelight (because wood alone is cheap); and using a coffin stool (an ancient piece of furniture suggesting former status). She has the door open (the chimney smokes). Later, she will hang a curtain (to stop neighbours knowing she is working late). This first house we see embodies in all its selected detail a way of life, built from trees, once substantial, now extremely poor; a palpable decline.

Even this tiny village has two large houses – also both past their prime. First, the Melburys' home:

It formed three sides of an open quadrangle, and consisted of all sorts of buildings, the largest and central one being the dwelling itself. The fourth side of the quadrangle was the public road.

It was a dwelling-house of respectable, roomy, almost dignified aspect; which, taken with the fact that there were the remains of other such buildings thereabout, indicated that Little Hintock had at some time or other been of greater importance than now. The house was of no marked antiquity ... looking at you from the still-distinct middle distance of the early Georgian time, and awakening ... instincts of reminiscence more decidedly than the remoter, and far grander, memorials ... from the misty reaches of medievalism ... great-grandfathers and grandmothers who had been the first to gaze from those rectangular windows ... reverberations of queer old personal tales were yet audible, if properly listened for, and not, as with those of the castle and cloister, silent beyond the possibility of echo.[17]

That would be a wonderful survival, if the Melburys' fortunes looked better (shares in the coach roads and the port they lead to; just the one daughter). Far grander is Mrs Charmond's house, often standing unused, because she cannot stand the remote life:

> ... it stood in a hole. But the hole was full of beauty. From the spot where Grace had reached, a stone could easily have been thrown over or into the birds-nested chimneys of the mansion. Its walls were surmounted by a battlemented parapet; but the grey lead roof were quite visible behind it, with their gutters, laps, rolls and skylights, together with letterings and shoe-patterns cut by idlers thereon.
>
> The front of the house was an ordinary manorial presentation of Elizabethan windows, mullioned and hooded, worked in rich snuff-coloured freestone from Ham-hill quarries. The ashlar of the walls, where not overgrown with ivy and other creepers, was coated with lichen of every shade, intensifying its luxuriance with its nearness to the ground till, below the plinth, it merged in moss.
>
> Above the house was a dense plantation, the roots of whose trees were above the level with the chimneys. The corresponding high ground on which Grace stood was richly grassed, with only an old tree here and there. A few sheep lay about, which as they ruminated looked quietly into the bedroom windows.[18]

Keystone, ashlar, laps, rolls, Ham-stone: Hardy is still educating his readers in architectural terms, and again, he is talking partly in *section*. This rich house is

Vanished houses: Turnworth House, a model for
Hintock House, burnt down in the 1950s.

often left empty and will be closed up by the end of the book: it is probably based
on Turnworth House,[19] itself burnt down and rebuilt.[20] Most important of all is
Giles's house: old and uncomfortably homely when we see it first, but, once his
life-hold lease falls in, vanishing with astonishing speed:

> Even in the gloom he could trace where the different rooms had stood; could
> mark the shape of the chimney-corner in which he had roasted apples and
> potatoes in his boyhood, cast his bullets, and burnt his initials on articles that
> did not belong to him. The apple trees still remained to show where the garden
> had been ... Apples bobbed against his head, and in the grass he crunched
> scores of them as he walked. There was no-one to gather them now.[21]

The disappearance of these little bubbles of architecture (the houses 'built by frogs
or mice', according to Ruskin) is a key working part of this decline. Once the
houses go, so does the society that lived on and with the woods; which planted as
well as cut. The famous scene of Marty and Giles planting was written around the
time of planting at Max Gate:

> The holes were already dug, and they set to work. Winterborne's fingers
> were endowed with a gentle conjurer's touch in spreading the roots of each
> little tree, resulting in a sort of caress under which the delicate fibres all laid
> themselves out in their proper directions for growth. He put most of the

Vanished houses: a woodland cottage, from
The Truth About Cottages.

roots towards the south-west; for, he said, in forty years' time, when some great gale is blowing from that quarter, the trees will require the strongest holdfast on that side to stand against it and not fall.

How they sigh directly we put 'em upright, though while they are lying down they don't sigh at all, ... She erected one of the young pines into the hole and held up her finger; the soft, musical breathing instantly set in which was not to cease night or day till the grown tree should be felled – probably long after the two planters had been felled themselves ...[22]

The Woodlanders shows a tiny moment in the defeat of this ancient way of life. Grace gets lost in her native woodlands; she can no longer tell John-apples from Bittersweets: we know neither. Marty's hair, Giles's house, Hintock House, the departure of Grace and Fitzpiers, Melbury's worthless shares are all grains of sand in this environmental tipping point. When Giles dies, Hardy makes the woods sensible of their loss:

> The whole wood seemed to be a house of death, pervaded by loss to its uttermost length and breadth. Winterborne was gone, and the copses seemed to show the want of him; those young trees, so many of which he had planted, and of which he has spoken so truly when he said he should fall before they fell, were at that moment sending out their roots in the direction he had given them with his subtle hand.[23]

This is a kind of parable of the saintly death of the intimacy of man and environment, extended (by implication) through a million tiny stories like this, in the great drift to the towns. Hardy had never written so immersively, or in such detail of the skilled ecosystem of the past. This is the collateral decline of the countryside in a world busy elsewhere. And to some extent, mourn as we will, we *accept* it. Giles's death, and Marty's lonely and bitterly hardworking life are glimpses of an uncomfortable life and poor education, not the things to which we would want to return. It is part of Hardy's great paradoxical achievement. He summons up a world just as he tells you it has gone. He makes you mourn, while recognising your own complicity in its death.

*

Interestingly, *The Woodlanders* was placed in a magazine which did *not* publish illustrations and even Hermann Lea's later photographs are not memorable. Dragging the long-lens camera that he and Hardy would use through the vegetation would be hard to manage (although there is an intriguing, poor image of a saw-mill buried in trees: I strongly suspect a badly conceived crop of a photograph originally framed to be largely of and through trees). But perhaps Hardy was *not* seeking to reconstruct the past. Many of Lea's photographs for this book are almost polemically bare. The landscape of *The Woodlanders* – and Hardy knew now that his readers would go out looking for it – was not to be found. Here is his 1912 preface:

> I have been honoured by so many inquiries for the true name and exact locality of the hamlet 'Little Hintock' ... that I may as well confess here once for all that I do not know myself where that hamlet is ... To oblige readers I once spent several hours on a bicycle with a friend in a serious attempt to discover the real spot; but the search ended in failure, though tourists assure me positively that they have found it without trouble and that it answers in every particular to the description given in this volume.[24]

Hardy is never more acute than when he is teasing or perverse. He had come to realise that it was vital that we should look for the settings – and even more essential that we should be unable to find them. He was deliberately creating a vast immersive understanding of the past; and yet reminding you that it was lost – and could only be partly recovered in the misty, tangled thickets where reality joins fiction.

WESSEX COPYRIGHT

The Place on the Map

Wessex was changing shape. Hardy was expanding its territory – moving into Hampshire and Wiltshire with *Tess of the d'Urbervilles* and Berkshire with *Jude the Obscure*; and enlarging and developing the form it was taking, the way it was working. His idea of Wessex, as a place both real and fictional, was growing increasingly clear and ambitious. He was extending his authorship over the whole territory in, and beyond, his writing.

Others were recognising, and joining in with Hardy's great reciprocal work; for example, George Eliot sets *Daniel Deronda* (1876) partly in Wessex. Hardy also had some (rather unsatisfactory) early experience in theatre adaptations of his books. And he was seeing the start of a remarkable stream of secondary tourist literature, recognising the 'public role' of Wessex.[1]

By 1888, Hardy was writing to his publishers:

> ... could you, whenever advertising my books, use the words 'Wessex Novels' at the head of the list? I mean, instead of 'By T.H.', 'T.H.'s Wessex Novels'? I find that the name Wessex, wh. I was the first to use in fiction, is getting to be taken up everywhere: & it would be a pity for us to lose the right to it for want of asserting it.[2]

The idea of an architect-writer claiming *copyright* of a written and published place is irresistible for architects. For that is what they naturally do: take creative and curatorial control over the places, buildings and things they create: built or unbuilt, real or imaginary. But claiming architectural 'copyright' is hard to do. Writers and artists have reasonably clear ways of establishing authorship: architects, less so. They are working in a collaborative world, where 'ideas' elude ownership, and may not have come from the named architect nominally in charge – so historians are chary of claiming Turnworth as Hardy's independent design because he was working under Hicks/Crickmay's name.

And architectural ideas are *naturally* copied: emulation is part of how the profession works. Design is hard to protect as intellectual property: any new building, however much it seems like another (in style, detail, structural method, appearance, arrangement of spaces, for example) inevitably differs from it too (in site, client, cost, time, condition or circumstance). All architects learn from each other, by 'reading' built and published works by others; and it is hard to establish where the authorship lies. Yet architects *do* claim intellectual property of their buildings, of details, and ideas; of whole movements in building or planning. Architectural authorship is part-working fiction, part-lost cause. A deliberate, knowing, often misleading line in the sand.

Hardy was clearly *interested* in all this. When, in A *Laodicean*, the maverick Will Dare incites the plodding architect Havill to copy Somerset's designs, it is not the simple-sounding matter of Dickens's Martin Chuzzlewit having his Grammar School design pinched by his employer.[3] Hardy shows instead that Havill is *inspired* to a good design of his own: exploring the richer questions of how all this copying, inspiration, vision and creative control actually *works*.

Books are by far the easiest way architects can claim intellectual property – especially in unbuilt projects and ideas (or indeed their role in the development of popular building types). In his 2004 book *Content*, Rem Koolhaas, by then a world-famous architect, drew and claimed his 'patent' for ideas within building projects which other architects were using elsewhere: including 'Variable Speed Museum (1995)' or 'Skyscraper Loop (2002)'. These are ideas which can be lucidly understood by other architects – but are not necessarily obvious to others (they include ideas about shape and structure as well as how people move around buildings).[4] This idea was only partly polemic: Koolhaas had successfully defended an intriguing court case about plagiarism in 2001 and he went on to file actual patents on some of his designs. But Koolhaas's famous architectural books (notably *S,M,L,XL*: an architectural 'blockbuster') would remain his strongest way of broadcasting and claiming ownership of his own, highly innovative and influential, architectural thinking. When architectural authorship matters, books (by yourself or others) are almost essential. And from Palladio onwards, architects have used them.

Koolhaas is an exceptional architect by any measure – theory or practice[5] – but once again, Hardy is a century ahead of the field. Like Koolhaas, he is not trying to close down the secondary versions of Wessex – quite the reverse. He is claiming other people's writings on 'Wessex' precisely as part of the outreach of his great project, and asserting his right to be recognised as the generator of the secondary work too.

The Wessex of which Hardy is claiming ownership is not, exactly, the name. He is deliberately adopting the historical one, and is about to underline that, consciously expanding into the historical capitals of the Anglo-Saxon kingdom beyond Dorset (Winchester in *Tess*; Wantage in *Jude*). He is actually increasing its historical grounding – while signing his name firmly to it. Hardy is claiming what any architect would see as theirs: creative authorship of this imaginary-real Wessex as it was now working, both in and beyond his works. He is claiming Wessex, as Koolhaas claims the architectural 'ideas' in his work – Wessex, as it exists in our personal and collective imagination, influence and all. And he does it exceptionally well. To recognise the influence of Palladio, Le Corbusier or Koolhaas – architectural giants – requires special knowledge. But *Wessex* is still known today – even by a great many who have not read his fiction or poetry – to be Hardy's construction.

*

Hardy was now working on poems, plays and short stories. *Wessex Tales* was published in book form in 1888 (although some stories date from the 1870s). As with his first collection of poems, he would place his new branch of work firmly *inside* Wessex, the imaginary entity he had made and claimed. He was clearly turning the form of Wessex over in his mind. His remarkable essay, 'The Profitable Reading of Fiction' (also 1888) shows him thinking expressly about what Wessex was *doing* for its readers:

> A sudden shifting of the mental perspective into a fictitious world, combined with rest, is well known to be often as efficacious for renovation as a corporeal journey afar.

> In such a case the shifting of scene should manifestly be as complete as if the reader had taken the hind seat on a witch's broomstick. The town man finds what he seeks in novels of the country, the countryman in novels of society, the indoor class generally in outdoor novels, the villager in novels of the mansion, the aristocrat in novels of the cottage ... our true object is a lesson in life, mental enlargement from elements essential to the narratives themselves.[6]

Hardy is utterly clear how he thinks novels work. They 'take' us somewhere we could not visit otherwise: partly Dorset; partly the past. The 'profit' of reading his novels, he says, is our capacity to *visit* the Wessex he is making for us, in our imagination. And gradually, partly in reality too.

*

In the fascinating essay, 'Thomas Hardy and the Literary Pilgrims', W.J. Keith comments on Hardy's obsession with exact topography: 'no other major novelist, it may be observed, has concerned himself so minutely with issues which the literary critics consider to be at best peripheral.'[7]

Peripheral to literary critics perhaps, but this is central to architects. The topography of Wessex, its names, pictures and maps, its attachment to and difference from the real places, are part of the working substance he was using to make Wessex. And he is not just taking control of them in his own books (as a successful author, he had much more control of them now) but, whenever he can, in the remarkable stream of specialised, literary tourist literature written by other people.

Literary tourism was not new: the first visitors to Haworth came during Charlotte Brontë's lifetime (after her father's death, one even stole a piece of her window glass); and when the museum opened in 1928 Haworth was awash with visitors.[8] So were the sites of Sir Walter Scott's novels, which have their own intriguing real–imaginary histories. But Hardy's direct involvement in the beginnings of Wessex tourism is really remarkable.

Hardy was right to claim copyright in 1888, because a little publishing boom had begun: a still-flowing torrent of guides to, and books about, Hardy's Wessex. J.M. Barrie wrote one of the early essays, himself fascinated by, and (Piers Dudgeon says dangerously) seminal in, the use of imagined places to both generate and imagine, to read *and* write, books and plays.[9] (An interesting article on Victorianweb describes Lulworth Cove as the 'original' of Neverland.[10]) By 1894 the first two books had appeared, and these were not principally about the novels, but about the *place* Wessex, and many of them included maps.[11] Keith says: 'In bulk these far outnumber the more traditional literary critical studies of the period. Even more significant is the fact that a considerable number of them claim Hardy's approval.'[12]

Keith argues this 'late 19th century group of enthusiasts' effectively 'forced' Hardy in a direction he had avoided,[13] in getting him to specify which bits of real countryside his novels related to – and how closely. These writers, he concludes, got Hardy to open his realm up to us all: a new ability for us to visit, experience, imagine, know and 'see' Wessex. I agree that Hardy was starting to see Wessex as a partly collaborative construct, but few modern critics take Hardy's 'reluctance' at face value – much less being 'forced'. When Hardy turned down a request for a map (by H.E. Rideing) in 1893, elliptically saying 'a map of the scene of my novels is just what I should not like to be published just now, or indeed at any time, by anybody but myself', Keith understands Hardy was unaware of the *Bookman* map – the first map of Wessex – two years earlier. Now, we read it as confirmation that the *Bookman* map was by Hardy himself.[14]

Hardy's map. Wessex Novels edition, 1895–1896, and clearly by the
same hand as the *Bookman* map (but without the railways).

The *Bookman* article (1891) was, Gatrell shows, written by its editor, Robertson
Nicholl, in consultation with Hardy and in guidebook tone: 'Wanderers through our
south and south-western counties … will find few better guides than Mr Hardy'.[15]
Gatrell also quotes a letter where Nichol asks Hardy to provide a map, which had
obviously been discussed[16] – presumably, the one published: 'No-one has discovered
an earlier', says Gatrell.

Because it is not decorative like later Wessex maps, the *Bookman* map is
sometimes called a 'sketch' or 'rough' which is far from the case. It is careful, precise
and probably traced. 'Sketch' normally suggests a work of Hardy's origination,
and it certainly looks like Hardy's map. Even if re-engraved for publication, it is
very architectural in its lettering; its careful, traced, accurate drawing; its lucid,
confident sense of priorities; and in its tendency to draw things too small for print
purposes. The coast and geographical features are shown; so are the principal towns,
the locations of the novels, and the railways, and there is confident, assured white
space in the places between.

To an architect, this is the best type of Wessex map. Hardy's later map pasted
into his scrapbook[17] is the basis of the Osgood McIlwaine editions of 1985–1986,
following the same hand, with the confident repetition of understood characteristics.
They are more professional, and at the same time more conceptually abstract, than
the later versions, with a clear precise vision. Most notably, it seems to be the
same map, drawn in sketch form, for a magazine article on *Tess*, that apogee of

Wessex vision. The fact that it is taken from a *railway* map is important. Rail travel is linked with the rise of the English conservation movement,[18] with maps themselves, and with tourist trips to 'fictional' locations. That uneven, reciprocal link between Wessex and the cities was the lifeblood of the Wessex project: the water forced uphill; the seekers after scenery; the milk drunk by people who never imagined the milkers; the half-Londoner. The new and old worlds intimately linked – both through the experimental imagination, the sense of the past, and the modern ability to visit (and own detailed maps of) the 'real' place.

The railways would vanish in later maps (until *Tess*), but they must be a key part of how Hardy himself *saw* Wessex – otherwise, he would not have drawn them. They are its real context, its underlying modern structure – and paradoxically, the route 'seekers after scenery' could take to visit it.

The Wessex maps which followed – generations of them – are different; more like treasure island maps, with no railways. I would be inclined to say generic (with the exception of the lovely Edmund New map, on which Hardy collaborated), if the genre itself was not so largely of Hardy's own shaping. They all seem to be based on his own drawn version, and he even specified the fancy lettering, ships and so on, which appear in full florid form. If that made them popular, so much the better. Venturi and Scott Brown would say something similar of their second, cheaper 'ugly and ordinary' edition of *Learning From Las Vegas*.[19] Widening readership was the point.

As a teenager, I found those maps rather dull. I remember searching for markings showing the 'witch's ride' taken by Waterston Manor, or the vague, blurry constellation of villages which might have formed the vanished Hintocks. But that would require abstract and conceptual representations, or the capabilities of Google maps (possibly both). And in any case, my reader's mind was doing the job for me. Those maps were for those who might want to *visit* Wessex. They were part of the reciprocal dialogue Hardy was now having with his vast public – the people who wrote, or turned up at Max Gate and were annoyed if asked to come back a bit later. Of course they could visit Wessex, to see the place for themselves. Hardy himself had given them directions.

It was Bertram Windle, in *The Wessex of Thomas Hardy*, 1902 who hit the jackpot.[20] Windle had written a thoughtful letter:

> I have, I think, identified most – at least many of them – but am unable to feel quite sure about the others. I do not know whether you wish that all of them should be known, but if you have no objection, you would confer a great favour upon me if you would permit me to ask you to solve a few of my difficulties.[21]

Hardy replied equally considerately:

> I will with pleasure give you any information that you may require as to the
> real names of the places described in my Wessex novels. Such information
> in the Handbook will perhaps relieve me of the many letters I receive on the
> subject and perhaps serve to correct the erroneous identification of places by
> journalists and others.[22]

He offers to answer questions, and (so as not to put Windle to 'unnecessary
trouble before my return') adds a list of 'rudimentary notes': masses of them, giving
chapter and verse on all the major place-names. He also 'co-operated' on the map,
drawn by Edmund New. It was stylishly graphic, combining priority, precision, a
certain popular panache – with a still recognisable architectural style in its elegant
lettering and scale: a properly authorised, probably closely directed and definitive
map. The illustrations too, are very lovely, many of them also suggesting the uses
of some form of photography or lens-capture drawings; and they were probably
highly directed by Hardy; not only because the settings illustrated are so precise,
but because they follow Hardy's classic sparse and detailed vision.

Some Hardy critics are surprised by Hardy's willing cooperation; and as his life
goes on, they are more surprised, even puzzled, by the extent of work, effort, time
and discomfort Hardy took on, to assist selected representations and extensions of
Wessex by other people, including watercolours[23] and postcards.[24] Sets of postcards

The Edmund New map, 1902; authorised (probably directed) by Hardy.

Hardy's Wessex: the decorative 'populist' map from
the Wessex Edition, based on Hardy's drawing.

would later be available from Hermann Lea's first publication in 1906. (If anyone
finds any, please let me know.)

As an architectural critic, it is unsurprising that Hardy was sympathetic to
'seekers after scenery'. These writers were helping the public construction of
Hardy's Wessex, both as something read and imagined by many, many people, and
as something you could (more or less) visit. And all architects know their ability to
imagine a place depends on their ability to actually visit and experience a real one.
(Peter Zumthor once refused to show slides of his work at a lecture at the RIBA,
insisting that pictures could not stand in for real experience.) Of course Hardy was
making Wessex available, even at some personal cost.

Later this would include Hardy hosting annual marquee teas for journalists; bus
drivers shouting "Ome of Thomas 'Ardy, famous novelist', outside Max Gate; and
a London theatre critic accommodated during building works. He had *made* this
phenomenon, and made it for people to experience. He was sharing his project
in all ways he could. Those tourists were (in part) doing his bidding, following his
choreography to visit and see the land itself. He was teaching us how to look at
Wessex and at rural England. However inconvenient it could be, all these visitors
meant his remarkable project was working.

This phase of tourism and mapping around 1888 is what Gatrell calls the 'first evolutionary leap' of Wessex. His own remarkable book itself uses architectural ways of imaginative reconstruction: 'working from the accumulated detail of Hardy's revisions – reading Wessex as Hardy shows reading and reconstructing old buildings, through the imaginative assembly of real fragments.'[25] 'Wessex meant a structure of thought as well as a place and a history', says Gatrell.[26] He even fixes on a *picture* as the driving idea of his book: Hardy's vision of his countryside, through his glasses – a really quintessential picture of how architects and their theorists *see* architectural thinking: Ledoux, Le Corbusier and so on.[27] 'Hardy taught me to read Wessex ... not as a place but a way of thinking', says Gatrell.[28] Hardy, like the highest of high architects, is trying to *illustrate* how a vision of a place is itself constructed. He is devising, and delivering, a very extensive, very architectural, very modern education – but in remarkably popular form.

Hardy now begins to write and revise his novels so that parts read *and* work like a guide book. Using 'his best guidebook tone', he gives lucid, clear, directions within the novels, for readers to find the places for themselves: even to lie in the coffin where the sleeping Tess is placed. 'Fiction and reality, Wessex and England, can come no closer without merging', says Gatrell.[29] However bizarre, this is an architect's home ground, as visitors lie on the recliner-wall by the bath at Le Corbusier's Villa Savoye: they are after the architectural experience.[30]

Wessex, by the late 1880s, is a fully developed imagined place. It is described, drawn, named, mapped, its authorship claimed, and its author developing increasingly strict control of images and publications – and providing good directions on how to get there into the bargain. Hardy had made a new way of seeing and understanding the countryside, and he was helping shape the tourist industry he had generated, so that we could use it in the way he wanted us to. He was doing this very particular, peculiar thing, because besides being a novelist and poet, he was an architect too.

*

Wessex has never stopped working. Although an imperfect measure, an interim search of the Amazon website for 'Thomas Hardy Wessex' in the midst of this project brought up 1,028 titles, of which only 284 were fiction. These included reference books and study books; travel and holiday books; history books; poetry, drama and criticism books; society, politics and philosophy books; biography; antiquarian, rare and collectable, art, architecture and photography. 'Brontë Country' only pulled 244 titles in total, and 'Dickens's London' only 112. And if that is because of the classificatory power of Hardy's use of 'Wessex', it is worth noting that Hardy set out to do that, deliberately.

None of this – the intellectual property, the working with participants, the maps – was new territory for Hardy. Any architect hearing about that claim of copyright would understand it. Wessex was *his* project; he had imagined, conceived, and constructed it. He was behaving in a perfectly 'normal' way – if you can call anything about imaginary architectural projects 'normal'. And his grasp of authorial control was done with a skill, speed and effectiveness which leaves our most exceptional equivalents standing.

This too has irony. Hardy's actual built architectural work is often treated with caution – but in his fictional place, using maps, names, secondary writers and branding, he had by the 1890s established an unquestioned authorial role over Wessex. He had staked his role in the public access and tourist guide elements of this secondary publishing boom, stamping his name on it, from the start. As with the Dorset County Museum, whose opening and ongoing public role is so closely tied to Hardy's work, Wessex was now open to visitors.

14

VISITING WESSEX

Real and Imagined

When you visit Wessex – when, as any good architectural student should, you visit the *place* – you find something distinct and peculiar. This is not, or not only, like visiting Dickens's London or Brontë Country (and those are strange enough places). It is not just that you can imagine the world of the novels, or see the places from which Hardy made it. It is how closely real and imaginary places are grafted together. It is how many real aspects of Wessex there are: how far they extend; how hard it is to separate them from their imaginary version. It is that so much of Hardy's Wessex was really shaped (in one way or another) by his own hand.

*

I will start with the most speculative suggestion of all, about the place that Hardy scholars go: the Dorset County Museum. It is a wonderful institution, in a characterful building with marvellous special collections. Most emanate from Hardy's era, his peers and collaborators: William Barnes, Henry Moule, the Archaeological Society, the collections of fossils, of rural artefacts and Dorset painters. And of course, the Hardy collection itself, visited by scholars from all around the world.

The building is part of a listed group in the middle of town, with St Peter's Church (where the young Hardy worked on Hicks's restoration), and the Dorchester Corn Exchange by Benjamin Ferrey (who also designed All Saints, a few doors down). Hardy later criticised Ferrey's destruction of the older All Saints, as we've seen.[1] But Hardy and his colleagues were more central – and had a longer outreach. They were effectively establishing Dorchester as the centre of a form of local history – and All Saints, with poetic justice, is now used for museum storage.

During one particular visit to the museum, I found my eye seamlessly moving from Hardy's drawings to the building itself: its generous, detailed, always-varied Victorian-gothic windows; its varied, idiosyncratic staircases; its attic rooms; its corner study-windows; the careful detailing of every working space. And I found myself reading them, quite accidentally, as something designed by Hardy himself. That was fantasy; I had no evidence that Hardy worked on this building. But architectural critics are *invited* to make accidental leaps of imagination; to describe their instincts and then test them out. It was an idea worth considering.

Dorchester had an established historical and conservation culture. The Dorset Field and Archaeological Society was well established; the Museum and County Library established in 1845, housed in a series of older buildings. But since 1884, the purpose-built museum has been Dorchester's heart: a building embodying and enabling the cultural reach of this small town, accommodating almost 50,000 visitors a year. A building, a town, whose outreach was extended around the world, mainly by Hardy himself.

The building was designed by *Crickmay* – Hardy's most recent employer. Who wrote the brief, or chose Crickmay? Hardy was certainly collaborating with Moule and Crickmay on conservation campaigns for SPAB at this time. He is called a 'founder' of the museum;[2] Andrew Leah[3] believes he contributed to its funding too. Hardy was living at Colliton House, just behind the museum building works. He would have walked past it, on site, almost every time he left the building, and on the way to his own project at Max Gate (also on site 1883–June 1885[4]). It is inconceivable he would not have been, at the very least, dropping in to see how work was going, discussing ideas, making suggestions, getting ideas himself: for that is what architects do. The family similarities of rich, varied windows; complex staircases; the attic workplaces and corner windows are no coincidence: those who have worked together naturally do things in similar ways. Architectural influence passes in all directions; ideas are generated in discussing and seeing other projects.

Architectural critics are allowed instinctive hypotheses, but this needs proper investigation. I am not suggesting Hardy designed the building (he would not have had the time or the experience), but I am suggesting he probably had, at the very least, some kind of significant role in the client body. He was involved with both client and architect; he was influential; he was an architect himself; he was good at making modest 'suggestions' behind the scenes, as we have seen with SPAB. He was right on site. And he would be thinking as a future user too.

Crickmay did a good job. The museum is a lovely piece of architecture: contextual, allusive, irregular and exciting, an under-recognised member of the genus of wonderful museums like the Oxford Museum. (Augustus Pitt Rivers, founder of the Pitt Rivers Museum at the Oxford Museum gave the opening speech when the DCM was opened on 7 January 1884; Hardy was a friend, and we will be returning to Oxford.) Surely this was a job in which Hardy had some hand.

These speculations come because, in those attics, you are immersed in boxes and folios of Hardy's *real* architectural work of all kinds. Fragments, details, references; notes copied, written or sketched; letters in which Hardy casually delivers a detailed, working specification for drainage or repairs. There are incomplete sets of drawings from known, built buildings and peculiar unknown ones, including a half-finished pragmatic set for a mystery farm. This is the work of an architect whose thinking remained hands-on throughout his life.

Beatty spent a lifetime chasing and placing these fragments: he tells us which drawings were copied from which books; which were surveys of real places; whose house plans Hardy was sketching; where real, banal, late, tiny, unproven buildings might have been, or still be, and he identifies several 'composite' Hardy fonts in churches round Dorset. More recently, a Hardy *reredos* at All Saints, Windsor has been physically uncovered, in pristine condition.[5] (Beatty says he was on site with a similar project in Wales.) One cannot help feeling there are more fragments, patches, still to come. From inside my critic's natural conspiracy theory, I was struck by a familiar-looking wall in Fordington: it looked like the one Hardy drew, and built, for Max Gate: just a Dorset type, surely. But Beatty says Syward Lodge (much-altered, and now demolished) in East Fordington *was* designed by Hardy or an employer. They *might* be 'his' walls.

Beatty, Hardy guidebooks, instinct, gossip; the mass of information, books, knowledge in the Dorset County Museum and its wonderful staff; fragments of work, drawings, descriptions: exploring this, with generations of others, you become bewildered as to whether any boundary exists between Hardy's real and imaginary worlds. As Desmond Hawkins says, 'It is in the end the dream worlds ... that draw us to explore the haunted and haunting countryside, where his name seems to be written everywhere, yet invisible.'[6] Max Gate, itself an ongoing project, sits in the middle of an intimate, tough, transparent web linking the real and the imaginary countries of Wessex together.

Stinsford is particularly hard to categorise. It is his family church, where his grandparents, parents, Emma, Florence, Hardy's own heart, and his sisters and brother all lie buried, along with characters he described. He drew the big house, described the churchyard and lanes, designed and redesigned his real family gravestones using those full-size masking 'trait' drawings – including his own (which had to be adapted when his body was included in Poets Corner). A full rough plan of the church, heavily scribbled on tracing paper, is stuck between pages

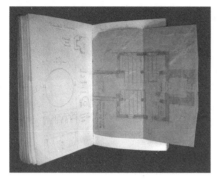

Stinsford Church: sketch plan; and drawing of the vanished musicians' gallery.

115 and 116 of the Architectural Notebook, showing where Lady Susan had sat, and Mrs Pitt; and the dotted line showing the position of the old musicians' gallery, and the old entrance path. This must be drawn from his father's or grandmother's memories: it is called 'Stinsford Church before the alterations about the year 1842': Hardy was only two years old.

The whole plan is measured (Notebook, page 114), for restorations or for comparison with West Knighton. There are rough detailed drawings of the composite font, which Beatty shows he restored in 1920.[7] On page 25 is a nice drawing and measured plan of a column detail, and overleaf (suggestively), a remarkable drawing of a choir in full voice.

As a critic, there is something niggling here. Stinsford is the strongest example of Hardy's desire to really conserve Wessex – but it is an imperfect work of conservation, as it stands. It had already been destructively restored in the 1840s and again in the 1870s (by Crickmay). Much was already lost: fine old pews, the gallery, the way it worked. Imaginatively, the drone of the ring-road is most damaging of all.

Hardy keeps returning to the demolished gallery. There are several 'finished' plans (included in the *Life*) showing where the musicians sat, including the Hardys. There is a sketch view too (and a suggested comparison with that vivid notebook tracing drawing, from an unknown original, of a village choir). It is the resonant core of his obsession with church galleries. Making good acoustic space is a specialised architectural and human skill: musical and technical, learned through experience. It cannot really be drawn, or fully predicted, but built and then 'tuned up' through testing (as the Irish architect and fiddle player Steve Larkin tunes houses for his musician clients). In a way, being a musician makes you read spaces, intensely, as architects do – yet without using drawing at all. As a traditional musician-architect, Larkin describes a strong sense of a modern performer in the long human tradition of collective, improvisational skill: a variant of the same sense in both music and architecture.[8]

In 'Notes on Stinsford Church', addressed to the restoration committee in April 1909, Hardy says:

> If an organ be really required, I should say, speaking for myself alone, that the old west gallery should be re-erected for it. Such west galleries, which were unadvisedly destroyed in the last century, are now getting replaced in some churches, there being no point in the edifice which so completely controls the singing of the congregation as the west gallery.[9]

And in 1996, a gallery *was* put back (the original north entrance has also been reinstated). Hardy's wishes have a long, slow outreach.

*

Just down river is Kingston Maurward of *Desperate Remedies*, where Hardy's father and grandfather were the retained builders; where his grandfather helped clamp on the fake stone, and where Hardy had seen one 'model' for Tess, the milkmaid Augusta Way. In a letter to the DCM, Beatty suggests this was also the site of the mystery farm building whose rough working-out drawings – cattle pens, farmhouse and drainage plans – are held in the museum.[10] And Beatty discusses the rough, measured sketch of the 'Fane' or temple and pond (described in *Desperate Remedies*) – the last of the 'chronological' drawings in the *Notebook*. Beatty checked the measurements against those at Kingston Maurward: an exact fit. He suggests Hardy (again a friend of the owners) may have designed the water lily pool,[11] perhaps as late as the 1920s. The temple figures in the miniature scenery were designed by Henry Tilley with Hardy for the Hardy Players productions too: and perhaps painted by Hardy himself.

Going on, through the fields, you reach Bockhampton. Built by his grandfather and extended by his father (when Hardy may have helped 'puddle' the walls). One of his very last pieces of factual writing, 'The Ancient Cottages of England' (1927) describes the building of one of the last 'mudwall-cottages' – using clay, chalk and straw:

> ...mixed up into a sort of dough-pudding by treading and shovelling, thrown up with a pitchfork till a rise of about three feet – left to settle for a day or two. When the wall had dried a little, the outer face was cut down to a fairly flat surface with a spade, and the wall then plastered outside and in ...[12]

These buildings lasted well, he says, if maintained, kept thatched and dry: thatch lasts better if not threshed but 'drawn' by hand. He continues: 'I never heard of any damp coming in through these mud-walled, plastered and lime whitened on the outside.' They are also much easier to keep warm than new, colder and damper, thin-walled, high-ceilinged buildings with large, single-glazed windows – like Max Gate, except for its cavity walls. Again, that sounds personal, and the precise date matches Bockhampton.

> I would therefore urge owners to let as many as are left of their old cottages remain where they are, and to repair them instead of replacing them with bricks, since, apart from their warmth and dryness, they have almost always great beauty and charm. Not only so, but I would suggest their construction might be imitated where rebuilding is absolutely necessary.[13]

Hardy's birthplace is one of the National Trust's gems: its beautiful cottage garden, its thatched loveliness, its unconverted authenticity, its well-captured history, and its immediate, beautiful access into some unspoilt fragments of England. And that is no coincidence either. Hardy organised his friend Hermann Lea to take on the lease after Jemima's death. The cottage, so often part-described ('Domicilium', *Under The Greenwood Tree*, 'The Self-Unseeing'; and many, many others) is a key piece of prescient, living conservation work. It is a demonstration of how to preserve, and maintain; of how to live in old buildings – not that he was doing it himself. He 'advised' Lea on how to replant the garden, manage the maintenance, take the photographs. Lea had to deal with the visitors too. Hardy had arranged the whole thing.

That whole setting, arguably, is part of his outreach. The woods his grandparents planted, reinstating a fragment of vanished woodlands, are protected under his aegis; the heath too. The Egdon of *The Return of the Native* is still genuinely wild: it is surprisingly easy to lose yourself in the head-high bracken and the directionless, ancient high landscape, although it is much smaller than its older, fictional avatar: as Hardy says. Recent documents say it is fifteen per cent of what was recorded in 1811; the strategy to preserve it draws both headlines and inspiration from Hardy's writing.[14] Further downriver[15] is Lower Lewell, the farmhouse standing for the idyllic Talbothays in *Tess*, in its wide, flat empty valley. Beyond is Woodsford Castle, that lovely restoration, near to West Stafford, with the other Talbothays: the large, plain, comfortable-looking house Hardy built for his brother and sisters. It is the *name* that seems shocking, taken from that rare and beautiful Hardy idyll. But the name predated *Tess*; it went with the *land*, which the Hardy family historically owned. In his usual close shifting of real names, that awkwardly noticeable name draws our attention to Hardy's real inherited place.

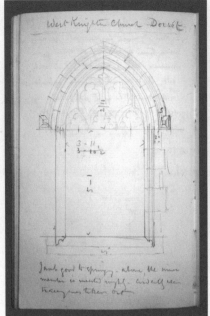

Left: West Knighton: Hardy's Notebook; right: Hardy's 'repairs'.

And so on. The Talbothays cottages over the road, another possible, now demolished house nearby. A name, Hardy Row, on pretty nineteenth century cottages, in West Knighton. And I could go on, between Beatty, inference, local assertion and guesswork. The trail of possible tiny fragments, patches, details and ideas of real Hardy architectural work does not stop, and generations of us keep following it.

I would say that was intentional. Hardy is deliberately making us *look* at this place, whether or not he actually authored bits of it. And then, he *was* an architect playing an active, covert role in the conservation movement; he *was* the member of a close family with a working building firm; he *was* helpful to those who sought advice. The bigger idea, of a Wessex dotted with tiny patches of lime-free mortar, drains, 'light and strong gates', hinges, ideas, names by Hardy, is not only a way of seeing the landscape he generated for us – but certainly, also partly true.

The best of all this cloud of possible, 'real 'work is clearly authored, lovely, and all but invisible. The restoration of West Knighton church in 1894 is entirely authenticated, although still very little known. An article in *The Builder*, written by Hardy himself (though anonymously[16]), begins:

The ancient church of West Knighton, which was closed for repairs in August last, has just been re-opened. The chancel roof, which was decayed, has been removed and a new roof with stone tiles been re-erected. The inner walls have had all the old plaster cleaned off, and been cemented throughout. Mullions and tracery have been added to the windows on the North side, and both windows have been made uniform...

The churchyard is exquisite. Unlevelled, containing a depth of healthy greenery; yew trees; the damp-proofing slot dug between church and risen graveyard (I am sure he loved this everyday grave-digging detail – like a section through time). It has that strong sense of life and death which is spoiled at Stinsford by the ring-road rushing past. The heavy stone slate roof (of which much remains) is really lovely, and unusual for the 1890s. So are the walls, deliberately, visibly patched. It is a lottery, walking into an old church in England: normally, you find yourself inexplicably in a sterilised nineteenth century, the past swept away. This is so much not the case at West Knighton that it is almost a shock. This is a lovely, welcoming church. There is a powerful sense of how it is, and has been, used. It is a palimpsest: ancient stonework (for example, a squint and part of an arcade) has been opened up and left exposed; so have remarkable fragments of frescoes, including an unusual one in Hebrew, for this was a Knights Templars' church.

The strong sense, when you walk in, is not just visual; and it is hard to capture in photographs. It is social, acoustic, spatial, and old: an assembly of physical conditions. You can *tell* this church is principally a social and human space for singing and music, for christenings, weddings, funerals, harvest festivals and other things, together, and that it has been for hundreds of years. You can *tell* the acoustics are good. Describing this church makes you remember how much deeper our knowledge of human environment is than in appearance alone.

Hardy's new West gallery must organise the acoustics. It is not a copy, not a statement, but simple, plain, well-crafted: designed for excellent sightlines and acoustics. You can see, and hear, well into the church; it has a good rooflight (galleries were often too secluded for the general good, a factor leading to their removal, as Dorothy L. Sayers shows in her detective novel *The Nine Tailors*). And the new West window makes the tower stair light and pleasant. The main church windows – neatly-glazed, clear glass, a bit of colour – maintain the wonderful 'prayer-book' church relationship of the congregation with the world outside. Awkward, irregular doors and roof trusses are carefully retained. Almost any other architect would have tried to reconfigure these fragments of diverse history into a new, coherent vision – but remarkably, this has *not* been done. This church is left as a loose aggregate of work over time.

149

West Knighton, Hardy's 'repairs': a rich assembly of fragments.

This is all Hardy. *The Builder* details it all: reglazing gallery, rooflight, uncovering of the arch and pillar, frescoes, font, encaustic tiles.[17] Beatty suggests Hardy is treating West Knighton as a kind of forgery: a restoration so 'authentic' you would not know it was new – just what the SPAB and William Morris argue *against*; although, Beatty says, the church 'emerged enriched rather than ruined ... Hardy was no botcher'.[18] Beatty's praise is right, but his interpretation inexact. The old, hand-worked stones are exposed in all their irregular glory, while the new windows are clearly fresh Victorian work. As Hardy later says of such work: 'The old form inherits, or has acquired, an indefinable quality – possibly some deviation from exact geometry (curves were often struck by hand in mediaeval work) which never appears in the copy.'[19]

What Beatty *is* recognising, I suggest, is that sense of continuity, which makes this church remarkable of its age, and exemplary in ours. You can sense how this building has changed through the centuries; been built, extended, reconfigured, re-thought over a huge timeframe. It will hopefully outlive us, doing so, old as it is. It has *not* had a new framework forced over it. That restraint, that collaboration with buried and unborn users, is a very unusual thing for an architect to do.

This is *not* signature architectural work: it is even more modest than Turnworth; almost polemically so. With notable exceptions it is almost unheard of for any architect to resist the temptation to make any job look all of a piece, finished, right, *now*. This is such a good restoration job that the architect has, deliberately, disappeared.

Or rather, he almost disappears. There is a lovely key, too, large, plain but with small flourishes in the metalwork which must date from this time, and which recalls Hardy's other ironmongery designs. And he *does* sign this work, both in *The Builder* – and by annotating Hutchins's history of Dorset, which says that the church 'contains nothing remarkable'. Hardy adds 'This statement is not now correct. Recent examination & repairs have uncovered much interesting early architecture.'[20] And this approach is *exactly* what Hardy described, nine years later, in his 'Memories of Church Restoration': 'The Protection of an ancient edifice against renewal in fresh materials is, in fact, even more of a social – I may say humane – duty that an aesthetic one.'[21] This, he says, means the architect with an 'antiquarian bias' is 'pulled in two directions': by his wish to 'hand on or modify the abstract form' (that means redesign, or 'Restoration'), and by 'reverence for the antiquity of its embodiment' which means leave alone. And he comes down firmly on the side of patching:

> If I were practising in that profession I would not, I think, undertake a church restoration under any circumstances. I should reply, if asked to do so, that a retired tinker or riveter of old china, or some 'Old Mortality' from the almshouse, would superintend the building better. In short, the opposing tendencies excited in an architect by the distracting situation can find no satisfactory reconciliation.[22]

Even allowing that he meant capital 'R' Restoration, this is extreme, disingenuous Hardy. He has already *done* this job, and with just such restraint, in exactly the way of the 'riveter of old china'. He is 'repairing', not 'Restoring', and he makes the same distinction in *Jude* – which he was writing at the same time as doing the church. He is not re-visioning; not reclaiming and remaking authorship of the building, but joining its long skilled vernacular tradition of imaginative care. And he must have told the clients something to this effect, too, for them to let him do what he did.

*

I am struck by the level of collaborative work Hardy appears to be doing – which is natural, for architects, but hard to trace. The SPAB campaigns, the work with Henry, the patching and repairing of ancient buildings which have traditionally been made in just this way. Hardy moved out of 'normal'

151

architectural practice in two directions. In one, he was operating in a highly visible, highly authored, very popular imaginative world – which also prefigured the most radical projects of a century later. In another, he was invisibly working back into a time when architects were not artists, authors and the elite; where they were master technicists, working and living collectively, part of an unnamed, instinctive, skilled, ongoing human construction of the environment.

West Knighton is special because it is *unusually* typical; a type which is hard to find. It matches some ideal of the past, in your head. A sense of continuum, of a palimpsest, has been carefully uncovered, reconstructed and made good: the architect leaving only traces (that signature, composite font, the key, the glazing). But then, Hardy could afford to be modest. He was claiming named authorship of the whole imaginary country in which it lay.

And this was while he was writing *Jude*. There is one particular vision in it which is rightly linked with West Knighton:

> For a moment there fell on Jude a true illumination; that here in the stone yard was a centre of effort as worthy as that dignified by the name of scholarly study within the noblest of the colleges. But he lost it under the stress of his old idea. He would accept any employment which might be offered him on the strength of his late employer's recommendation; but he would accept it as a provisional thing only. This was his form of the modern vice of unrest.[23]

I believe his 'small country town architect' idea probably came from here. The satisfaction in the making of physical things was, in later life, present to him in a way he had probably undervalued in his youth. I believe Hardy *had* found his 'satisfactory reconciliation'. He had developed a means of 'practice' where his dilemma, between architectural vision and the wonderful 'patching' of the skilled, invisible everyday worker, actually worked. He had constructed a vast, imaginary, reciprocal project in which his authored, copyright visions were realised (without ruining himself with architecture). And *within* that, he was arguing for, and actually exercising, an older, anti-architectural, skilled human practice. The contradiction between opposites, intimately balanced. The more famous the imaginary project, the more invisible the everyday craftsman could be.

PART 3

EXTENSION

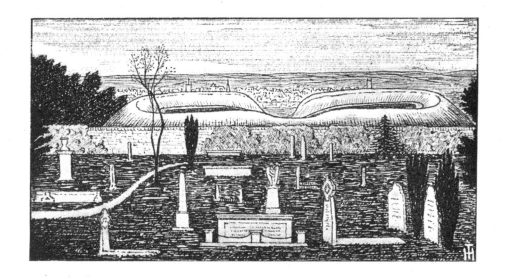

Overleaf: *Wessex Poems*: Maumbury and Dorchester.

15

TIME AND PLACE

Subject and Method

Hardy was born into not just changing times, but a change of time itself. 1840, the year of his birth, was when Railway Time was introduced to Britain: a moment when the age-old conception of time as a local reality determined by the position of the sun was snuffed out. A standardised time was imposed all over the country, to allow train timetables to work. Bristol was no longer ten minutes behind London, for example, and a consciousness lasting thousands of years was overridden by a new, modern, legally imposed way of telling time. Hardy was, as Michael Millgate says, born just in time to catch a last glimpse of a thousand-year rural lifetime, about to vanish forever.[1] And in his work, there is always a sense of his double-exposure of time: the speculative, modern vision used to frame the ancient, physical past. An intensely imagined older world, imagined through frames of photography, moving image, the telegraph, and modern thought – a deliberate shift between our older senses of time and our newest.

All novels use time as a structuring device. Back in *Desperate Remedies*, Hardy was already underlining the strangeness of novels' conventions: 'The Events of Thirty Years' and 'The Events of Eighteen Hours', used as chapter titles with sub-sections broken down into hourly slots. Time is a normal-seeming device, which authors manipulate all the time. But for Hardy, it is also his great subject matter: the losses of countryside; of village choirs, woodlands, cottages; of local sensibilities, histories and skills; of the intense understanding of one's own environment passed through generations. The abstract ideas too: the almost unbearable sense of the quantum, of parallel lives that might have been; and Tess's memorable sense, in the repeating cycle of the year, of the unknown date of her own death.

Remembering stories in places, stroking stone, valuing old and well-used buildings, imagining, through knowledge and instinct, the working environment of the past: the 'art independent of written history'; the ongoing polemic for a conservation sensibility. The sense of time as perception, and stories embodied in place is everywhere in his poems, one of his defining traits: one can choose from hundreds of examples. This is part of 'The Self-Unseeing':

Here is the ancient floor,
Footworn and hollowed and thin,
Here was the former door,
Where the dead feet walked in ...

And this is a fragment of modern and cinematic perception, from the less-known 'Nobody Comes':

A car comes up, lamps full glare;
that flash upon a tree;
it has nothing to do with me
And whangs along in a world of its own
Leaving a blacker air

He would use this sense of repeating time in the outpourings of verse written after his first wife Emma died, obsessively overlaying the romantic and vivid past over more alienated and bitter recent events, in place after place. He would keep that study calendar set to the day he met her. Even the titles of the collections of poems which he wrote throughout his life: *Poems of the Past and the Present*; *Late Lyrics and Earlier* are assembled from work over time, and those names help structure and shape his work. He called himself a 'Time Torn Man'. He would greet Quantum Theory like an old friend.

As a designer, he was most at home and most remarkable in buildings like Turnworth and West Knighton, which are themselves accretive; where his architectural 'vision' is about continuing the works of nameless others. It is probably fair to say he should have converted a building to live in: even Woodsford looks exquisite. But he would treat Max Gate the same way, immediately starting to rework it as though dealing with an old building: leaving the shapes of walled-up windows and doors expressed and even emphasised. He was designing in the constant, conscious tension of age, newness, return. There is the framed mirror in the sitting room of Max Gate: a Hardy frame setting it over the fireplace, around an early nineteenth-century frame, around an eighteenth-century piece of dark, mercury-processed glass[2] which has reflected life through history. There is a possibly related poem, too, 'Moments of Vision'. In all, it is a miniature conceptual domestic artwork in itself. Hardy can, literally, make you see back through time.

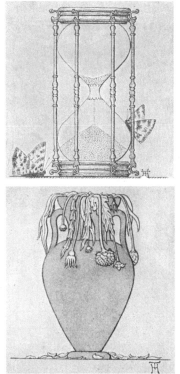

Left: *Wessex Poems* drawings: time visualized; right: the composite, dark eighteenth-century mirror, framed and reframed, which Hardy set in Max Gate: Hardy can make you see time.

*

And that is only the content. Trying to date the *development* of Wessex is like flying through a thick, volatile cloud. Hardy wrote and re-wrote his novels, edited and changed them throughout his life. He linked them together, wrote related essays, expanded their context, added and re-wrote prefaces, footnotes and work in other media. The identity of Wessex kept changing and growing, its structure becoming deeper, more complex, different, year on year. He would go on developing Wessex decades after the last novel had been completed.

Hardy's tiny edits can change things a lot. They shift the tone, shape and substance of the Wessex in your mind. He was expert at editing and shaping material to get it round publishing 'censorship'.[3] For instance, he published controversial bits of *Tess* as short stories, separately from the 'family' serial, re-assembling his full version for book publication in more liberal American editions. This cloud of publication adds to the shape-shifting sensation of Wessex as something not altogether *contained* in the book you are reading. Hardy's great palimpsest shifts with every new addition, edit or revision, as Gatrell shows. As a committed re-reader, you can find yourself inadvertently reading an earlier *Trumpet Major*, grounded in real Weymouth and a simpler oral-history, or regretting that the cheerful living Casterbridge of your projected imagination has been punctured by the pessimistic 1912 footnotes.

Writing this book has also made me acutely aware how unreliable bracketed dates may be. Victorian novels were published (usually) first in serial form, and in book form later (the bracketed date). Dates are often misleading, and usually overlapping. *Tess* (although both serial version and novel were published in 1891) overlaps with at least three other books: *The Woodlanders*, *The Well-Beloved* and *Jude the Obscure*, and was subject to Hardy's typical overwriting afterwards. Dates gather round any piece of his work like insects, and wander away again too. Whichever modern edition you read has already been reconstructed by an editor, selecting from the many print-ready versions Hardy prepared. The idea of any of his novels (and by extension, of any novel) as a dateable, definitive text starts to shimmer and evaporate like a mirage. Wessex has a chronological life all of its own.

That relates to architecture too. Dates are a badly-fitting measure of a slow, unpredictable, iterative process, where buildings are imagined, drawn, published, redrawn, delayed, built (and changed in the process), used, rebuilt, demolished, and remembered. Dates might denote design or publication, start or finish of construction – and rarely specify which. Published dates (mistakes and all) get *re*published, along with 'original' or finished drawings or 'perfect' unoccupied photographs (sometimes taken while the builders are still there), feeding an artificial idea of architectural 'completion'. A whole branch of fairly recent architectural theory discusses this. In *A Laodicean*, Hardy shows architecture as a different way of understanding time; he calls written history 'charlatanism': once again, his vision was radical, and ahead of ours.

For *all* design is necessarily time-based: an ingredient with which architects naturally work; considering how materials or details will age, how a building's needs, functions, contexts will change. It works in a projective tense; a subjunctive mood. The wonderful architects O'Donnell + Tuomey, in their Gold Medal speech at the RIBA in 2015, described this projective way of thinking as using the 'future perfect'. Architects project, as a working method, a vision of the future (and the past) as a guide to how to make and do things, now.

*

So dating Hardy's work is an elusive pursuit. *The Well-Beloved*, or *The Pursuit of the Well-Beloved*, the last of Hardy's novels to be fully published in book form, is the strangest of all. Two different versions of the story were published over a five-year period, from 1892, when the series was commissioned, making that bracketed date (1897) especially uninformative. That chronological blur continues in its content: the disturbing tale of a man who jilts a girl, only to fall in love with her daughter, then her granddaughter – all called Avice Caro – and who tries to marry all three of them. Its unsettling chronology includes its section titles: 'A Young Man of Twenty'; 'A Young Man of Forty; 'A Young Man of Sixty'. I have noted this irony shifts with the reader's age: obviously creepy to the confident teenager; painfully accurate to the older reader.

The Well-Beloved is itself a kind of model of Wessex (as Wessex is a model of England: an allegorical miniature, a barbed tail on the map). It is geologically grounded in the stone quarries, castles and cottages of the Isle of Purbeck – the strange Dorset peninsular from which London's famous Portland Stone comes. The whole isolated community works through the sense and skills of its geological substance: even the poorest cottages are finely detailed; even Jocelyn, the middle-class (anti)hero, is a sculptor. Stone seems a specially native and meaningful medium for Hardy, both epic and introspective. Proust wrote of Hardy's sense of stonework, in The Remembrance of Things Past: 'all of those novels which can be laid upon each other like the vertically piled houses upon the rocky soil of the island'.[4] As Beatty says, Hardy left his 'mason's mark' on The Well-Beloved.[5]

Again, this fascination is extended factually, in the remarkable article Hardy wrote for the Society of Dorset Men in London (1908–1909): 'Its façade thrills to the street noises all day long, and has done so for three or four hundred years. But through what a stretch of time did it thrill all day and all night in Portland to the tides of West Bay, particularly when they slammed against the island during the south-west gales.'[6] Son and grandson of masons; predictor of cinematic vision, watching trainloads of stone passing Max Gate on their way to London: the older England being emptied out to build the new. Hardy was in fact a brilliant experimenter in turning the essential linear form of text, which packs so neatly into novel form, into embodied, imagined form too, making time work like the far more intense, variously perceived, abstract, embodied, repetitive, instinctive, infinitely present mind's-eye phenomenon it really is.

*

Yet following Hardy's work as it developed is architecturally familiar too. The leaps of vision and imagination, the improvisatory assembly of any material happening in your mind at the time. The critical revisiting of past projects, the response to critics, the sense of adjusting, experimenting and remaking the whole assembly of work. Of work, both noun and verb.[7] The recognition of a slowly-emerging structure and substance; of a vision, outlasting its age. This is a familiar place for an architectural critic to be – although expressing it is fairly unusual.[8] But Garbett does it; Gatrell's 'evolutionary model' of Wessex describes the same process; as does Dalziel's study of the *Wessex Poems*. It is roughly the process that schools of architecture (like the AA) use to actually teach architectural design: through those imagined, drawn, illustrated design projects; those 'enabling fictions'.

Those 'fictions', like the development of Wessex, mirror the process of architectural work itself: the period of survey and experiments, the drawing and re-drawing, the gradual, trial and error development of the parts and the whole, the assembly of complex things to form a big, working whole. And then the processes of standing back, testing, discussing, revising, deciding which things work and which do not, almost always in some kind of public form. These things are not exactly written down, and they do not exactly happen all in separate batches, but shade through the whole working process: generally more experiment, survey or research at the start; generally more assembly and synthesis in the middle, and ideally leading eventually to a more tuned-up, critically lucid working whole at the end.[9]

It is also the process Hardy appears to be attempting to discuss with Albert Richardson: 'Hardy said architecture taught him to place one thing upon another … it refers back to the old method of building, the walls first, the beams and the roof-lithic construction.'[10] Lithic means to do with stone, but I suggest Hardy was talking far more widely than has been thought here, of the whole iterative design process of trial and error, improvisation, refinement and learning, all of it in some way collective, working with others, through which architects actually manage to do their incredibly complicated job.

And Hardy has now reached the third 'evolutionary' design stage, where the experienced practitioner has developed a great ability to stand back and look at the whole body of their work: to re-describe it, test it, challenge and improve it. This usually takes time: Garbett suggests a few years for the working practitioner; RMIT suggests seven years as a working requirement for its PhD by practice. Or it may come more or less in parallel, by giving lectures, by responding to the criticism of others – and often by writing and publishing a more analytic version of your own work. (Koolhaas set up a separate research arm of his practice to do just that.[11]) The publication, and the response to criticism, which Hardy is sometimes criticised for following too slavishly, is an absolutely fundamental part of this collective, improvisational, critical, inventive process at its highest level.

Experienced critics, tutors and architects can see this process working, chronologically. Although the processes are (inevitably) unique and unexpected, 'simple' chronology reveals things which do not appear when work is grouped thematically. The way that Hardy's different types of work interact show this; the inevitable, working connections between novels, buildings, drawings, conservation, factual essays, poems and plays, fragments of restoration and polemic. The range of experiment, the way he is drawing from his critics and his peers; the constant testing, developing, changing, rethinking and visualising of his great project can only be seen working *together*, when you take that artificial cross-section through 'simple' dated time.

*

With *Tess* and *Jude*, Wessex reaches that third level; they mark a kind of sea change. Although written close to *The Woodlanders* in time (and place; each was written in a different room in Max Gate), they are very distinct works. Hardy and Florence's own *Life* is split between the writing of *Tess* and its publication. Other writers agree: 'The Wessex cycle of novels really concludes with *The Woodlanders*, and *Tess* as a whole is a very different novel from its predecessors,' says P.N. Furbank.[12] Hardy himself listed both *Tess* and *Jude* as part of his definitive Character and Environment group of novels: heartland of Wessex, with *Tess* at the top. *Jude*, only a little further down the list, so outraged his audience that Hardy claimed it stopped him writing novels altogether. Terry Eagleton, in his foreword to *Jude* says:

> With *Tess of the d'Urbervilles* and *Jude the Obscure*, Hardy had brought his long exploration of the human condition of society to a point of mature complexity ... these two novels have a sense of imaginative resolution about them which makes their status as last novels logical rather than fortuitous – something more, anyway, than a submissive bowing to bad reviews.[13]

Eagleton is right: these two books feel not like a thwarted project, but a fully completed one. They seem distinct from their close neighbours; and part of the final 'evolutionary' stage of Wessex – each, in their own bleak way, around a deeply idealistic and visionary core. They are so highly achieved, so profoundly different, that they can be taken as alternate conclusions of what the Wessex of the novels had become.

They are both spectacular, tragic, consummately achieved – and entirely different. In *Tess*, the great description of Wessex, the fully imagined *place* would be triumphantly delivered. And *Jude* – surprisingly – is the resolution of Hardy's outrageously polemical experiments, the 'novels of ingenuity', although Hardy does not put it in that category. And although it has scarcely been noticed for this strange quality, it is the most outspokenly architectural of all.

THE CENTRE OF THE MAP

Tess of the d'Urbervilles

Blackmoor Vale, Hermann Lea.

Something happens, in *Tess of the d'Urbervilles*, which is crucial to an architectural 'vision' of Wessex. It is as though two ways of looking at Wessex: one architectural, one more broadly human, suddenly overlap. Indeed, it is only now (where it pauses) that we can see that such double-focus *was* more or less characteristic of Hardy's vision before. For in *Tess*, those focal lenses converge. Wessex itself appears: lucid, coherent and whole.

Tess of the d'Urbervilles, Gatrell says, is *the* Wessex novel. If all the others 'were to vanish from human consciousness overnight and *Tess of the d'Urbervilles* were saved, then Wessex could survive, not intact, but in essence'.[1] That is true architecturally too, despite the lack of architects, builders or building work. Despite, even *because* I would argue, its organising vision is of a bleak and empty landscape.

An overview, a view from high ground, or a map, is a key moment in an architectural project. When one picture or structural idea starts to *contain* others, to act as a key to understanding them, architectural critics and teachers start getting excited. However long it takes to make or to recognise, however much debate it takes to agree, this is the strong, familiar sense of an architectural project. It is what enables architects to construct buildings at all. You *have* to be able to work out details and locate them, to stand back and assess how they work together in the as-yet-unreal places you are designing. It requires the practised skill of imagining the same thing at different scales; the relationship of parts to the whole. It is an unspoken skill that architects learn, in school and in practice, by doing their job.

And *Tess* gives us a fully-imagined place, startlingly visual, mapped, measured and meaningful. We know what that place is like, how it works, how it affects the experience of people's lives, practically and imaginatively. Wessex *looks* right, now; *feels* right, in form and content. And that is because we know how to put it all together. Hardy has shown us substantial places in intense analytical detail before: in *The Return of the Native*, in *The Mayor of Casterbridge*, and in *The Woodlanders*. But he has stepped back here to make a sketch map of the whole thing, linking the places we already know, adding the many missing elements: the uplands, the farming valleys – and the infrastructures, old and new, which connect them. He is showing us how these environments fit together; the hidden means which make them work as they do, rich or poor, fertile or harsh. *Tess* is not just wonderful in itself, but a lucid, coherent vision of Wessex itself.

*

There are two key *Tess* maps remaining. One, 'Tess's Wanderings' is Hardy's own, marked-up copy of 'Cruchley's Railway and Telegraphic Map of Dorsetshire', a highly detailed railway map, with Tess's routes and destinations drawn on it by Hardy, in detail. It is a story largely contained in a single map sheet with Tess's walks drawn in red and with crosses also identifying key navigational points – often hilltops and viewpoints. For although Cruchley's map is very detailed, the topography – the shapes of the hills – can be sketchy.

The other, 'Tess's Country' (published in *Harper's* magazine in 1925), is a smaller, retrospective map. It is of the familiar Wessex type: drawn freely and confidently, in proportion, with an assured sense of what matters – as architects *do* retrospectively

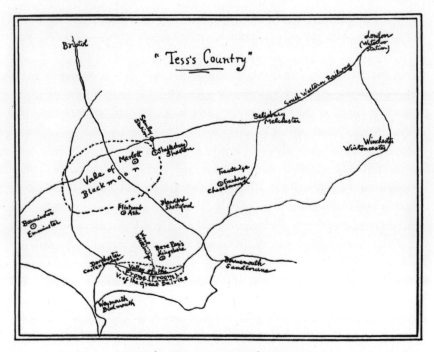

HARDY'S OWN MAP OF TESS'S COUNTRY

A hitherto unpublished map drawn many years ago by Mr. Hardy for
Mr. and Mrs. Lorin F. Deland (Margaret Deland)

'Tess's Country' map.

'sketch' their fully achieved projects. It is a return to *The Bookman* map – and specifically, to being a *railway* map. It even updates the network, adding the new South Western line through the vale of Blackmoor. Like the drawings in Vladimir Nabokov's *Lectures on Literature*, this is both a map of a place, and the structure of the story. Tess's 'wanderings' – literally – describe Wessex.

Yet the book only touches those railways. The main parts of the story happen in the spaces between them: the unnamed range of hills and the broad, open valleys. But the *map* clearly shows a network of lines as the organising structure: the infrastructure which set out the conditions of the story. Hardy is showing the framework between which Tess's life fell.

*

Written in the late 1880s, *Tess* is set in recent memory and, I would say, an utterly accurate landscape. There are no 'witch's rides' for Tess: her fruitless thirty-mile, day-walk to Angel's parents, half of it wearing the wrong shoes, stretches endurance: it is realistic, precise and measured. The most overtly epic of Hardy's novels – invoking the Gods, fate, Homer, King Lear and human sacrifice – it is also the most strongly grafted to a visitable land. Hardy puts it at the top of the Wessex list: the most important of all. So to follow Tess around – as Ralph Vaughan Williams did[2] – is instructive.

We begin roughly where we left off: the country of *The Woodlanders*, but 'the forests have departed'.[3] Marlott is her childhood village and the teenage Tess has scarcely visited the local town. 'Every contour of the surrounding hills was as personal to her as that of her relatives' faces.'[4] Tess belongs to the generation educated to aim for better things but struggling with the near impossibility of doing them.[5] This is the age of 'The Dorsetshire Labourer': a generation dependent on short-term work, vulnerable to exploitation, homelessness and destitution. Sent to seek wealthy 'relatives', Tess finds: 'a country house built for enjoyment pure and simple, with not an acre of troublesome land ... beyond what was required for residential purposes and for a little fancy farm ... The crimson brick lodge came first in sight ... Everything looked like money.'[6]

Note that bitter joke: 'troublesome land'. This is the shift to a modern countryside: wealthy incomers with token farming interests and local workers with nowhere to live. We will see Wessex at its most bleak *and* its most idyllic and heady here. But on the ground, each environment is completely immersive. After the death of her baby, the story unexpectedly takes Tess to work as a milkmaid in the beautiful water-meadows of the Frome:

> Not quite sure of her direction Tess stood still upon the hemmed expanse of verdant flatness, like a fly on a billiard table of indefinite length, and of no more consequence to the surrounding than that fly. The sole effect of her presence upon the placid valley so far had been to excite the mind of a solitary heron, which, after descending to the ground not far from her path, stood with neck erect, looking at her ...[7]

The Talbothays part of the book is filled with delight: sensual, visual, erotic, dreamlike. Tess's profile pressed on the flank of the cow like a cameo; the flooded stream stopping girls in their best dresses getting to church; a butterfly trapped in a layer of gauze. The writing is saturated with concupiscent metaphor – moist, fecund, filled with creatures; you wonder how he got away with it.[8]

> Amid the oozing fatness and warm ferments of the Froom Vale, at a season when the rush of juices could almost be heard below the hiss of fertilization, it was impossible that the most fanciful love should not grow passionate. The ready bosoms existing there were impregnated by their surroundings.[9]

Wellbridge/Wool Manor, site of Tess's disastrous honeymoon, Hermann Lea.

Tess is filled with scenes which are both emphatic metaphors and acute, visceral descriptions: the primeval forest; the wounded birds in the woods; Tess shaken bodily on the threshing machine; the evicted family camping in their ancestral churchyard (their bedstead making an 'excellent tent' against the traceried window[10]); the crypt where Tess is literally driven to the wall: 'why am I on the wrong side of this door!'[11]

Hardy is showing his mastery of calling up *any* kind of environment and our reactions to it, from the romantic charge of youngsters working at lush Talbothays to the brutal, hard work of Flintcomb-Ash. He even describes how modern incomers like Angel Clare experience rural work:

Unexpectedly, he began to like the outdoor life for its own sake ... He grew away from old associations and saw something new in life and humanity ... he made close acquaintance with ... the seasons in their moods, morning and evening, night and noon, winds in their different tempers, trees, waters and mists, shades and silences, and the voices of inanimate things.[12]

This is no fictional conceit, it is an analysis of the real conditions of post-rural England.

The startling clarity of sensory vision is everywhere. Tess was Hardy's favourite character, and we have a surprising amount of information from which to construct our own picture of what she looked like. Hardy drew the 'grotesque caricature' drawings in Wool Manor (perhaps for use in the stage version), and named several real-life models: Agatha Thorneycroft; Augusta Way, the Kingston Maurward milkmaid, whose daughter would act the part of Tess herself in the Hardy Players.

But the place (I would argue) is entirely precise. Here is the famous description of Flintcomb-Ash, the harsh, chalk upland farm where Tess works after the collapse of her marriage to Angel Clare:

> There was no exaggeration in Marian's description of Flintcomb-Ash as a starve-acre place. The single fat thing on the land was Marian herself; and she was an importation. Of the three classes of village, the village cared for by its lord, the village cared for by itself, and the village uncared for either by itself or by its lord (in other words, the village of a resident squire's tenantry, the village of free or copy-holders, and the absentee-owner's village, farmed with the land) this place, Flintcomb-Ash, was the third ...

> The swede-field in which she and her companion were set hacking was a stretch of a hundred odd acres, in one patch, on the highest ground of the farm, rising above stony lanchets or lynchets ... loose white flints in bulbous, cusped and phallic shapes ... the whole field was in colour a desolate drab; it was a complexion without features ... The sky wore, in another colour, the same likeness; a white vacuity of countenance with the lineaments gone. So these two upper and nether visages confronted each other all day long; the white face looking down on the brown face, and the brown face looking up at the white face, without anything standing between them but the two girls crawling over the surface of the former like flies.[13]

This is the unromantic land, condensed in one of the greatest, most-used of Hardy quotations, a brilliant, economically drafted description: visual, graphic, informative, allusive – note the reference to King Lear,[14] the scrupulous information, and the joke. This writing renders illustrations unnecessary.

Yet Flintcomb-Ash, at the centre of both book and map, has a surprisingly disputed location. Hardy's own directions are crystal clear: 'A farm near Nettlecomb-Tout'; 'a mile south of Nettlecomb-Tout.'[15] Yet generations of writers have failed to identify, or have disagreed about, the 'remains of a village'. Doles Ash, Alton Pancras, Church Hill and Plush have all been suggested, none of them meeting that precise direction. Most confusingly, Hermann Lea, Hardy's 'authorised' guide and friend, calls it 'unidentifiable', but also mentions Church Hill. This is *not* Hardy's wry, polemically missing woodlands in *The Woodlanders*, and it is important that

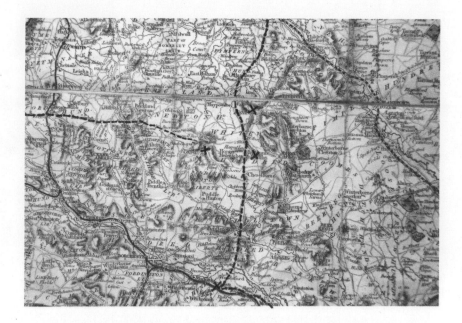

'Tess's Wanderings', detail. Hardy's map, highlighted to show
location of Hardy's faded red marks round Flintcomb-Ash.

such ambiguity has grown around it. The problem seems to be that these secondary
writers were looking for a *village* – so they plump for Plush or Alton Pancras,
overlooking the scant remains of one of Dorset's *real* vanished villages: precisely in
the farm, marked clearly on the Cruchley map, where Tess's marked trail runs out
and with viewpoint crosses on its high fields: 'Liscombe Farm', exactly a mile south
of Nettlecombe Tout.

Lyscombe Farm is made up of the great bowl (or 'shallow depression') of Lyscombe
Bottom, the valley opening out from it, the coombe further down, and the high
ridges all around them: Nettlecombe Tout (until 2014) was on Lyscombe land. The
farm is named, its buildings marked, by Cruchley, and Hardy's red line stops here,
with two red crosses marked on the high ground. It is precisely fifteen miles from
Beaminster, as Hardy says – and has an all-but-vanished mediaeval village in its
farmyard into the bargain.

The mediaeval village or grange of Lyscombe was once a meeting place, on the
pilgrimage route between Milton Abbas and Cerne Abbas, with a small eleventh
century chapel, a medieval fishpond (paying dues of twelve trout a year to Milton
Abbey), a sixteenth-century priest's house, and a large, late mediaeval barn.[16] The
important crossroads of the Dorset Gap, a crossing of 'hollow-ways' or deep droving
and packhorse tracks, lies just over the shoulder of the hill, used from at least the

Middle Ages and probably much earlier, and Lyscombe is ringed with cross-dykes and ancient earthworks, still roughly visible in the high fields. But by the mid-nineteenth century, it was an almost abandoned landscape. An article by Jo Draper in *Dorset Life* (not mentioning Hardy), says:

> There is no road through the valley, so all visitors must walk. Until the 1880s access was even more difficult, [maybe that's why Lea didn't find it] with only a rough track (now a footpath) leading to the hamlet. Lyscombe was sold in 1880 (along with 1,320 acres of Plush) and the sale map shows that there were only three buildings in the hamlet then – the late medieval barn, and across the river the cottage and chapel. Lyscombe was an out-farm, with just the barn and cottages. The land was farmed as part of a much larger area, and the farmer lived elsewhere. Indeed in 1880 Lyscombe must have had even fewer buildings than it did in medieval times. By 1900 a new access road (the current one) had been built, along with a big farmhouse and more farm buildings.[17]

This dovetails with Hardy's description to an extent suggesting the same source – perhaps the 1880 sale document had drawn Hardy out for a walk. For the vision of *Tess* is that of Wessex Heights: the sense of distance, of isolation. Hardy clearly never brought Lea here; as the poem says, he comes here alone.

Even today, restored and repaired, the 'remains of the village' are hard to see. The chapel and priests' house were in use as cottages until the 1950s, when they quickly became ruins, the thatch and building decaying; the chapel covered in ivy and corrugated iron. The whole thing was camouflaged by the more recent farmyard, often a precursor to the end of such vanished villages, as Linda Viner describes.[18] The other house-plots, across the stream, can only be seen as irregularities in the land.

But I happen to know Lyscombe, and the views Hardy describes are all there. There is a model for that wide exposed swede-field, on Thorncombe land, overlooking lynchets, as described. There are many views into the Blackmoor vale, and from some of the eastern high fields, you can see the valley of the Frome, where Tess hoped to catch a glimpse of Talbothays: Hardy's two crosses on the map above Lyscombe might record these points of vision; the contours of the map are too far from reality to be sure. The sea, Sandbourne and the Isle of Wight can also, sometimes, be glimpsed from here, weather permitting.

You do not see *Tess*'s high views together; they are from different places. But put maps and views together, as architects do, to imagine a place in their heads, and *Tess* gives you a vision of a complete landscape, stretching to the edges of vision. This is an assembled view, of an ancient place, left behind by a modern world, only discernible on the fringes of our vision and knowledge, and

Lyscombe: 'the remains of a village'.

a suggestive centre in an old, empty settlement and crossroads which has all but vanished from sight or knowledge.

Flintcomb-Ash is the middle of the book, the middle of the map which Hardy himself drew. To an architectural critic, *Tess* seems *organised* by this empty view of Wessex, looking out from high up, on the old tracks, well away from the railways. As a practiced architectural reader, I can see or perceive the infrastructures which make or made it work: the railways hidden in the flat valleys; the old, high roads, now deserted; the sprawling new town creeping over the horizon of this empty-seeming world.

This is not a single picture. But for architects, used to assembling such information, it feels very complete. Bournemouth, Poole and the railways on the horizon or hidden in the valleys; the traces of older inhabitation all around. Architects are used to drawing out what cannot quite be seen. Even Drakes Lane, the Piddletrenthide to Cheselbourne road, was unbuilt on the Cruchley map: this ancient human landscape was truly hard for nineteenth-century visitors to reach. Tess, leaving the railways and fertile valleys for the deserted upland trackways, had fallen through the holes in the map, into a world whose infrastructure has turned inside out.

*

If you then start looking, systematically, at the places which make up this 'Director's Cut' of Wessex, you find this environmental argument everywhere.

170

Here is Tess's native Marnhull, as described by Hermann Lea: 'Marnhull was once quite a considerable place: the remains of many streets may be traced where the houses have entirely disappeared. The dwellings are now curiously disconnected, many wide gaps intervening ... the old cottage in which Tess was imagined to have been born ... all seems to have been swept away ...'[19]

Chaseborough, where Tess spends her fatal night out, was, Lea says, a famous town in Norman and Saxon times, 'much decayed'.[20] Another vanished village, Knights Mayne, lies between West Knighton and Lower Lewell – the Talbothays of the book. There are more near Emminster/Beaminster, Angel Clare's family home. Trantridge/Pentridge is surrounded by earthworks; Tess passes through Shaftesbury/Shaston during major depopulation (when 350 families emigrated to Canada).[21] The d'Urberville 'seat' is in the 'decayed old town'[22] of Bere Regis/Kingsbere; with holdings in the Wool/Wellbridge of Tess's honeymoon. There are even *two* vanished villages in the parish of Bingham's Melcombe/Stagfoot Lane, just over the hill from Lyscombe – and also marked firmly with a cross on Hardy's map. (The rector, Charles Bingham, was the model for Parson Tringham; the Binghams too married into the Turberville family.) And so on. *Tess's settings* – almost all of them – are the architectural, archaeological, economic, social and environmental evidence of the decline of Dorset.

Arguably, that is inevitable. Dorset *was* hugely depopulated; vanished or shrunken villages have been uncovered everywhere: Bardolfestone, at Hardy's mother's native Puddletown or Winterbourne Faringdon in William Barnes's parish (which features in *The Trumpet Major*). Yet they are not famous, they take knowledge and attention to find, and according to Linda Viner, the *study* of them only really began with Maurice Beresford's *The Lost Villages of England*, 1954.[23] But if you followed Tess's *footsteps* – as Hardy knew by now that many would – you would naturally pick this up – with Stonehenge as its monumental destination, where Tess is hunted to her sacrificial death. Tess and Angel hear, feel, sense it, in total darkness:

'What monstrous place is this?' said Angel. 'It hums' said she. 'Hearken!' ... Clare felt the vertical surface of the structure. It seemed to be of solid stone, without joint or moulding. Carrying his fingers onward he found that what he had come into contact with was a colossal rectangular pillar; by stretching out his left hand he could feel a similar one adjoining. At an indefinite height overhead something made the black sky blacker, which had the semblance of a vast architrave uniting the pillars horizontally ...[24]

Stonehenge was not just the monumental presence of a vanished past, but itself then threatened with complete obliteration. *Tess's* map of Wessex is, precisely, a walk from one vanished settlement to another, through a landscape of epic depopulation.

But critically, *Tess* shows us this stripped countryside as umbilically *linked* to the modern cities of England. Talbothays – that miniature Eden – thrives because it has fertile land near a *railway*. Tess and Angel drive the milk to the station, where it will, Tess says, go to London to be drunk by people who never see them:

> They crept along towards a point in the expanse of shade before them ... a spot where, by day, a fitful white streak of steam at intervals upon the dark green background denoted intermittent moments of contact between their secluded world and modern life. Modern life stretched out its steam feeler to this point three or four times a day, touched the native existences, and quickly withdrew its feeler again, as if the touch had been uncongenial ...[25]

For Wessex is the corollary of Hardy's (and our) modern, urbanised life. There is an amazing description of the booming new metropolis of Bournemouth/Sandbourne (laid out by Benjamin Ferrey): 'a city of detached mansions; a Mediterranean lounging-place on the English Channel',[26] where d'Urberville sets up Tess as his mistress; where Angel – too late – runs her to earth:

> This fashionable watering-place, with its eastern and its western stations, its piers, its groves of pines, its promenades, and its covered gardens, was, to Angel Clare, a fairy place suddenly created by the stroke of a wand and

Bournemouth/Sandborne: surreal modernity on the edge of prehistoric Egdon Heath.

then allowed to get a little dusty. An out-lying eastern tract of the enormous Egdon Waste was close at hand, yet on the very verge of that tawny piece of antiquity such a glittering novelty as this pleasure city had chosen to spring up. Within the space of a mile from its outskirts every irregularity of its soil was prehistoric, every channel an undisturbed British trackway ...[27]

This surreal modernity, on the edge of the ancient land, is not so much hostile as extremely strange, dream-like – less real-seeming than those emaciated villages and trackways. Angel (the guilty 'I-figure' of the book) is surprised to find Tess the milkmaid expressing 'the ache of modernism',[28] but the ache of modernism, seen from a decimated countryside touched by those 'steam feelers', is exactly what Tess is about.[29]

And the book does not end at Stonehenge. The final vision of Tess is that 'isometric' high architectural vision of Winchester, seen by Angel and Liza Lu – bright, beautiful, but terrible to them. Hardy's great realisation of Wessex has, somehow led him to an unexpected, high architectural viewpoint: he was already working on Jude.[30] And with that, the stereoscopic frames, the old human senses and the constructed architectural ones, slide apart again.

Perhaps Tess, where those visions converge, shows how an architectural vision itself works. P.N. Furbank, arguing that Tess gives us 'partial visions', seemed wholly wrong to me, in this most fully achieved 'vision' of Wessex, until I realised how architecturally accurate it was.[31] For architects and their critics have to recognise

Stonehenge, late 1880s, showing the 'altar' stone.

that *all* visions are partial. Any picture, model or construction is inevitably selective, biased; including some things while leaving others out. Plans, sections, details, photographs, isometrics, sketches, all show different things and not others; and almost all drawings exclude thing like acoustics, human behaviour, climate and views. Architects learn to put such things together in their heads, test them against reality, past experience and future possibilities. Of course *Tess* is built of partial fragments. That is how architects work. Hardy made it up.

And in *Tess*, Hardy's intensely analytical, architectural constructed vision of Wessex is resolved. He is describing perceived, imagined experience, the immersive working detail; the sense of collective overview, which assembles his great, analytical, critical interpretation of Wessex. He is showing us what modernity has *done* to this countryside, its structure and infrastructure – and how this has re-shaped humans' lives upon it. If Koolhaas, Venturi and Scott Brown and the Smithsons are recognised as radical in their great, analytic, provocative re-readings of found places, it is time we started recognising that Hardy's Wessex, drawn from the same imaginative culture, should be given the same kind of status.

Tess is a completely realised architects' working vision of Wessex during the 'great change' from rural to urban-dominated life. Mapped, visualised, visionary, informed, sympathetic and biting; it is Hardy's great analytic criticism of the processes of modernity itself, seen from the land it left behind. *Tess* is Hardy's definitive (if not last) vision of Wessex, complete from infrastructure to imagination: a depopulated countryside of 'troublesome land', turned inside out to fuel the booming towns beyond the horizon.

OBSTRUCTED VISIONS

Jude the Obscure

Fawley/Marygreen Church by G.E. Street. Photograph by Hermann Lea.

'The schoolmaster was leaving the village and everybody seemed sorry', starts *Jude the Obscure*.[1] This is not the opening we would expect, and we go on finding the unexpected. Despite the achievement of *Tess*, Hardy had serious unfinished architectural business.

Jude, remarkably, does *not* use Hardy's famous cinematic scenes. There are scarcely any views of isolated figures crossing vast landscapes, and some of those you think do exist (Jude in the field of rooks; Christminster on the skyline) shimmer like mirages and vanish from the page. The landscape scenes – many of them – occur inside the characters' heads.

That is startling in itself, and it has a further peculiarity. Those views are far more architectural than anything Hardy has done before. Not because they are technical, but because they are *visionary*. They often describe an idealised city, in ways that Ruskin does in *The Stones of Venice*, for example. But *Jude* is, centrally, showing how drastically those visions fail, when working craftspeople believe in, and try to enact, them.

Hardy was actually reading *The Stones of Venice* while visiting Venice in 1887: for he calls it 'Humbug'.[2] A short critique – but precise. *Stones* is humbug, for all its visionary writing; its range and scope; its discussion of ways to look at architecture; for all its role in making people value the great city which was then sinking into the lagoon. He 'treats truly on the imagination', as Garbett says.

All these are Hardy concerns too. But *Stones* is riddled with sweeping generalisations about the everyday, working practices of building; about the lives, instincts, moral dilemmas, joys, sorrows, skills and satisfactions of the people who build. Its whole construction is drawn (sometimes brilliantly) from the 'self, self, self' of young Blomfield's cartoon, yet Ruskin makes absolute moral and aesthetic judgements everywhere: about fundamental links of obedient morality, good architecture, the nature of masonry and the happiness of the workman. I do not attempt any appraisal here of Ruskin's vast, influential, infuriating, famously contradictory work.[3] But I do point out that Hardy, clearly, has already done so.

For it cannot be a coincidence that Jude is a stonemason; that *Jude* shadows the arguments, and even 'real' projects, in the architectural high-ground of its day. Or that it is set in Oxford, where Ruskin, *the* leading figure in artworkers' education and the first Slade Professor, had now given two series of controversial lectures, challenging the 'feverish idea' that anyone could be 'a gentleman and a scholar'.[4] By 1885, he was effectively telling his art-worker students to stop trying to raise themselves through education and get back to the obedient pursuit of the trades they were born to – just as Jude himself is told.

This book cannot possibly have done all this accidentally. It is written by an architect, the son of a mason, a reader of Ruskin, a self-taught classicist, an outsider in Oxford in 1864,[5] where Ruskin's attempt to realise architectural ideals had just crashed into comic reality. Written by a working architect, fresh from reading Ruskin, in Venice in 1887, soon after those last notorious Ruskin lectures, and on site, doing stonework, at West Knighton at the time. It had to be deliberate.

Hardy tells us specifically in the Preface that he was 'jotting down' notes for *Jude* in 1887. By April 1888, he has sketched a short story of a young man who tries and fails, and commits suicide. He says there is '... something in "the Oxford world" that ought to be shown and I am the one to show it to them',[6] although he adds that he could possibly have got into Cambridge. This was clearly personal.

In the 1912 Preface, Hardy, discussing the furore of attention to the marriage and religious issues of the book's publication says firmly: '... the shattered ideals of the two characters ... had been more especially, and indeed almost exclusively, of interest to myself.' He adds: 'I was informed that some readers thought these episodes an attack on venerable institutions, and that when Ruskin College was subsequently founded it should have been called the College of Jude the Obscure.' That is classic Hardy: he is making the main point, in an aside, putting words in the mouths of others. If you want a detailed appraisal, criticism, evaluation and partial demolition of Ruskin's arguments, and an epic projection of the heartbreak their outreach can cause, try *Jude*. Hardy has pointed it out.

*

Right from the start, *Jude* is laced with biting architectural criticism and content. It starts in the village of Marygreen:

> It was as old as it was small, and it rested on the lap of an undulating upland adjoining the North Wessex downs ... Many of the thatched and dormered dwelling houses had been pulled down of late years ... the original church, hump-backed, wood-turreted and quaintly hipped, had been taken down and either cracked up into heaps of road-metal in the lane, or utilised as pig-sty walls ... a tall new building of modern Gothic design, unfamiliar to English eyes, had been erected on a new piece of ground by a certain obliterator of historic records who had run down from London and back in a day. The site ... was not even recorded on the green and level grass-plot that had immemorially been the churchyard, the obliterated graves being recorded by eighteenpenny cast-iron crosses warranted to last five years.[7]

This is St Mary's Church, Fawley, 1864–1866 by G.E. Street. Hardy would get Lea to photograph it; his sister Mary (and possibly Hardy too) drew the curious vanished original. That devastating bit of architectural criticism was also against the workings of his own profession: 'running up and down in a day' was almost exactly what he had done himself.

The book is peppered with architectural placement. Street had lived in Wantage (Alfredston, where Jude learns his trade). William Morris and Philip Webb met while working in Street's Oxford office, and the Fawley church includes a Morris & Co. stained-glass window (although Morris would criticise Street too). Jude later works on Salisbury Cathedral (Lea says on Gilbert Scott's 1870–1880 repairs: Hardy would be his source), and even on a museum in Casterbridge;[8] that is, the real Dorchester County Museum itself. Jude is linked directly, in detail, to the real world of architecture, and he is circling round a parallel Oxford – with a parallel professor. If you were reading this book as an architect, or art-worker (those keen, engaged students) you would be quite capable of picking all this up.

If you re-read *Jude* looking for Hardy's 'typical' visual descriptions, you find something new. 'Architectural' visions of towns (Winchester, Sherborne) have dotted the novels until now: Hardy kept subliminally linking his world to a high architectural vision. Now they have moved centre stage, and he is *demolishing* them. Here is a Ruskin vision of Venice: 'For truly, every pinnacle and turret glanced or glowed, overlaid with gold, or bossed with jasper ... it must have seemed to them as if they were sailing in the expanse of heaven, and this a great planet, whose orient edge widened through ether ...'[9]

Hardy shows these are a kind of marsh-gas. He gives (handwritten) directions to Jude's exact viewpoint on the Wessex Ridgeway,[10] where a tiler, working on a barn, describes seeing Christminster when 'the sun is going down in a blaze of flame'. Like 'the heavenly Jerusalem', says Jude. At sunset he climbs the roof:

Some way within the limits of the stretch of the landscape, points of light like topaz gleamed. The air increased in transparency with the lapse of minutes, till the topaz points showed themselves to be the vanes, windows, wet roof slates and other shining spots upon the spires, domes, freestone-work, and varied outlines that were faintly revealed. It was Christminster, unquestionably; either directly seen, or miraged in the peculiar atmosphere.[11]

You could hardly draw this miasmatic impression; there is nothing to draw. It is very like Turner's extraordinary paintings of vision itself. *Late* Turner, the work Turner's old champion Ruskin called 'indicative of mental disease'. 'The much-decried, mad, late Turner', who Hardy specifically revered.[12]

Jude is about fifteen miles away: around the limits of distant vision, although high enough to see further. He returns at night: '... what he saw was not lamps in rows, as he had half-expected, only a halo or glow-fog over-arching the place against the black heavens behind it, making the light and the city seem distant but a mile or so ...'[13] Hardy is exploring the edges of perception.

But *Jude* is, centrally, about ideal visions crashing into reality. All kinds of characters have their own interpretations or tall tales of Christminster, from Phillotson to the mendacious peddlar and Jude's practical aunt (who warns him it is not for him). Jude himself seems to echo John Donne's 'The University is a

Wessex Poems: The limits of vision.

Paradise ...':[14] 'It is a city of light', 'The tree of knowledge grows there' ... 'It would just suit me.'[15]

Yet when Jude – as experienced stonemason, separated from his wife, gets to Oxford, his vision *does* at first appear. In a marvellous, proto-modern passage Jude walks the streets and goes into the colleges. As night falls, shut out onto public streets, he debates with the ghosts of alumni emerging from the gloom:

> During the interval of preparation for this venture, since his wife and furniture's uncompromising disappearance into space, he had read and learnt almost all that could be read and learnt by one in his position, of the worthies who had spent their youth within these reverend walls, and whose souls had haunted them in their maturer age ... The brushings of the wind against the angles, buttresses, and door-jambs were as the passing of these only other inhabitants, the tappings of each ivy leaf on its neighbour were as the mutterings of their mournful souls, the shadows as their thin shapes in nervous movement, making him comrades in his solitude. In the gloom it was as if he ran up against them without feeling their bodily frames.
>
> The streets were now deserted, but on account of these things, he could not go in. There were poets abroad ...[16]

Jude debates with the great figures who appear, until he is sent home by a policeman. In the morning, he sees that the buildings he dreamt would welcome him are designed to close him out: 'he found that the colleges had treacherously changed their sympathetic countenances: some were pompous; some had put on the look of family vaults above ground; something barbaric loomed in the masonries of all. The spirits of the great men had disappeared.'[17] That is acute architectural analysis. Oxford is a city of closed, walled paradises; they call you from a distance, but also lock you out; and it's no surprise that the 'other world' children's classics of Alice, Narnia and His Dark Materials all come from this city of physical and imaginary other worlds and wonderful environments behind high walls and locked doors. Until the 1970s, when the sandstone buildings of Oxford were first jet-washed, it was a black city, too; more grotesque and suggestive of its mediaeval battles between 'town and gown' than it feels today.

This shifting from the physical to psychic writing is remarkable in *Jude*, and it is almost always located in the architecture. It moves from aesthetics and material description to the visionary and the critical. It is far better writing than Ruskin's *Stones*. Indeed, it exemplifies and refines what Batchelor calls Ruskin's 'daring proposition' or reading architecture to find 'central political and social truths about the civilisation which created the buildings'[18] and extends it through real architectural and craftsman's experience in the realm from which it came. But that is normal in architectural writing. Ideas and details; views and theories; details of stonework, are always explored as part of an intimate, elusive but critical entity. Ruskin had reinvented it, reached a new audience, and explored its freedom of forms – but that fusion of technical thinking, instinct, theory, history and imagination is the working fabric of architectural thought. And Hardy is not a normal architectural writer – he is a superlative one. Jude is one of the most astonishing and little-recognised pieces of architectural critical writing ever. This is how architectural criticism works: by analytic, speculative close reading of embodied physical qualities, extended by technical, social and historical knowledge, aesthetic, imaginative proposition, and actual, physical possibilities. Quite normally, it considers how social possibility is enabled, or restricted, by how and what we build, who does it, and who controls it.

Next morning, Jude observes that the stoneworking done in Christminster is patching and repairing, not new building:

The numberless architectural pages around him he read, naturally, less as an artist-critic of their forms [guess who] than as an artisan and comrade of the dead handicraftsmen whose muscles had actually executed those forms. He examined the mouldings, stroked them as one who knew their beginning, said they were difficult, or easy in the working, had taken little or much time, were trying to the arm, or convenient to the tool.

What at night had been perfect and ideal was by day the more or less defective real.[19]

That is surely a direct reply to Ruskin's twelve-page disquisition on stone-working in *Seven Lamps*.[20] Jude *does* find work as a stonemason. He is really skilled, able to work with eye and brain and hand, using just that intelligent fusion of abilities which fascinates current researchers.[21] But his 'true illumination' (the one we have already linked to West Knighton and will see discussed again in 'Memories of Church Restoration') is lost under the 'stress of his old idea' and 'modern vice of unrest'.[22]

Strange hopes and dreams; imaginary arguments with your mentors; ideas embodied in buildings; knowledge springing from one's own trade. Jude does not come to see his trade as a liberation, but as something which holds him in the position of his labouring forefathers. Just where Ruskin was telling Hardy's generation to stay. Jude does not comply either. He sets himself a punishing course of self-education, and writes to several colleges. Finally, he hears from the Master of Biblioll, T. Tetuphenay: 'Judging from your description of yourself as a working man, you will have a much better chance of success in life by remaining in your own sphere and sticking to your trade.'

Just what Ruskin would tell a whole generation. Tetuphenay is Greek for 'to have beaten'. Slayed. Slade. Could this even be a disguised quotation from a real letter?[23] Hardy's comments on Oxford sound personal, and in any case, Ruskin was addressing a whole generation. Jude takes to drink, and marvellously, beats down a student in his knowledge of the Nicene Creed in Greek. Hardy's arguments against Ruskin are far too strongly laced into the story to be coincidence.

Jude's cousin, Sue, a nervous freethinker, works in the Gothic engraving business. Jude, idealistically, imagines this (as Ruskin and Pugin would): 'a sweet, saintly, Christian business ... !'[24] Sue disabuses him. She has lived with a male student in London; attended lectures; is well-read. She leaves her lodgings when her religious landlady breaks up her classical Greek statuettes. She would certainly know Ruskin's strictures against Greek architecture:[25]

'Wardour is Gothic ruins – and I hate Gothic!'

'No. Quite otherwise. It is a classic building – Corinthian, I think; with a lot of pictures.'

'Ah. That will do. I like the sound of Corinthian. We'll go.'[26]

As a well-informed art-worker, Sue is expressing a wholistic, passionate response to the debates of the age. Without Ruskin, her fearsome battle against Gothic does not make sense. Putting this story into an easily identifiable Oxford, Hardy is taking the battle into the enemy's camp.

For Oxford was also the site of Ruskin's theories coming back to bite him. Ruskin had at first been critical of plans for the Oxford Museum (by Benjamin Woodward, completed in 1861), but became the building's most influential supporter, calling it 'the first truly Gothic structure to be raised in England since the fifteenth century.'[27] The project was led by Henry Acland, a friend of Ruskin's,[28] and was filled with iconographic carvings and imagery: statues of Aristotle and Bacon, Darwin and Linnaeus, flowers, fruit and leaves; its cast-iron columns had unfurling leaf-fronds in the place of capitals, like those in Hardy's notebooks, but rich, fine, full of hidden life. Hardy, on site for Blomfield in 1864, would surely have visited as Beatty suggests.[29] It is the leading example of the museum type built at Dorchester. Its biblical snake amongst the leaves surely generated the native response of the sand lizards in Turnworth's sandstone. Even the pillars of the gallery were curated as a geological exhibition of different stones – with many from Dorset. The whole thing was a cathedral to the belief in a natural, scientific and gothic enlightenment – and the role of the craftworkers making it. It was right up Hardy's street.

But what Ruskin said was not what Ruskin did. The most famous stonemasons of their day, the O'Shea Brothers and their nephew (who worked on Trinity College Dublin), were employed between 1858 and 1860 – and then sacked, Ruskin says, for the 'unnecessary introduction of cats' into a window-carving. Another account says James O'Shea, told to stop work for lack of funds, immediately carved parrots and owls into the main doorway, to caricature members of the client body, the 'Convocation'. The offending owls, cats and parrots were hacked off again: the façade remains stripped and plain today. Ruskin said (in a lecture in 1877): 'When I said the worker should be left free to design his work as he went on, I never meant that you could secure a great national monument of art by letting loose the first lively Irishman you could get hold of to do what he liked to it.'[30]

Hardy must have known this story; must have admired the superbly skilled O'Sheas. In his mason's dress, the photograph of James O'Shea looks like Hardy's uncle Antell, the self-educated shoemaker, who drank himself to death and is known as a model for Jude.[31] Perhaps Hardy had seen the picture: he was friends with Pitt Rivers, who opened the Dorset County Museum,[32] and Hardy was himself involved in the Dorchester museum client group. And remember the prominent owl and hidden lizards appearing at Turnworth, a few years after the Oxford owls were obliterated. A coincidence? Hardy's work and life *are* dotted with sympathetic animals,[33] but Hardy, working in Blomfield's gossipy, well-informed

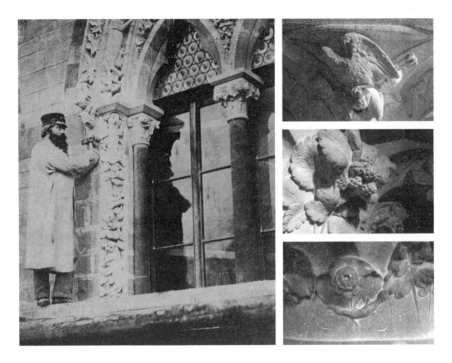

James O'Shea at work on the Oxford Museum;
and Hardy and the Boulters' capitals at Turnworth.

practice, with a critical view of Ruskin, could hardly have avoided this story. That prominent owl has to be a direct response: 'stonemasons welcome here.'

There is another Ruskin stone-working experiment too. In 1874, Ruskin cajoled Oxford undergraduates, including Oscar Wilde, into building a road between the marshy North and South Hinksey villages, just outside Oxford, as an exercise in the dignity and excellence of labour. Here is Wilde:

> So out we went, day after day, and learned how to lay levels and to break stones, and to wheel barrows along a plank – a very difficult thing to do. And Ruskin worked with us in the mist and rain and mud of an Oxford winter, and our friends and our enemies came out and mocked us from the bank. We did not mind it much then, and we did not mind it afterwards at all, but worked away for two months at our road. And what became of the road? Well, like a bad lecture it ended abruptly—in the middle of the swamp. Ruskin going away to Venice, when we came back for the next term there was no leader, and the 'diggers', as they called us, fell asunder.[34]

183

Ruskin's 'diggers' at North Hinksey.

The schoolmaster was leaving the village. The sense of a vision betrayed runs right through the book. Walking in to Oxford from the south-west (at sunset) from the art-worker's town of Wantage: (Hardy describes it specifically[35]) Jude would have walked roughly along the route of Ruskin's abandoned road.

*

But skilled craftsmanship *can* be a means of self-education: Hardy himself managed it. All Sue and Jude's moments of self-empowerment, however fragile, are *architectural*, from the model they exhibit of Cardinal College, to their 'Christminster cakes' – architectural models made in pastry. (Pastry-work: architectural slang for much-abused non-structural decoration.) In their co-work in repairing churches[36] Sue and Jude are told: "'It is not a very artistic job ... the clergyman is a very old-fashioned chap, and has refused to let anything more be done than cleaning and repairing." "Excellent old man!" said Sue.'[37]

Sue and Jude are dismissed from this job when their unmarried state (Sue is pregnant) is discovered. The moral code was Ruskin's too: 'good art inseparable from the moral virtue of the artist and the moral life of the society ...'[38] Sue and Jude are in direct protest against Ruskin. Most expansively Sue takes issue with such ideas while in Salisbury, trapped in a miserable teachers' training college (she should certainly have stuck to artworking):

'Shall we go and sit in the Cathedral'? he asked when their meal was finished.

'Cathedral? Yes, though I'd rather sit in the railway station', she answered, a remnant of vexation still in her voice. 'That's the centre of town life now. The Cathedral has had its day!'

'How modern you are!'

'So would you be, if you had lived as much in the Middle Ages as I have done these last few years! The Cathedral was a very good place four or five centuries ago, but it is played out now ...'[39]

Salisbury Cathedral was, almost exhaustingly, discussed as the ideal of English architecture at the time and Ruskin does not like railway stations at all: 'better bury gold in the embankments, than put it in ornaments of the station' or 'no-one with any sense of beauty would travel by train.'[40]

This is only the start of a cross-reading of Hardy's work against the great architectural writings of the Arts & Crafts: a detailed comparison between *Jude* and William Morris's *News from Nowhere* should clearly be done too, and the whole relationship of Hardy's work to the movements of late nineteenth-century and early twentieth-century architecture begs to be done in far more detail.

But modernity *does* offer Sue and Jude a better chance. In the booming town of Aldbrickham/Reading they pass the happiest part of their lives (undescribed, but they conceive several children), in a small house, unmarried, drawing no comment. They briefly achieve the anonymity which allows nonconformity[41] – unlike the morally loaded stasis Ruskin was re-advancing. They are both wrong only in looking back: Sue, into Ruskin's inflexible morality; Jude, to his old ideal of Oxford.

They started in quest of a lodging, and at last found something that seemed to promise well, in Mildew Lane – a spot which to Jude was irresistible – though to Sue it was not so fascinating – a narrow lane close to the back of a college but having no communication with it. The little houses were darkened to gloom by the high collegiate buildings, within which life was so far removed for that of the people in the lane as if it has been on opposite sides of the globe, yet only a thickness of wall divided them. Two or three of the houses had notices of rooms to let ...[42]

This is a real, bad architectural condition (like Dickens's Marshalsea): the oppressive use of buildings themselves to enforce social divisions. Sue and Jude should have headed for the anonymous terraces of the Cowley Road. It is modernity, and not tradition, which offers what little hope there is in Jude – the sense that the future might, sometime, deliver on its promises.

It is impossible to end Jude on a good note. It is a bleak, unredeemed, horrific book, brilliant as it is. Jude dies while 'illustrious gents' are cheered for their prizes outside. (Ruskin got his Newdigate Prize at the same time as Wordsworth's honorary degree.) Ruskin and Pugin's lives did not end well either; and Wilde would return to stone-breaking in Reading Gaol. The high idealism of architectural polemic almost has to fail. It is the working, imaginative compromise – as Hardy says in 'Memories of Church Restoration' – which has the best chance of success.

Yet Hardy's wide, human sympathy probably extends to Ruskin too. The parallels, although everywhere, are not explicit. His name is not mentioned until 1912, well after Ruskin's death. There are enough overlaps in Jude, with Hardy's own life, marriages and romantic obsessions, and visionary, humanitarian engagement with a reading public, to suggest a continued fellow feeling. But if one takes Hardy's work seriously, as the profound and sophisticated architectural writer he surely was, then Jude is clearly his great reply to Ruskin: possibly the greatest piece of architectural criticism there has ever been – in popular, fictional form.

POEMS, PREFACES, PHOTOGRAPHS

Horizons Open

Wessex Poems: the view is of Portland Bill. A coloured version,
without the figure, was used for the cover design.

Jude the Obscure was the end of the Wessex novels. Between *Tess* and *Jude* – realised place and bitter polemic – fictional Wessex was now working. By 1890, Hardy was lying awake, imagining the freedoms of poetry: he said 'new horizons seemed to open, and worrying pettinesses seemed to disappear'.[1] He had, for the first time, enough money to live on. American copyrights for foreign authors were put into law in 1891; money was flowing in from *Tess*. He told Robert Graves 'that he could sit down and write novels by a timetable, but that poetry came to him by accident, which perhaps, was why he prized it more highly'.[2]

But this in no way stopped his startling architectural innovations. Wessex was moving into a newly sophisticated phase of development as a project. And in his first collection of poems he was about to do something which most closely foreshadows architectural experiments of a century later, working exactly in the projection of 'new horizons'.

The *Wessex Poems*, published in December 1898, was 'unique in being extensively illustrated by its author'.[3] What is riveting, architecturally, is the way Hardy *made* the book, obsessively generating the pictures as a way of realising and assembling the poems – some of which he had written decades before.

He called it 'A mysterious occupation.'[4] 'I told nobody I was doing the sketches as I was by no means sure that the attempt would come to anything', he told his friend Florence Henniker.[5] There are 30 drawings in the book (or 31 if you include the 'frontispiece' in some imprints[6]) and he may have done others which did not make the cut. To another friend, Edward Clodd, he called them 'a sort of illegitimate interest – that which arose from their being a novel amusement, & a wholly gratuitous performance which could not profit me & probably would do me harm'. It is notable that he was working in private. I have already suggested at least some of these might be the working up of pictures for which he already had, in some form (tracings, sketches, photos, Camera Lucida outlines or others) rough images from earlier in his life.

He apologises for the drawing quality, citing his 'years of unpractice':[7] presumably as an architectural draughtsman, possibly as a user of various drawing techniques too. He specifically says it was the drawings which *drove* him to revise the poems 'so perfunctorily collected'.[8] This is an experiment both in drawing, and in publication, and in the greater ideas generated when you put pictures and texts together as architectural books always have.

Pamela Dalziel describes: 'detectable tension between Hardy's personal, creative commitment to the drawings', and his 'uncertainity as to their value either in themselves or as enhancements of the poems'. Hardy never seems to have resolved it, she adds; 'and it was "responsible for several curious aspects of the work's publication history".'[9] That is another remarkably observant description of the working processes of design thinking. Hardy had by now delivered his working fictional-real Wessex, and was drawing out (in both senses) the various ways of imagination in which he could see Wessex – and try to project it to others too.

The pictures in themselves are startling. Many have the wide horizontal frame of vision which would only become normal with cinema and car travel (both the Smithsons and Venturi and Scott Brown describe this mode of travel as re-framing experience). But they are also the wide horizons of Dorset itself: the sense of elevation and distance from its long, flat-topped ridges of hills, which Hardy could now see from Max Gate and explore by foot and bicycle (and later by car). The 'new horizons' of imaginary Wessex are precisely what he is imagining, drawing and constructing, in both content and form.

These drawings stretch the limits of vision. They show darkness, disappearance, the dazzle of low sunlight bleaching sight. They are also *constructed* inventively, as drawings. The vault drawing is set up as a conventional section, but humans, alive and loving, dead and decaying are drawn too. The coffin drawing is even more peculiar, with the stairs depicted in a flattened 'planometric', with shadowy outlines through the ephemeral coffin bearers: the coffin is solid. The 'Tryphena' drawing of the shrouded body is another surrealised 'architectural' drawing – the elevation of a sofa; the imagined corpse which suggests both monument, body and landscape – rather like Madelon Vriesendorp's paintings of recumbent skyscrapers in *Delirious New York*.

Many of the drawings are composed and rendered exactly like photographs – with strong shadows, figures in silhouette and other photographic peculiarities: it seems unlikely that an architect would draw all of the accurate detail of Sherborne and not include the top of the arch. Many may have been set out by camera lucida: the landscapes in particular are peculiarly flattened. Others trap fragments of abstract thought in visible form: the image of Napoleon, hovering above a mass of bayonets as though in a song; or dance notation springing to life. As already mentioned, the vase of dead flowers takes its brief exactly from Ruskin 'It would be curious to see ... a painting of dead flowers.'[10]

Others are more impressionistic, more like paintings: the view of San Sebastian at night (another unsettling body-landscape vision, discussed by Shires) or the shaded vision of the fiddle-player at the pub window (another picture of music). Many have a single, shadowy pre-Le Corbusier occupant, or the image used by Robin Evans of his own shadowy reflection in the Barcelona Pavilion: all itself suggesting an imaginative double-take: am I watching that figure, or *am* I that figure? Some are ravishingly successful; some look clumsy. But they could hardly be clearer evidence of someone thinking and working like a conceptual architect of the twentieth century.

They try to capture projected vision itself, to stretch and combine architectural drawing techniques to cover things they normally omit: time, death, darkness, shadow, music, ancient graffiti. One even shows a view through Hardy's glasses in a type of picture of the *act* of imaginative vision itself which echoes through the architectural high ground – St Jerome in his study; Ledoux's theatre reflected in the eye; Le Corbusier's photographed glasses – which is deliberately ambiguous, as Keith Wilson says.[11] Either there was nothing wrong with Hardy's eyesight or he was suggesting that Wessex exists both through his eyes and outside them. Tschumi says of his own similar drawings:

Developed in the late '70s, they proposed to describe an architectural interpretation of reality, to this aim they employed a particular structure

189

involving photographs that either direct or 'witness' events ... At the same time, plans sections and diagrams outline spaces and indicate the movements of the protagonists, intruding into the architectural 'stage set'. The ... explicit purpose was to transcribe things normally removed from conventional architectural representation, namely the complex relationship between spaces and their use, between the set and the script, between 'type' and 'program', between objects and events.[12]

Which could stand, word for word, against Hardy's illustrations. The date alone is wrong.

All this is *entirely* on the home territory of experimental projects: the images which stick in the memory, the strange or inventive drawings, the testing and uncertainty. Pamela Dalziel turns drawings round to consider their different effects, which architects often do,[13] and describes how in different publications they were rotated or trimmed (I had been doing re-organisations myself to explore groupings or visual narrative). Even if such reconfiguration of pictures is rarely described (outside the specialisms of architectural research) this is native experimental architectural behaviour – and theory. Linda Shires, exploring speculative and ambiguous constructions made between picture and text, hits another architectural key idea in William Mitchell's 'Image X Text'. Pictures do not *add* to text, they multiply it, generating all kinds of possible readings. This is central to architectural theory and practice: how humans generally, and architects professionally, put pictures and words together to imagine working places, in their heads, all the time.

The *Wessex Poems* fall eerily into architectural prediction mode too. Shires is describing 'Heiress and Architect' with its coffin drawing:

Wessex Poems: 'Thoughts of Phena'.

The woman requests the architect build a palace for her with "high halls" and "wide fronts of crystal glass" ... As he refuses each request, she reduces them to "[a] little chamber" or "[s]ome narrow winding turret ... Rejecting such notions entirely", he states that he will build, instead, just space enough to "hale a coffined corpse adown the stairs" ... The poem states but cancels her vision of the future and narrows space in the imagination.[14]

Emma had retreated to her attics around this time, when *Jude* was published; she would leave, by coffin, down that specially designed stair. As Shires, and many, many architectural writers quote from Deleuze and Guattari, 'texts hold virtual potentialities for their future reading'.[15]

*

The *Wessex Poems* drawings vastly expand the experimental substance of Wessex. Claire Tomalin, who often represents a kind of lay view of Wessex, says:

> ... it was a difficult collection to review. The inclusion of his own illustrations was a distraction. They are the work of a skilful draughtsman, but some are distinctly weird, especially the drawing of a dead woman lying under a sheet accompanying the poem addressed to his late cousin Tryphena, and the blank humanoid shapes manoeuvring a coffin on a staircase to illustrate a grim architectural joke in a poem addressed to Blomfield. You have to admire Hardy's determination to extend his range by providing decorative drawings, but it is a relief he did not repeat the experiment.[16]

Weird, naturally; a grim architectural joke, of course: this is *Hardy*. Calling them decorative illustrations is inaccurate, but experiment is right, as Keith Wilson

Wessex Poems: San Sebastian.

191

Wessex Poems: the shadow of the viewer.

argues. Like the poems themselves, they are both self-contained and open-ended. They do not seek to control what you imagine, but to provoke you to assemble the unexpected pictures, framings and oddities Hardy himself was seeing, to your own construction of Wessex.

Actually, many critics of the time were extremely acute. *The Westminster Gazette* says the effect 'is curiously in advance of their technical merits'; the *Glasgow Herald* that they not only gave force to poems but 'were themselves poems'. Arthur Quiller Couch describes their 'intrinsic beauty', revealing 'something which the poems they decorate are also trying to reveal': all exact.[17] From an architectural viewpoint, the *Wessex Poems* was a complete, experimental, architectural project in itself.

That is not to say that the *Wessex Poems* pictures were perfect. Hardy's vision had long outpaced his drawing/making skills, and the conventional book format is too fixed for the pictures. The reader gets too few clues of how freely they might read them. But you could say much the same of *Towards a New Architecture*, itself radical thirty years and a world war later and indeed, critics did.[18]

Hardy intended this experiment. He offered to indemnify Harper and Brothers against any loss,[19] and 'at this major turning point in his career was deeply anxious as to the reception of *Wessex Poems* ... sent out an unusually large number of presentation copies to friends and fellow authors.'[20] Dalziel wonders about Hardy's uncertainty, continually revisiting the images and insisting on their inclusion – yet eventually allowing the publisher to decide whether to include them in the next edition. No architectural critic will be surprised by Hardy's commitment to his experiment – or that the publishers did not include them again. Or that Hardy would find other ways of continuing the experiment.

To an architect, the *Wessex Poems* drawings are the visual key to Hardy's ambitious construction of Wessex: definitely visual, architectural, cinematic;

certainly by him, certainly experimental, fragments from which Wessex was being assembled. It is a brilliant, unexploded architectural bombshell. These remarkable pictures have never appeared in architectural publications of the work they clearly predict. They are an only partly recognised literary provocation – and an utterly overlooked architectural one.

*

Hardy's immediate control of Wessex was through the successive editions. The mix of shocked and delighted reviews of *Tess* fuelled its success,[21] giving him a new control and financial liberty to go *on* working on the novels – entirely on his own behalf. Through his Prefaces, he could respond to his critics – and he had final call on the illustrations too.

The first complete editions appeared in 1895–1897: they were nicely produced, with a Wessex map by cartographer Edward Stanford and *landscape* illustrations by Henry Macbeth-Raeburn 'drawn on the spot' – that is, working to Hardy's directions. In the Osgood McIlvaine 1895–1897 version, the place-names were made consistent – a huge shift for Wessex, but with little effect on the individual stories. Then followed a Macmillan 'Uniform' edition (1902, not illustrated); parts of 'pocket' and 'luxury' editions; the authoritative Macmillan's Wessex Edition of 1912–1913 (with revisions and footnotes by Hardy and frontispiece photographs by Hermann Lea); and the Mellstock edition, in 1920.

I would also suggest that the overall design of these books: the lucid typography, the notable cover designs of the Wessex Poems (1899 US edition Harper & Co.) and of Tess (Osgood McIlvaine, 1891), would by now be showing at least some of Hardy's direct design input too. Hardy could do more or less what he liked for Macmillan by 1912; and this area too would repay further investigation.

Throughout all these editions, Hardy kept working on his web of tiny changes, toughening Wessex's fabric. The first editions gave more realism and detail: they helped the now-steady stream of visitors find (roughly) the right spot. Gatrell suggests Hardy moves the sleepwalking scene in Tess so that Angel lays her in a publicly accessible tomb.[22] The sea changes in the fine grain edits moved from 'realistic dream-country' into the 'Partly real, part-dream country' of the Preface of 1902, to the more abstract, conceptualised 1912 version, where Hardy's despair at the failures of the conservation movement is close to the surface – and where he asserts a Prospero-like control of our imagination. The 1912 Preface reads like a legal document: imaginative ambiguity could not have been more firmly stated.

The region was known but vaguely, and I was often asked even by educated people where it lay. However, the press and the public were kind enough to welcome the fanciful plan, and willingly joined me in the anachronism of imagining a Wessex population living under Queen Victoria; – a modern Wessex of railways, the penny post, mowing and reaping machines, union workhouses, Lucifer matches, labourers who could read and write, and National School children.[23]

The Prefaces are essential reading and they too are fragmented: they work as one essay cut up. Like the *Wessex Poems*, they do not offer a single, definitive picture. You have to carry them in your head, to keep *assembling* Wessex, that ongoing work of projective imagination, as any architect would. Even in the Prefaces, Hardy's memorable descriptions of his England have a way of sticking in your memory, like the outhouse doors 'riddled with bullet holes which had been extemporised by a solitary man as a target for firelock practice when the landing was hourly expected'.[24] This is one of those images which falls deep into the imagination and never gets out, showing you how to read history in buildings themselves.

The famous quotation prefacing *Far from the Madding Crowd* belongs to the whole of Wessex:

> ... the geographical limits of the stage here trodden were not absolutely forced upon the writer by circumstance; he forced them upon himself by judgement. I consider that our magnificent heritage from the Greeks in dramatic literature found sufficient room for a large proportion of its action in an extent of their country not much larger than the half-dozen counties here reunited under their old name of Wessex.[25]

It is an extreme claim: placing his hay-trusser and milkmaid on a level with Greek heroes. But historical Wessex was the birthplace of England, of English law, language and literature; the early mediaeval Anglo-Saxon Chronicle was the first written record in English. And Britain was, in Hardy's day, sitting on its own vast empire, so far around the world that the sun never set. And there is something suggestive in the idea of great human narratives calling to each other through the ages.

This sounds grandiose, but Wessex was, as Hardy conceived and developed it, certainly not modest. In calling up Lear, perhaps even Homer, challenging Ruskin, claiming ownership of his partly real country, echoing Prospero, too, Wessex was an ambitiously formed, developed and assertively authored construction; a whole imagined world. He meant it.

*

John Fowles suspects Hardy 'had divided feelings' about photography; he calls it 'that inartistic species of literary produce'.[26] In fact, that is a misinterpretation: Hardy is describing the limits of translation: the 'written picture'.[27] And he was certainly using and drawing photographs himself. A whole new collaboration was beginning.

Hermann Lea was an enthusiastic local photographer who met Hardy while producing A Handbook to the Wessex Country of Thomas Hardy's Novels and Poems. They kept working together, remaining friends for the rest of his life, forming 'a real working bond': 'Lea was unlike most others who came at all close to Hardy: he was not gentry; he was not a woman; he was not literary, and he seems to have experienced a side of his friend that was less public and less reserved than most people were offered.'[28]

In my terms, this is a key collaboration.[29] Lea was surely a better technical photographer than Hardy and he would do a mass of time-consuming work which Hardy would not have had time for. But the vision is clearly Hardy's: it is what he has described in such detail, in writing, and in the Wessex Poems drawings: location, subject, focus, extremes of weather; framing, emptiness, the obsessive pursuit of the limits of vision, of vision itself – which he had already tried drawing through the Wessex Poems pictures. Hardy had effectively found a way of shaping the precise visual framing of Wessex.

Lea went on to produce the more obviously collaborative Thomas Hardy's Wessex for Macmillan in 1913. It was published in the same format as the Wessex novels – Hardy was firmly authenticating, even perhaps claiming it, and Lea's photographs were also used as frontispieces for the novels' Macmillan Wessex Edition.[30] I would suggest that this collaboration was, like much of Hardy's later and more inventive work, a rich, productive way of working; in which architects naturally cooperate and collaborate to get their visions realised, just as Hardy did on the maps and guidebooks.

This is not to deny Lea's remarkable achievements and his really wonderful pictures: rather the reverse. Collaborations are a key form of creative practice: individual authorship remains an open question, and classically, in the successful ones, each person extends the other further than either would have gone by themselves. This is the multiplication, rather than addition, of creative work.

Lea went on to take many other wonderful photos – including the staged portraits of rural people, and some trick photography shown in Draper and Fowles's wonderful book. But I had puzzled over the repeated use of the classic Wessex photographs (there were many published variants, including a popular motor-touring guide) since they often looked so dull and dumb. That was before I saw the collection of the photographs held by the Dorset County Museum, the ones sent off to the printers for Thomas Hardy's Wessex, with Hardy's own

Maiden Castle, Hermann Lea.

captions written on the backs – and returned to him with the printer's mark-ups (drawn in the china-clay pencil used for layouts in the days before computers). These are the physical photographs, which Hardy saw (and Lea gave back to him) – and they are profoundly beautiful photographs, with *astonishing* levels of detail.

This was because of Lea's remarkable camera – the home-made super-zoom which finally could capture Hardy's long-lens vision of his emptied landscapes. Lea's book does not describe the development of this extraordinary device, but Hardy had inherited a telescope from a 'collateral ancestor', and he had certainly researched telescopes for *Two on a Tower*, as well as possibly using a 'graphic telescope' and other lens devices himself. His telescopic vision, most notably in *The Woodlanders* and the Wimborne drawings, and his lifelong obsession with lenses certainly pre-dates Lea's involvement – although it was only now fully realised.

This collaboration, and these photographs have been vastly underrated. For generally, they have been reproduced incredibly badly – muddy, greyish, and *terribly* poorly cropped. You can see from the printers' marks how and why this was done. The sub-editor tended to chop out sky, or unoccupied land, when sky and unoccupied land were precisely what Hardy was showing us. He tried to crop these down into normal pictures: as though the meticulous, peculiar framing and focus

Hermann Lea with camera.

of Hardy's vision were not *exactly* how Wessex was constructed. Again and again, the reproduced, banal photograph is a travesty of Lea and Hardy's carefully framed, intensively zoomed view. Hardy had finally found someone who could capture the scale and detail of his view, the value of vast, empty places – and a pragmatic sub-editor who chopped them all out again.

These are telephoto pictures of often empty landscapes; in often bad weather, showing the limits of vision with incredible clarity. Some are taken in deliberately appalling weather, like the amazing one of Wareham Heath which became the frontispiece to *The Return of the Native*. It is a good, moody picture in its full-page reproduction, but the *print* shows it was taken in a torrential downpour, water pouring along the track (p. 68). Hardy must have had Lea out photographing, miles from anywhere, in all weathers. They were both, clearly, and rightly proud of that photograph – and I bet the sub-editors thought they were mad.

This was a preposterously ambitious endeavour. Lea had to cycle that massive lens around on a special trailer, behind his bicycle, to remote and distant places (until he got a car). It is no wonder Flintcomb-Ash, on the top of a hill, and way off the road in the 1880s – could not be found by Lea alone.

But there is no question we are seeing Hardy's vision here. It is exactly the picture of the *Wessex Poems*, *Tess* and the *Return*: dazzle, distance, detail; absence, disappearance, a landscape emptied. He is taking us, always, to the very limits of visual perception. Lea called his own book *Hardy Through the Camera's Eye*: that vast double-barrelled thing seems to be an SLR camera; they would both have been looking through the 'Camera's Eye' – and they both enjoyed a pun. As in the *Wessex Poems*, Hardy is *not* just asking Lea to illustrate the stories or their settings: he is building up his assembled, diffuse, coherent view of Wessex as a whole.

The places photographed are personal as well (Fordington, Puddletown and Wimborne for instance) and he would continue to extend this photographic survey adding (and photographing) 'local' settings in his remarkable play, *The Dynasts*. The

Faringdon Ruin, Hermann Lea.

photographs – like the *Wessex Poems* – are a key part of the assembled construction of Wessex. They do not just show us pictures of the places. They show how to focus our own vision, to see Wessex the way that he did.

So the best ones are works in themselves. The exquisite photograph of Maiden Castle, taken in dazzling sunlight, looking as far as the eye can see, and further than history can remember. The strange image of Faringdon Ruin in its plain field: a key awkward remnant of such 'vanished villages'. Or the view from the Wessex Ridgeway, looking towards Dorchester.

That photograph is a type of picture Hardy always returns to. It is a road, empty, running through an empty landscape, out of sight: *the* vision of Wessex. They are almost always old roads and they often open the books: Roman roads through Egdon Heath, Iron-Age ridgeways, sometimes mere tracks made by the passage of humans, or signified only by the fluttering of birds getting out of their way. It is the pedestrian's view of an old human landscape, forensically recovered, through a modern frame.

You can see the human occupation of the landscape, used in a similar way, stretching perhaps twenty minutes ahead by foot, back beyond written history. Those drawings, photographs and descriptions are pictures of time and place itself, of the human in the world, seen through an inventive long-lens camera.

View from the Wessex Ridgeway towards Dorchester.

Rather like Patrick Keillor's film essays,[31] they show us how much we can read from an apparently empty view, if we really look at it, for long enough, as architects have to.

Lea's work is central, architecturally, because it is a clear, constructed, highly experimental and clearly directed vision of how Hardy actually *saw* Wessex. It is another body of work in which Hardy, working closely and creatively with others, extends the substance of Wessex itself. These pictures evidence a very particular *type* of vision, from obsessively close detail, to vast visions stretched to infinity – empty roads; buildings lost in the mist, rain or sunlight – where we see the passage of humans across an empty land. This is what Wessex looks like.

Like the *Wessex Poems*, these photographs have not been seen in the way that a modern architect would see them. Mostly, they have not been seen at *all*, rarely reproduced well enough to show the remarkable way they were made, or how they stretch our vision to the edge of experience.

*

I know it will feel as though I have turned off the architectural highroad, but the obsessive, curatorial construction and creative control of a partly imagined,

199

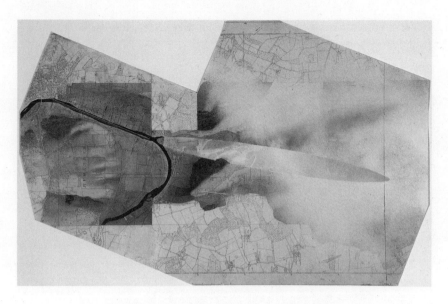

Temple Island by Michael Webb. *Jude*'s Fawley lies in
the clouded area above the curve of the river.

partly interpretative, partly real environment, is architecture's highest ground. Michael Webb is the most elusive of the famous group who revolutionised architectural thinking in the 1960s, Archigram. Their speculative, visionary projects predicted our own emerging world: with its hand-held technology; pop-up events; strange mix of consumerism and challenge. But Webb's most remarkable project is the extraordinary Temple Island, which he has never stopped making, quoting Barnett Newman: 'an artist spends a whole lifetime working on one picture.'[32]

Temple Island is an unended series of imaginary and very abstract paintings obsessively surveying a real place. It is in the Thames near Henley – actually in the parish of Fawley (the Estate's house is called Fawley Court). It has a classical pavilion, designed by James Wyatt, much photographed when the annual Henley Regatta passes it. So a landscape composed for a classically framed picturesque landscape view is continuously re-photographed, using the fastest and longest lenses, to capture time, speed, event, distance, as it passes this epitome of the fixed picturesque vision.

Webb's wonderful, bewildering paintings and drawings are an obsessive exploration of how these different modes of perception meet and do not meet – the classical vision with its fixed, perspectival Arcadian dream, the age of fast photography; cones of vision; flood levels: photographs blanked out where they would be hidden from the fixed eighteenth-century view. They are a remarkable, deliberate attempt to re-draw our own, infinitely uncertain views, pictures and projections of time and space.

Again, we are on several kinds of home territory: just down the hill from *Jude's* Fawley and in one of the most ambitious, beautiful and existential of architecture's speculative projects. Webb replies to my email, late at night: 'Henley is but 8 miles from Aldbrickham ... All of which brings us to Temple Island, referred to in an unpublished MS of Hardy as the Lake Isle of Innisfree.'[33] Just a joke, but architecture's imaginary worlds do have a habit of joining up, into a wider and shared cultural imagination. It is just that Hardy's great experimental project, somehow, was delivered into a wider world too.

19

MAX GATE CONTINUED

An Ongoing Project

Between 1894–1895, Hardy used his new prosperity to expand Max Gate too. He had said he 'didn't want to ruin himself with architecture',[1] but a few years in, the whole household was back in the turmoil of building works. He virtually doubled it in size, and he kept adding bits throughout his life. If Max Gate was his most famous building, it was the one he never finished. Or perhaps, one which challenged the idea of buildings being 'finished' at all.

The most important move was made straight away. He built a new, substantial back extension, in a slightly different manner – freer, more interesting, with some good rooms. He totally remodelled the front, too, but it was the extension which turned the way the whole house worked around: who used which parts, what views they saw, how they worked. He changed how any architectural critic would understand it. Virtually, it was a new project.

Max Gate extended: a whole new project.

And this may be his least known building of all: hidden in plain sight. People tend to treat extensions as subsidiary parts of architecture: it is rare for them to be considered more important than the original, especially when done by the same person.[2] Moreover, this is a *kitchen* extension – a remodelling of services: a new kitchen, better drainage, a study, and more attics, all of which are too easy to dismiss as scarcely architectural at all.

But those prejudices – downgrading services and alterations – are the antithesis of Hardy's thinking. He was, anyway, of an age which profoundly connected architecture and servicing in all parts of the vast new infrastructure of Victorian Britain: its drains, housing, transport and institutions. And Hardy was always designing from the servicing outwards: you can see it in his novels quite as clearly as his drawings. His attention always goes to the kitchens, details, drains and flues. There is quite a careful drawing of the extension to the drainage and grey water system, coloured up for future reference or for interested viewers. There is something called a servant's bath in one of the lower back attics, too: it is clearly inaccessible to humans and must have been a kind of hot water tank, for bailing into the more normal portable bathtubs. The new apple store and the Single Man's room above it are lovely, as are the servants' attics in the older part. The whole of Max Gate has had detail and care lavished on all users.

The new kitchen must have been a vast improvement. The National Trust have set it up as a kind of 'family kitchen' with honesty-box cakes and a jigsaw for visitors, and films about Hardy's music: a welcoming place on a rainy afternoon. It would not have worked quite like that in Hardy's day – cooks had dominion over

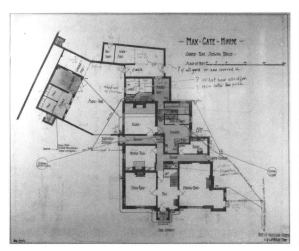

Max Gate. Left: obvious accretions; right: third and final study.

the kitchen – but Hardy often visited in search of stories, turns of phrase and dialect words. He naturally wanted to access all areas.

So Max Gate phase 2 was arguably *more* important for Hardy in being a functional, accretive extension rather than a new house. He was increasingly valuing the richness acquired by buildings over time, and Max Gate, with its deliberate, expressive accretion shows a building improving with age entirely. Every addition, or walling up, blocked window or moved doorway was framed and visible – every addition takes its own shape (that zigzagging plan shows it); the trees were growing, the brick mellowing. And his commitment to 'inside out' design was now so confident that he did not draw the overall elevation at all, even for the remodelled front. This project is, in its own way, rejecting the idea of a finished, 'perfect' architectural ideal in favour of the working everyday place.

A deliberate focus on additions is an unusual position for an architect to take, and an extension is rarely considered high architecture. It was deemed remarkable when Witherford Watson Mann won the Stirling Prize for the rebuilding of ruined Astley Castle as a Landmark Trust holiday house. WWM strongly join, add, patch and occupy the ruin – and resist making it pretty from the outside. Hardy would surely have been interested.

But most fundamentally, in Max Gate phase 2 the struggle between 'served and servant' gets reconfigured. Hardy takes that Arts & Crafts double stair, and swivels the whole working of the house round it, like twisting a Rubik's Cube. The back of the building, the 'servant' areas, now has all the best parts. Emma gets a sweet little pair of attics, just where you would expect the servants to be, with her own pretty stair, featuring that 'coffin turn' window. Hardy, below that, gets a big, confident study – with a huge, idiosyncratic double window looking south across the kitchen garden: the grandest space in the house, and rightly so. A new, confident sense of what this house represents has emerged. It is a working building, with that study as the key room – somewhere between the study of a master of a college and Henchard's office overlooking his workyards in Casterbridge. Hardy is privately overseeing the working operation of Wessex.

Partly, this is pragmatic: it is easiest to put these new rooms together at the back. But it is also more idiosyncratic. With Hardy's growing fame came an irregular, intrusive trickle of visitors, known or unknown, hoping to catch a glimpse of the famous novelist at home, and always treated with extreme courtesy. But visitors invited into the front rooms need not know that Hardy's study or Emma's boudoir existed. That grand, confident, south-facing study is fully screened behind walls and trees, and especially the Nut Walk, planted by Hardy and Emma, which divides the front garden from the side one (which has Hardy's gate for slipping away from unwanted visitors). The extension is a complete, camouflaged, private 'back' house tucked away behind the formal front, in which guests were generously hosted to those comedy meals – with dogs or cats sitting on the table.

If you were *drawing* this twisting around of the main rooms into that 'servant-space', back-house, you would have to use exploded axonometric – something like a flat-pack assembly drawing, also beloved of Tschumi. That would reveal something else that happens with this move. While the back extension becomes looser, more confidently rural and 'inside out', the front becomes *grander*. And, if anything, worse. Not internally, though: the lower rooms lost their east-facing windows in this extension, but Hardy liked dual aspect, so a new bay was added on to the music room, culminating in a second turret – for the cook (they were doing everything to keep a cook). Later still, he would add a conservatory and other details for Florence. The old window openings were walled up but left visible in Hardy's deliberately accretive manner.

The new front, though, is both grandiose and lumpen. The awkward effect of two not-quite-matching towers may be a by-product of Hardy's inability to set out perspective or three-dimensional drawings (and indeed, his lack of practice in new design at all). Hardy also re-worked the porch – probably as a draft lobby from those vicious south westerly winds, but no prettier than the original. And there are a few details on the pleasant south side which would have been improved by an edit, too.

But the back house extension has a new sense of real confidence. Its refusal to work as a formal composition (there is no drawing of the extended elevation) paradoxically generates a far better composition. The more extreme range of window sizes helps: Max Gate, with a classic Victorian deep plan and steep roof, needs the huge study windows to give a proper sense of proportion and scale; the other (actually substantial) windows around them make it feel more 'cottagey'.

Originally, the two attic dormer windows were the same size, but on Emma's request, Hardy enlarged one: a good compositional touch, which offset her workspace and presence against his nicely in asymmetrical elevation – she was still writing and drawing. But it is a shame – symbolically and practically – that he did not make that 'short window' longer, giving a seated view. For now that Emma had her private space, and with her distaste of Hardy's critique of marriage in *Jude*, she retreated there, leaving, finally, by coffin, down that stair. Texts 'hold potentialities for their future readings', as we have already heard.

But this is a better house now, functioning more like a farm than a villa, moving beyond the problems of architectural expression into something more rambling, working on its own terms. Something *older*. Hardy has felt his way into this project using the adaptive skills he was best at. While less manifestly 'architectural', this has a new freedom of architectural expression. It is a shift towards the freer style of the turning century.

And perhaps, even Max Gate's grandiose front did the defensive job intended. Here is an aggressive comment from a later visitor, Arthur Benson: 'a red house dimly visible, bordered by turnip fields. It is a structure at once mean and pretentious, with no grace of design or detail, and with two hideous flanking turrets with pointed roof of blue slate.'[3] Maybe, after all, the Bensons were exactly the people Hardy was perfectly happy to put off, architecturally speaking.

Because other, famously creative, people kept coming (and writing about it). The strangeness, the animals, the gloomy comedy; the idea of this odd house as the gateway to Wessex. (The National Trust embraced this, studding the rooms with quotes.) When the writer Rebecca West came, her lover H.G. Wells did a captioned sketch of the conversation. Hardy is explaining that the house is 'built on Skellingtons'. Rebecca says: 'Lovely! Lovely!' Florence (who seemed 'depressed') says 'Skellingtons may be healthy, but they ain't gay'.

West was one of many of Hardy's visitors who themselves conjured up powerful places in novels: her fictionalised autobiography *The Fountain Overflows* contains astonishing evocations of vanished houses of childhood. Virginia and Leonard Woolf came too. Leonard Woolf, looking back, described how Virginia tried to talk about books – but Hardy kept 'reverting to the dog'. He says the house 'with its sombre growth of trees, seemed to have been created by him as if it were one of his poems translated into bricks, furniture and vegetation'.[4] J.M. Barrie, author of *Peter Pan*, inventor of Neverland and mentor of Daphne du Maurier[5] – the man who described how to imagine yourself into fictional life through imaginary islands and who was involved in Hardy's stage productions – came often, and became a friend. So did E.M. Forster, who makes places do everything in his novels: plot, atmosphere, mythic appearances, sex, marriage, beauty. And whose own architect father worked (after Hardy's time), for Blomfield's and also designed his suburban house. Forster would lovingly describe (in *A Room with a View*) a comically suburban house, with a 'small turret like a rhinoceros's horn': for watching carts going up and down the road.[6] Forster himself sought 'real' sources for his fictional house: Max Gate may have been considered.

There was Robert Graves, who ended *Goodbye to All That* with a visit to Max Gate. There was Siegfried Sassoon, who became fascinated with the elision of the wizard of Wessex with this suburban householder in his poem, 'At Max Gate', in *Common Chords*, 1950. Even better, he wrote in his diary in 1921:

Some day this evening will be a miraculous memory, as if I'd spent six hours with Ben Jonson or John Milton. Now I ask myself again, 'Was it the author of The Dynasts who went up the dark stairs in front of you carrying a silver candlestick, and showed you, with a touch of pride, a new bathroom which has superseded the previous hip-bath brought into the bedroom before breakfast?'[7]

This is something of an achievement. Max Gate – 'pretentious' suburban Max Gate – has permeated into the whole of the overlapping atmospheres of imaginary worlds of Wessex and of England.

Yet Max Gate does not feel quite like 'architecture', while Wessex does. It does not meet the unspoken, part learned, part instinctive shifting cultural criteria critics use to identify and discuss 'architecture'. It is not exactly beautiful – although one can become obsessed with what it is like. It does not invent a new style or exhibit mastery of an existing one; its technical innovations (grey water recycling; cavity walls) are invisible. Its proportions – its detailing – do not exhibit much polemic or rationale. Its one major, lovely idea: the twisted interlock of served and servant, public and private, is hard to see, although, if Hardy himself had drawn the kind of diagrams Koolhaas used for his 'patent' applications in *Content*, I suspect the conversation would be different. Even the visible, complex double stair, where the idea is powerfully developed, is all but impossible to photograph. Then it is unfashionable. Its circulation, its exciting, poky staircases and closed rooms are roughly (with honourable exceptions) out of favour in the current fashions for open-plan, 'wow' spaces. Yet they are seductive, even that coffin stair, in an instinctive, children's novels way.

The qualities which distinguish art from pictures, and architecture from buildings, are elusive. In architecture, they require an idea or approach operating on many scales and in many ways: relating the detail to the overall form of the building, say. Usually, the drawings help us locate this quality, but Max Gate's drawings are nothing to write home about.

But if you have ever visited a house lived in by the same people for a long time, you will be familiar with Max Gate's power. The quality Bachelard describes,[8] or Alvaro Siza, in his depiction of the heroic business of living in a house, and battling with cold, damp, heat, wildlife.[9] It feels older than it is. Even the constricted circulation of Max Gate, that warren of rooms and passages and stairs – is somehow exciting, with the homely-unhomely sense of life and death. It is a spooky house, a slightly gloomy one, naturally. Max Gate can make your skin prickle.

Even in forcing me to write down these curious, invisible, dividing lines between 'architecture' and 'a house' (and they move culturally all the time), Max Gate manages to challenge those assumptions. Hardy designed a home which people seem loath to leave, which improves with age. Like his focus on sheer description in his writing (which architects have abandoned to their peril), Max Gate works in the circuit of our older, human, non-specialised senses. It is what architectural writers write *about* – but which is not quite what is usually called architecture.

Here's part of Hardy's bookend to 'Domicilium', 'At Day-Close in November', a poem written shortly before his death:

... I set every tree in my June-time
    And now they obscure the sky

And the children who ramble through here
    Conceive that there never has been
A time when no tall trees grew here
    A time when none will be seen.

Building houses, planting trees, vision. Hardy's writing was bracketed by these ongoing, working architectural ideas. Of course Hardy did not want to modernise it: Max Gate, with all its failures and flaws, works as a building tangibly evolving its own past where imaginary and real worlds cannot get away from each other.

So Max Gate – much visited, awkward, imperfect – covertly challenges what we think architecture is, makes us reconsider the curious line we draw between 'architecture' and buildings which, somehow, are not architecture. Does architecture include how a building is used over time? Not usually. Does it have to work foremost as an art-object? Many architects would think so; others would challenge it. Is the front elevation the most important thing? Does it have to be tangibly original?

Max Gate stumbles on the classic definitions but succeeds on its own, perverse alternatives. It was never a pure, polished, perfect design; it was, as a writer's house, continually occupied, always changing, imaginatively rich, perversely real; a workshop for the imagination. Something which, made by the great wizard of Wessex and imaginatively reconstructed by the rest of us, still shapes the real and imaginary worlds of England; a compelling irritant, the grit in the oyster, a catalyst. Max Gate is, surely, a great gateway to Wessex, just as the name suggests.

It keeps working too, rather expertly continued and extended by the National Trust. And this too is not quite beyond his outreach. Remember Hardy's immediate installation of Lea at Bockhampton, his sister Kate's swift purchase of Max Gate on Florence's death in order to pass it immediately over to the nation – she must have done it with money which had come from Hardy. Even the 'National Trust' (an idea, a name which he coined) and the phenomenon of opening houses of writers and artists to the public is a collective endeavour which, I would argue, Hardy in some part helped shape.

THE CONSERVATION OF WESSEX

'An Imaginary Story'

Hardy's involvement with conservation continued, even strengthened towards the end of his life. His support was sought in all kinds of campaigns, local and national. This was not because he was a 'dedicated case worker'. It was because he was the author of Wessex itself.

Rather like Prince Charles's position in British architecture of the 1980s, Hardy had become a 'source' to be quoted. An influential spokesman, a first call for journalists seeking opinions on rural life or building conservation. In both cases they were sought-after because of their fame – and then paradoxically treated as a sort of 'everyman', a spokesman for the layperson.[1] Media constructs are not always logical, but they had chosen well in Hardy.

Naturally, Hardy's campaigning was always discreet and covert. 'He never voiced his opinion on such delicate matters architectural in the local press, and rarely elsewhere',[2] says Beatty. Yet in Beatty's diligent work we can see Hardy directly using Wessex as a deliberate conservation campaign in itself.

This was still a huge struggle: 'Few occupations are more pleasant than endeavouring to re-capture an old design from the elusive hand of annihilation', he wrote in 1906, in 'Memories of Church Restoration'.[3] This was a barbed comment. Hardy had just been in a painful struggle over Fordington Church (the home of his friends, the Moules, and close to Max Gate), where far too many people had their own enthusiastic interpretations of what and how to 'recapture'. Hardy was nominated to the over-enthusiastic Restoration Committee in what sounds like contentious circumstances. The vicar, Sidney Boulter, backed his appointment, saying:

Mr Hardy was a name which had perhaps not so much weight locally as it had further afield, on the principle of the prophet being 'not without honour, save in his own country' ... If he joined them, they would find him a tower of strength to them, in that, having an intimate knowledge of church architecture, his views were listened to throughout the length and breadth of the country, more than they sometimes realized ...[4]

Hardy did at first seem to have some sway in this work. He got a clause inserted into the 'appeal for funds' saying that nothing would be done 'to interfere with the archaeological or artistic features of the church'.[5] But that was a famous last word. The architect, W.D. Caröe claimed the parapet and pinnacles were in a 'dangerous condition', and that the tower 'was intended to have a finial, and it has never been finished or more probably had been altered'. (Hardy commented bitterly 'it may have been removed after trial because it was unsightly'.[6])

Caröe drew up his plans and submitted them to the committee and SPAB. But then, at a committee meeting when Hardy was away, he rushed through the alterations, including a prominent 'pepperpot' finial – without any drawings at all. Hardy promptly resigned from the committee in 1903, politely but precisely saying he could not always attend meetings:

One result has been that I did not know such an essential change of the outline of the Tower was in contemplation as has been effected by carrying up the turret (which happened by accident while I was away from home) & upon which, if I had seen a drawing of the proposed addition beforehand, I should have expressed my misgivings ... I wonder if I, or anybody, ever told you that its proportions were so much admired by Sir Gilbert Scott that he sent a man to measure and make an exact drawing of it for preservation?[7]

That was outspoken, for the public Hardy. In a 'private' note to the vicar, Hardy added: 'Architects do go on in rather a high-handed manner, even nowadays, when they have had so much education. Between ourselves, I think this one needs looking after.'[8] Thomas Perkins also told SPAB: 'Mr Hardy ... did not feel safe in the architect's hands and did not want to have the credit of sanctioning work he strongly disapproves of.'[9]

Hardy's anger can be felt in his most polemic conservation argument, 'Memories of Church Restoration', the speech written for SPAB at the RIBA in 1906 – which he began composing at this time. As Beatty points out, it is typically read as 'memories' of his work in the 1860s and 1870s, but clearly includes both his reaction to the problems SPAB was facing, *and* his own 'patching' restoration at West Knighton. It opens:

A melancholy reflection may have occurred to many people whose interests lie in the study of Gothic architecture. The passion for restoration first became vigorously operative, say, three-quarters of a century ago, and if all the mediaeval building in England had been left as they stood at that date, to incur whatever dilapidations might have befallen them at the hands of time, weather and general neglect, this country would be richer in specimens today than it finds itself after the expenditure of millions in a nominal preservation during that period.

Active destruction under saving names has been effected on so vast a scale that the concurrent protection of old structures, or portions of structures, by their being kept wind- and waterproof amid such operations counts as nothing in the balance.[10]

Back at Fordington in 1906, *another* architect, Jem Feacey, and a *new* vicar, were doing more restoration. Feacey did not like the Kentish 'pepperpot' addition either – but he did propose stripping out the Georgian chancel. Hardy strongly objected:

It is quite the opposite of a 'mean erection', as the architect describes it in the lecture sent, having in fact considerable dignity; but of course it is true that it contrasts with the Gothic portion of the church.

It seems to depend upon how far down the centuries our sentiments of veneration extend, whether the Society should protest on grounds of antiquity. But it certainly could protest on the ground that there is no reason whatever for pulling down so substantial a piece of 18th century work merely to erect 20th century imitation in its place.[11]

The battles continued. Caröe attacked Feacey's restoration, saying 'a more deplorable and aggressive scheme in worse taste it would be hard to imagine'.[12] Hardy, although sometimes asked for advice, was ruthlessly ignored and his proposal to do the work himself turned down.[13] The 'drastic', expensive extensions went ahead. Fordington is a classic example of Victorian 'restoration': architects stamping their own ideas over the top of the existing building, effectively eradicating the character it had acquired over time. It would focus Hardy's thinking.

Hardy's deliberate use of his novels in campaigns is clearest in the campaign over Puddletown, or Piddletown church in 1910. This was his mother's hometown, the Weatherbury of *Far from the Madding Crowd*, a late campaign – and a church that Hardy and SPAB might have thought safe.[14] Writing to SPAB, the 70-year-old Hardy calls it 'the only one I know in the county which had not been tampered with'. Hardy deplores the proposed extension. He questions the idea that a larger church once stood on the site (which was being asserted as grounds for extending it). He mentions he had been round the church with Blomfield, and 'he, though a restorer, emphatically stated that this particular church was one which ought not to be touched'. He says the previous owner (at that time) had assured him that no alteration should take place.[15] Then, in classic understatement:

> ... I may add that, curiously enough, the church happens to be the village church of the novel, "Far from the Madding Crowd", which brings many visitors to it every year, particularly Americans. I may say privately, that I cannot help feeling that, if expostulation fail, & as soon as the Society feels sure of its ground, a letter to *The Times* on the matter, adding the fact that it is the church of this well-known novel, might be effective. You will quite understand that my own view on an imaginary story of mine makes no difference to the case, but as some of the public think otherwise, it would be well to enlist their sympathy even though we suppose it bestowed for foolish reasons.[16]

Clearly, Hardy believes his novels *could* influence popular opinion – and used them, deliberately, to do so. The letter *did* go to *The Times*;[17] there *was* an 'outraged' reaction – from a wide range of institutions including the RIBA, the National Trust, the Royal Archaeological Institute and SPAB. Beatty, comparing it with more significant acts of 'restoration' vandalism, is baffled. It is 'a mystery to understand' why far more devastating 'restorations' aroused a 'relatively low key' outcry.[18]

This would not have been a mystery to Hardy – that was why he suggested it in the first place. Or to his opponents: 'The fact that Mr. Thomas Hardy describes this church in his novel, "Far from the Madding Crowd" may or may not enhance the interest connected with the church; but it cannot justify such puerile tirades against the restoration of its demolished chancel, so necessary for convenience and worship.'[19]

Although it is impossible to firmly identify 'effects' in mass communication campaigns, this seems clear. Hardy knew he had a secret weapon – a pervasive, diffuse hotline to public opinion. His influence was way beyond the overtly rational; it operated on another level altogether – and he was using it accordingly.

And its outreach went beyond his actual involvement. When enthusiastic restorers stripped out the Georgian gallery at Symondsbury, SPAB's letter read: 'This is a Thomas Hardy Church and perhaps one, if not the only one left of the ones he writes about'.[20] Beatty says there is no evidence Hardy had *any* connection with Symondsbury. But SPAB – accurately – implies that stripping out a Georgian musicians' gallery; removing both ongoing heritage and social, musical working of a church, was a *type* of damaging restoration at the heart of Hardy's concerns. However vaguely stated, that was now well understood by all concerned.

On a case-by-case basis, and in the prophet's own country, there was little sign of success. Hardy had written, in the 1895 preface to *Far from the Madding Crowd*, that 'the church remains, by great good fortune, unrestored and intact'. By 1912, he had added 'this is no longer the case'. The *Mayor* similarly footnotes the loss of the houses of Casterbridge. The bleakness of those footnotes and arguments suggests a deeper sense of failure. Having reconstructed Wessex for us, in his novels, he was now seeing it demolished all over again, both in fact and (as his footnotes show) in the fictional surrogate too.

Yet conservation is arguably the area where Hardy's direct architectural influence has been strongest of all. For the tide was turning. The National Trust was set up in 1895 (using just that phrase from *A Laodicean*). The National Trust Act was passed in 1907, and in 1927, 1,400 acres of farmland around Stonehenge were bought after a national appeal. Stonehenge is not covered in Beatty's book, because it is not in the Hardy–SPAB letters, but his hand is here too. While the stones were well documented and published, there was nothing to protect it in the 1880s. Hardy, placing it so epically in *Tess*, his greatest and most successful work, now moving into amateur and West End dramatic productions, had it well framed in the public imagination, and as Gatrell argues, he underlines and reminds us of it during the First World War, in his poem 'Channel Firing',[21] where the guns 'disturbed the hour ... As far inland as Stourton tower,/And Camelot, and starlit Stonehenge.'

More directly, there is an article in the *Daily Chronicle* in 1899, where Hardy directly argues it should be bought for the nation:

> A nation like our own ought to have what may be called a final guardianship over any monument or relic which is of value to it as a page of history, even though the hieroglyphics cannot be deciphered as yet ... emphatically Stonehenge should be purchased by the nation ... A certain area – shall we put it at 2,000 acres? Must be bought as securing control of the surroundings of the monument.[22]

Apparently, this piece is written by a journalist telling Hardy that the stones are to be sold, with Hardy reacting in shock and dismay. But the strategy Hardy puts forward is very well worked out, saying exactly how many acres should be purchased: surely, he set this article up. The concept of preserving a landscape as a way of understanding our story as humans is laid out here – and that is just what the Trust would do (although it took another 28 years to buy the Stonehenge land and not as much as Hardy had suggested). But he had put the idea in our minds.

*

Hardy's conservation influence depends on the power of fictional environments in human imagination, and he understood this well. The campaign to restore

Stoke Poges churchyard in 1923 also sought the 83-year-old Hardy's backing.[23] This was the church of Gray's 'Elegy in a Country Churchyard', from which *Far from the Madding Crowd* takes its name. Hardy again was involved with the idea of 'patching' the church, and using the appeal to buy the surrounding land. When SPAB were seeking to stop a restoration project in Sherborne in 1919, a draft telegram from SPAB to Florence reads 'a word from your husband would sway the meeting.'[24] Oddly, that forecasts the telegram sent by SAVE Britain's Heritage to the Prince of Wales to help reverse the decision to demolish the area round Mansion House in the 1980s: '... another word from you Sir, at this crucial time, could help save London.'[25] Perhaps those erudite conservationists knew the story. For disingenuous media campaigns run by influential people downplaying their status to present a kind of 'public opinion' are *still* a characteristic of the conservation movement. In *Preserving the Past* (1996), several writers chart the growth of the English conservation movement through a series of purportedly 'amateur' special interest groups. Gavin Stamp (a key player in many of them) says: 'Architects have always been involved ... but leading lights have usually been interested amateurs (and often journalists) ... many of the founders have been architectural historians, a novel species.'[26]

Such groups, adds Andrew Saint, 'cultivated the image of the educated amateur but were proficient at pulling establishment strings.'[27] SAVE Britain's Heritage (which Gavin Stamp called 'a novel ginger group' and John Summerson called 'a menace'[28]) ran particularly high-profile campaigns throughout the last decades of the twentieth century – principally because its leaders occupied almost all the posts as 'architectural correspondents' in the broadsheet newspapers, generating an almost automatic 'consensus' of expert press opinion on any given case.[29] They too believed, like Hardy, in their power to affect the real world of public action on public affairs.[30]

But well before SAVE, Hardy had also set out with his colleagues to try to build an idea of the value of conservation as an unquestionable good: an idea which was still, in the 1980s, measurable in general newspaper coverage of architectural matters.[31] And although such cause and effect can never be proven, there is no question that Hardy developed Wessex, in part, to do exactly this. Indeed, the whole shape of Britain's unusually strong conservation history follows the pattern Hardy set; preserved lansdcapes, human stories, accretions, conservation histories based on international collection of local narratives.[32]

*

Hardy had always, from 'How I Built Myself a House' on, managed to deliver the architectural profession's most specialised ideas to an entirely non-specialist public.

He worked – consciously and deliberately so – *outside* the profession's own rarified forums and *for* a wider and inclusive public. Yet he is not to be beaten on even the highest ground of conservation theory. His work was always concerned with both abstract and practical dilemmas of conservation. It was the mainframe of his professional career, it was discussed in *A Laodicean*, and it is shown in his best built projects. His novels, factual writings, campaigns and letters discuss conservation's rapidly evolving areas of debate. They consider whether and when to rebuild or to leave alone. They argue against the selective destruction of unfashionable work (which in his day included Jacobean and Georgian). They debate whether new work should be 'an honest patch' (as Paula Power thinks). They question the idea of trying to restore an ancient building to an idealised 'original' state. They actively champion the value of accretion. These are well discussed in Hardy studies – but generally, to give the impression that Hardy was, in his own quiet way, quite a good conservationist. It is rare to find discussion of how *unusual* this was – or how inventive and influential it may have been. For Wessex is not simply SPAB's agenda carried out by other means, and Hardy is *more* than acute in identifying major conservation dilemmas of his own age – he is setting out the ideology, the highly evolved conservation consciousness of our own.

Hardy's 'Memories of Church Restoration', written straight after the Fordington debacle, was a rare foray towards the professional practitioners of the day. It was only written after repeated requests and not intended to be delivered in person.[33] But it is an open, direct, stinging and sophisticated challenge to the prevailing idea of conservation. It opens and closes with that absolute assertion that restoration has caused far more harm than good – and that the best thing to do is to leave as much as we can alone. It directly argues that conservation's true value is human or social rather than aesthetic – driven by an older human relationship with our environment – and of *more* value as social history than as art:

> It is the preservation of memories, history, fellowships, fraternities. Life, after all, is more than art, and that which appealed to us in the (maybe) clumsy outlines of some structure which has been looked at and entered by a dozen generations of ancestors outweighs the more subtle recognition, if any, of architectural qualities.[34]

This is ambitious, challenging thinking, overturning the received wisdom of aesthetic historical worth, in favour of human associations, memory and everyday working necessity:

> To the incumbent, the church is a workshop; to the antiquary it is a relic. To the parish it is a utility; to the outsider a luxury ... The quaintly carved seat

that a touch will damage has to be sat in, the frameless doors with the queer old locks and hinges have to keep out draughts, the bells whose shaking endangers the graceful steeple have to be rung.

If the ruinous church could be enclosed in a crystal palace, covering it to the weathercock from rain and wind, and a new church be built alongside for services ... the method would be an ideal one.[35]

This is deliberately iconoclastic. That 'crystal palace' (originally a term of abuse) was meant to provoke his professional audience (rather like Prince Charles's 'Monstrous Carbuncle' speech to the RIBA in 1984). It challenged his audience of architects and conservationists to think what, and who, conservation is *for*. It points out how peculiar and constructed are the ideas we use.

He *still* challenges us on the same questions today. His powerful arguments about the human value of long-used buildings is clearly of a type with Alois Riegl (1857–1905) who argued people esteemed 'Age Value' rather than 'Historical Value' in buildings and who Forty says offered a refinement of Ruskin's ideas about memory.[36] This is called one of the most modern of the ideas of conservation theory[37] – but it seems self-evident to those who have grown up reading Hardy.[38] As far as our very evolved, world-famous English conservation thinking has gone (with the human stories of gardeners, maids and cooks now foregrounded by the National Trust; the preservation of everyday houses as well as grand ones; the idea of leaving even major buildings like Calke Abbey as found, as far as possible, rather than faking a historic perfection), Hardy was there before us.

*

Following any oddity in Hardy's work always leads somewhere unexpectedly extreme. With the 'crystal palace' reference Hardy forces us to notice the contemporary framework of conservation. He is nudging us to see conservation as a fundamentally *modern* construct – a deliberate surrogate for, and exhibition of, our ruptured, older relationship with the environment.

The naturally modern nature of conservation is not quite what historians say – although many stop just short of doing so. Jukka Jokilehto says: 'modern conservation is based on some specifically modern concepts and values.'[39] Wim Denslagen quotes (but does not discuss) Foucault's argument that 'there is no such thing as a return'.[40] And Michael Hunter lists factors underlying the speedy development of conservation: the growth of mass culture; the demand for visitor attractions; the expansion of railways, cheap travel, car ownership, and the leisure industry.[41] It is modernity, and popular modernity at that. Exactly the framework of publication and travel through which Wessex operated.

Yet all Hardy's well-recorded conservation arguments seem to have stayed within literary, not architectural, studies. The long, interesting 'Memories of Church Restoration' paper is well quoted in Hardy studies – and typically not at all in conservation ones. Because it is *fiction*, Hardy's deliberate construction and critique of conservation thinking has been either professionally discounted or entirely overlooked. Conservationists have no more recognised his leading-edge contributions to their field than conceptual architects and even Forty, who regrets architects' 'neglect of the lessons of Proust', omits him.[42]

Yet Hardy probably chose the more influential path. He was, I would argue, surely the greatest conservation thinker and campaigner of all time, working in fictional and visionary form, and setting an imaginative background for one of the most sophisticated conservation cultures in the world. He was well aware of the limits of architecture's professional outreach, and was, with extreme sophistication, working beyond it.

Hardy's outreach: Winterborne Tomson before restoration,
preserved by the sale of Hardy's letters.

POETRY, PLAYS AND OTHER PROSPECTS

Inventive Traditions

Hardy valued his poetry over his novels, as he had told Robert Graves. He published not far short of a thousand poems, from his teenage 'Domicilium' to 'At Day-Close in November' written shortly before his death. It was his preferred medium, and at the end of his life, he was still making analogies between poems and architecture, and yet I have scarcely touched on Hardy's poetry.

At the start of this work, the idea of studying Hardy's poems in detail – one by one, in their collections, and as a whole, from an architectural point of view – would have seemed far from the point. Yet all his work seems to answer to architectural analysis, and major prospects for further exploration seem to be opening up now, for work beyond the limits of this book. And not only in poetry, but in the short stories, the maps, the book designs, the musical adaptations, the many plays and theatre adaptations, and certainly in the wider question of collaborative work too.

*

For Hardy, poetry and architecture were naturally close; he was still asserting it in the *Life*. Perhaps it was the sense of something both visionary and embodied which fused the media in his mind, something greater than the sum of its parts. And something, too, where high and low culture were one; something shared, passed from person to person, from one generation to another, and yet something never fully fixed, but inherently improvisational.

Linking 'Domicilium' to 'At Day-Close in November' suggests a bracket of poems about people making houses and planting trees which will outlast them. A negation of architecture's professional constructions – or its deepest foundation and real substance. They are certainly dealing with things both visionary and embodied.

There are the foot-worn steps, of 'The Self-Unseeing'; the drowned, hubristic Titanic in 'The Convergence of the Twain'; the animals kneeling in the barn on Christmas Eve in 'The Oxen' (Beatty mentions a mediaeval carving of a kneeling ox at Rampisham Church, which Hardy worked on for Hicks[1]); the handposts, cliffs, clothes, trees and landscapes of the wonderful, moving and distressing poems revisiting his first love for Emma against their later alienation written in grief and guilt after her death. But Hardy's poetry defies such generalisation. His poems are many and varied, pervasive, moving, bitter, tragic, visionary, uneven, resonant, and different. As Gatrell says, they have:

> many characteristics in common – a verse-form to fit the material (I haven't counted but he has hundreds of different structures), a sense of rhythm that incorporates many fractures of the pattern (too much regularity is dull, lifeless, he felt), a surprising use of strange words (I always think of 'wan wistlessness' to rhyme with existlessness), a fondness for ballad metres (music lies behind so many of them, even to his lines to the scherzo of Mozart's E flat symphony), and I could go on.[2]

The necessity for individual structure for purpose is fundamental to architecture too. Such analogies seem more fundamental than one might have assumed.

Often, the poems too predict ideas which emerge, famously, elsewhere. 'Drummer Hodge', the rural soldier buried in South Africa, predates (and surpasses) Rupert Brooke's famous 'there's some corner of a foreign field that is for ever England'; 'The Man He Killed' predates Wilfred Owen's 'I am the enemy you killed, my friend' and Yeats's 'An Irish Airman Foresees his Death'; 'Horses' pre-dates Michael Morpurgo's *War Horse* – to name just a few. They have Hardy's knack of lodging an idea in your imagination, which stays there, long after you think you have forgotten it. Like his deliberate use of the vanished dialect words, 'dumbledore' and 'hag-rid', Hardy has a way of snagging things in people's memory.

Hardy's first collection *Wessex Poems* had briefly taken a form close to a speculative architectural project, in its elusive and troubling assembly of pictures and texts, its awkward predictive vision of an ancient subject matter. The visual experiment was not directly repeated, but the speculative grouping remains. *Poems of the Past and Present* (1901), *Time's Laughingstocks* (1909), *Satires of Circumstance* (1914), *Moments of Vision* (1917), *Late Lyrics and Earlier* (1922), *Human Shows* (1925), *Winter Words* – grouped in counterpoise, across time and place: as flashes of illumination through Wessex; extending or taking us deeper into the places we know; adding ideas, details, voices, pieces of furniture (the mirror, notably, in

Moments of Vision); underlining and reminding us of others. They are many, diverse, condensed, diffuse, and different; they tune Wessex up, keep it moving, uncertain, alive. Ignoring his embargo on 'dragging in architecture',[3] Hardy says in the *Life*:

> He knew that in architecture, cunning irregularity is of enormous worth, and it is obvious that he carried on into his verse ... the Gothic-art principle in which he had been trained – the principle of spontaneity, found in mouldings, tracery and such like – resulting in the 'unforeseen' ... character of his metres and stanzas, that of stress rather than syllable, poetic texture rather than poetic veneer ... 'constructed ornament', being what he, in common with every Gothic student, had been taught to avoid as the plague. He shaped his poetry accordingly, introducing metrical pauses, and reversed beats; and found for his trouble that some particular line of a poem ... was greeted with a would-be jocular remark that such a line 'did not make for immortality'.

> The same critic might have gone to one of our cathedrals ... and on discovering that the carved leafage of some capital or spandrel ... strayed freakishly out of its bounds ... or that there was a sudden blank in a wall where a window was to be expected ... have declared with equally merry conviction, 'This does not make for immortality.'

> One case of the kind, in which the poem 'On Sturminster Bridge', was quoted with the remark that one could make as good music as that out of a milk-cart ...[4]

That was another piece of disingenuousness. Music out of milk carts was *exactly* what he was making: *Tess* was being set to music while Hardy was telling Florence to write this. Indeed, musical interpretations of his work by the moderns of his day (Gustav Holst's wonderful tone poem *Egdon Heath* [1918], for instance Holst's favourite work[5]) are the simplest parallel ways to understand Hardy's work – and its continual invention and abstraction of collected, vanishing traditions.

And as Charles Pettit shows, this is another area where Hardy too was often collaborating, behind the scenes but directly, on creative work by others: on Gustav Holst's settings of poems from 1903 onwards; Frédéric d'Erlanger's opera version of *Tess* (1906); Rutland Boughton's setting of the experimental play *The Famous Tragedy of The Queen of Cornwall* (1923–1924) – both showing 'the same mixture of public distance and private enjoyment'[6] and Holst's *Egdon Heath* (1922–1928) mentioned above. Vaughan Williams's Ninth Symphony and John Ireland's 'orchestral poem' *Mai-Dun* are also based on Hardy's work, and Edward Elgar also found Hardy keen to collaborate, though nothing came of this.[7]

There is a human tradition linking landscape and climate, music and architectural form, as the architect and traditional fiddle player Steve Larkin explores in his PhD: setting, for instance, a series of crafted gutter details against his own collaborative playing of traditional songs. The parallel is clear: this is an ongoing culture of skilled improvisation, the process Hardy seems to have been describing to Albert Richardson; a culture both traditional and spontaneous; a creative process of cumulative trial and error found in poetry, music and buildings, sometimes highly authored, sometimes anonymous, sometimes collective, sometimes individual. As one may enter a remote graveyard and find generations of stonecutting work of true genius. That is an idea taking us back to Gray's 'Elegy Written in a Country Churchyard', a source from which Wessex itself seems to have sprung, in that title from *Far from the Madding Crowd*. Larkin is not what would be thought of as a 'vernacular' architect: he can create fine, stark, almost Brutalist modern houses, often for other traditional musicians, of great beauty, tuned for interior acoustics as Hardy's church restorations seem to be. Both are reaching down into an older human tradition, a sense of the landscape, and of people, together in a place. It is (in part) the argument in *Church Restoration*: an inventive tradition both instinctive and professional, both abstract and everyday.

So we are indeed in the realm of the vernacular, as we might have expected, but of a perennially modern and inventive vernacular, which is not how it is always portrayed. Interestingly, the great authority on vernacular architecture, Paul Oliver, who compiled the remarkable *Encyclopedia of Vernacular Building*, also undertook parallel field research studies on Blues music in America – and on the suburban semi-detached house upon which so much professional distaste has been lavished in *Dunroamin*, the book which explores the anti-professional taste that the professionals disliked in buildings such as Max Gate.

Hardy, surely, was one of those who removed a barrier between high and native music and architecture, as between ancient and modern. He loved late Turner and Wagner: 'The "simply natural" is interesting no longer. The much-decried, mad, late-Turner rendering is now necessary to create my interest',[8] or 'Exactly the modern note of unease'; and indeed he heard in them the unsettling chants of old tunes as well as new ones. And, having established his fame, claimed his copyright, won his ability to determine how his works were published, I have the strong sense that Hardy is handing control of Wessex – elusive, yet portable; an unfinished, ongoing work – over to us, for our own continuing use.

With the vision of *Tess* and the idea of the architectural relationship of parts-to-whole in mind, 'Wessex Heights' seems one of Hardy's key poems. Strange, unpredictable, flawed, and somehow the stronger for it, it shifts from transcendent visions to rhythmic, low black comedy; from detail to overview. A rough path that leads to a place of vision:

> So I am found on Ingpen Beacon, or Wylls-Neck to the west,
> Or else on homely Bulbarrow, or Little Pilsdon Crest,
> Where men have never cared to haunt, nor women walked with me,
> And ghosts then keep their distance, and I know some liberty.

Though it is personal, it is also transcendent: shared, not quite your own. This is his own private vision (he never took Lea to Flintcomb-Ash) of the shared culture of how we humans (perhaps since creation myths began), both remember and imagine places. Those are the moments of vision we have found everywhere in his work; from detail to wide distance. Architecture inherently ties the overview to the detail (and vice versa). In moving us from folk rhythms, dialect, technical details, low comedy to transcendent overview. Hardy shows us an ongoing, working, visionary, inventive, uneven tradition of creative humanity of which we are all, more or less, a part.

I have no idea where a proper study of Hardy's work, poem by poem, collection by collection, as a whole and as a working part of Wessex would lead. To Gaston Bachelard's *The Poetics of Space*, perhaps; and to many other texts which attempt to study the relationships and broader cultures linking architecture with other creative human ways of working. To exploration of the uses of metaphors and spatial imagination; to discussing creation myths and the fundamental construct of another place in human imagination and belief. Somewhere dark, but with moments of illumination; somewhere old and new, between the inside of the mind and our understanding of the time and space in which we exist. Not somewhere comfortable, but surely revealing about how humans see, imagine, and make the world.

*

In 2013, the Dorset County Museum bought a small model theatre which a local builder Henry Tilley had made for the Hardy Players. They paid £2,000: two-and-a-half times what the sellers had hoped, but from an architectural point of view it was a bargain. For it is utterly clear that if Hardy did not actually draw and paint the sets himself (and my view is that he did), then he told Tilley exactly what to do.

Hardy was an enthusiastic, lifelong theatregoer; he even had a walk-on part in *Ali Baba and the Forty Thieves* at Covent Garden in 1866.[9] His annual trips to London always took in a range of productions, from Shakespeare to music hall and pantomime, George Bernard Shaw, Oscar Wilde and W.B. Yeats. He saw the London productions of J.M. Synge's *The Playboy of the Western World* in 1906. Both the new Irish drama and Shakespeare's fusion of visionary ideas and vernacular black humour was native to Hardy. And of course he relished (and ironically commented on) the role of translating his work from one medium into yet another.

In 1892, he was asked to contribute to a symposium in the Pall Mall Gazette. Accepting the question like a school essay, 'Why I Don't Write Plays' starts:

> Because in general the novel affords scope for getting nearer to the heart and meaning of things than does the play; in particular, nowadays ... when managers will not risk a truly original play ... when scenes have to be arranged in a constrained and arbitrary fashion to suit the exigencies of scene-building ... the presentation of human passions is subordinated to the presentation of mountains, cities, clothes, furniture, plate, jewels and other real or sham-real appurtenances, to the neglect of the principle that the material stage should be a conventional or figurative arena, in which accessories are kept down to the plane of mere suggestion ...[10]

Actually, Hardy had been (unsatisfactorily) involved in dramatisations of *Far from the Madding Crowd* in the 1880s.[11] And in 1889 he published a remarkable letter calling for 'a British Théâtre Libre'. This was a radical movement in Paris, begun in 1887, staging uncensored works (including Tolstoy, Strindberg and Toulouse-Lautrec), using provocative real props (meat carcasses, for instance) and 'ensemble' acting. Here is Hardy's remarkable design brief:

> The imagination should be appealed to rather than the bare eyesight. Could not something be done to weed away the intolerable masses of scenery and costume ...? The ordinary pit boarded over to make a stage ... the form of an old Roman amphitheatre, the scenery being simply a canvas hung in place of the present curtain, the actors ... disappearing behind it when they go off stage, a horizontal canvas for sky or ceiling; a few moveable articles of furniture or trees in boxes ... The costumes to be suggestive of the time and situation, and not exclusively suggestive of what they cost ...[12]

Hardy is, before the fact, re*designing* how theatre works. He is writing as a constructive design critic, *proposing* a design idea for others to do. He is considering theatre's native roots – mumming, the choir, the village band, the oral tradition, classical theatre – and reinterpreting them for his own time and ours. And once again, he is predicting the future: the world of physical theatre; of 1950s Paris, or our own Complicité theatre company. *Three Lives of Lucie Cabrol* feels very close to Hardy;[13] as do the puppet adaptations of *War Horse*. (Even the early London dramatisations of the 'overpacked' *Far from the Madding Crowd*,[14] won praise for the real expert sheep shearing and ensemble-singing:[15] very *Complicité*.)

'Why I Don't Write Plays', was a famous last word. J.M. Barrie immediately persuaded Hardy to adapt his short story 'The Three Strangers' for the London stage. Next was *Tess*: Hardy readily cut vast chunks and re-visioned the whole thing in a new medium: a kind of dialogue promenade – an almost mediaeval format. The three-act *Jude*, in its first version, also tells the story in three domestic dialogue ensembles: a scene when Sue leaves Phillotson; when Sue leaves Jude; when Sue returns, in guilt, to Phillotson, a structure not unlike the seminal 'Angry Young Man' drama of the 1950s, *Look Back in Anger*.

Within ten years, Hardy had completed the first part of his epic experimental play *The Dynasts*.[16] He wrote adaptations of most of his novels and some short stories; two major, highly experimental plays; and was intimately involved in an intriguing body of local amateur dramatics work. This was a whole new strand of creative work, building up from the moment of writing his 'disclaimer', and continuing, like the poems, until he was physically unable to do more.

Keith Wilson is another Hardy specialist bewildered as to why Hardy went to such lengths for an apparently ancillary occupation. Adaptations, staging, rehearsals, set designs, wrangles over rights, casting, accommodation and mollification of London critics – all for no profit (the money went to local charities), and an uncomfortable degree of personal publicity.[17] Wilson decides the Hardy Players embodied the 'generative and generous' basis of Hardy's sometimes difficult relationship with the people and places he had transformed into myth.[18]

While accepting the answer, there was never a question for any architect. Hardy had *created* Wessex, published it, drawn it, had it photographed, mapped it, claimed copyright of the whole working, elusive, influential construction. He would even name his aggressive dog after it (architect Tadao Ando called his dog Le Corbusier, perhaps for the pleasure of bossing him around). Now people were inviting him to extend it, in a native medium linking human performance, high art, visionary assembly and physical, detailed design, and ongoing, oral culture. Of course he would do it. This was a whole new body of work for Hardy to manage and create.

And we now see the curatorial, creative and modern side of his physical design imagination too. Visionary, abstracted, challenging, the ancient re-made in modern form – the design qualities some of us are surprised not to find in Max Gate. 'Why I Don't Write Plays' sets it out: a radically plain, abstracted backdrop; framing of vision and character; just enough design to enable 'the willing suspension of disbelief'. If the first London shows illustrated a predicable lack of authorial control, the local ones did not. Hardy's apparently dismissive statement, when he first saw the Dorchester Players, that their main interest was 're-enacting the lives of their own great-grandparents',[19] was surely another backhanded compliment. He would continue to insist, in public, on his own relative lack of influence, but a new stream of creative work had begun.

Hardy gives two local Aldermen, chemist Alfred Herbert Evans and Thomas Henry Tilley, a builder, mason and decorator, headline status. But that is his usual description of any collaborative work: look at Florence's billing in the *Life*. When interviewed, Evans and Tilley describe Hardy's absolute control over any and all decisions.[20] Even Harry Furniss's drawing of Hardy with Tilley in the National Portrait Gallery shows that Hardy is directing the whole thing; you can *see* it.

Hardy's adaptation of *The Trumpet Major* was received as a great success in Dorchester, and even, to some extent, in London. 'It was held in Dorchester that there was a play in it somewhere and Dorchester has proved to be right ... ' said *The Times* critic (judiciously hosted by Hardy even during the ongoing building works at Max Gate).[21]

A surprisingly cheerful series of annual events quickly became established. While endless debates about possible West End versions of *Tess* continued (actresses lined up to play this role), down in Dorchester the plays were simply enjoyed. Indeed, the annual performances (rather brilliantly), were performed in *London* each year for the Society of Dorset Men in London: regularly built up by London critics in advance, Wilson explains, and then critically demolished as they appeared.

*

The 'light entertainment' mood changed in 1915 with the death of Emma, and the arrival of Gertrude Bugler, a beautiful 16-year-old, talent-spotted by Tilley. Bugler was the daughter and doppelgänger of the milkmaid Hardy had recalled in envisioning Tess, and her presence in *The Woodlanders* focused both critics' interest and Hardy's own, beginning a new, more intense commitment to what was now called the Hardy Players.

Meanwhile, Hardy was writing *The Dynasts*; a truly radical theatrical experiment. Here are the stage directions:

The nether sky opens, and Europe is disclosed as a prone and emaciated figure, the Alps shaping like a backbone, and the branching mountain-chains like ribs, the peninsular plateau of Spain forming a head. Broad and lengthy lowlands stretch from the north of France across Russia like a grey-green garment hemmed by the Ural Mountains and the glistening Arctic Ocean.

The point of view then sinks downwards through space, and draws near to the surface of the perturbed countries, where the peoples, distressed by events which they did not cause, are seen writhing, crawling, heaving, and vibrating in their various cities and nationalities.[22]

In his introduction (1903), Hardy writes of his fascination as to how 'such plays of poesy and dream' could be rendered on stage.[23] This is 'not for performance but voice alone',[24] with stage directions *spoken* by a narrator: a whole spectacular vision of extraordinary aerial shots sweeping over Europe and zooming in to wildlife in the battlefield – constructed in words, with strictly minimal staging.

Hardy and Granville-Barker's
staging of The Dynasts.

'He wrote his huge work in accordance with conventions of an art that had not yet been invented: the art of cinema', says John Wain. '*The Dynasts* is neither a poem, nor a play, nor a story. It is a shooting-script.' Even then, it is a type only really feasible in the age of computer-generated imagery: Peter Jackson's films of *Lord of the Rings*, for example (though spectacular cinematic experiments like Max Reinhardt's *A Midsummer Night's Dream* [1935] explored parallel territory too).

Hardy collaborated with the actor-playwright-manager Harley Granville-Barker, known for his minimalist version of *The Winter's Tale* (1912), and the 1914 staging looks wonderful: very close to Hardy's vision. It also predicts the sparse, monumental Heaven scene in Powell and Pressburger's *A Matter of Life and Death* (1946) another astonishing wartime vision of earthly actors and immortal commentary, and right on Hardy's territory.

Unsurprisingly, the various performances of *The Dynasts* got mixed reviews. 'An old Polytechnic entertainment taken in hand by the Elizabethan Stage Society', says the *Morning Post*.[25] *The Stage Year Book* 1915 says that 'Wellington and Napoleon searching the dress circle for the disposition of enemy forces did not make an impressive spectacle ...'[26] But from our perspective all this sounds wonderful. Peculiar and mixed-mode then: contemporary, and even avant-garde, today. *Peter Pan* (1904) with its call to the audience 'do you believe in fairies?' would make modern audience participation famous, but yet again, Hardy was at least writing *The Dynasts* before Barrie's production took place. (With Lulworth Cove mooted as the original inspiration for Neverland, the collaborative links between Hardy and Barrie are another area worthy of further exploration.[27])

What Hardy did object to was one critic's analogies between *The Dynasts* and architecture. 'Analogies between the arts are apt to be misleading', he says, arguing that the critic had shot himself in the foot by deciding to:

> drag in the art of architecture. In mercy to his own argument he should have left architecture alone. Like those of a play for reading, its features are determined by no mechanical, material or methodic necessities ... that art, throughout its history, has capriciously subdued to its service, in sheer waywardness, the necessities of other arts ... Capitals, cornice, bosses and scores of other details ... borrow from the art of sculpture without scruple and without reason.[28]

Borrowing without scruple and without reason: another great account of architects' creative instincts, however furiously expressed.

Despite the mixed reviews, and surely through a grim prescience, *The Dynasts* ran through the First World War. There are odd parallels with Joan Littlewood's agitprop *Oh! What A Lovely War* of 1963. Littlewood worked with Cedric Price on the Fun Palace (one of architecture's most influential unbuilt projects), and she too promoted experimental, enabling provincial theatre. Melodrama, provincialism, ensemble acting and a healthy irreverence for the established order were rather the point, and Hardy steadfastly and rightly kept promoting them.

He made a new adaptation, 'Scenes from the Dynasts', in 1916 for the Hardy Players to stage in Weymouth and 'not only prepared the whole script but also provided Tilley with six sketches for possible stage settings'[29] all showing places close to Weymouth. 'Sketches' in this context, are not just drawings; they suggest his detailed and direct input.

The Dynasts was selected as the first post-war performance by the Oxford University Dramatic Society. Hardy wrote in new parts for his own best Dorchester actors, and clearly discussed the wonderful-sounding staging with Maurice

Colbourn: 'For outdoors we are having a very long backcloth, with land, sea and sky, the whole cloth being on rollers, so that by turning a handle, the scene can be a pure seascape, a landscene or a skyscene or either of these together'.[30]

The performance, at the New Theatre, opened the day Hardy was awarded his honorary D.Litt, with Barrie in attendance – a wonderful overturning of the end of *Jude*. Wilson says it confirmed Hardy's commitment to amateur and participative productions,[31] and marked a new sense of ownership of the plays and their productions.[32] And, I suggest, of the overall construction and design too.

Tilley was now leading the Hardy Players: he was 'far more congenial' than Evans.[33] As builder, painter, decorator and monumental mason (of gravestones) he would be used to working to architects' directions. He is credited with both the stage designs and the miniature theatre box used to test and agree them with Hardy who (naturally) said the plays were 'entirely the work of our respected alderman, Mr. Tilley':[34] his normal way of describing active collaboration. Tilley was certainly working to Hardy's orders. We know Hardy gave him 'sketches'. We also know the miniature theatre was made to discuss designs with Hardy and that Tilley refused to continue the work after Hardy's death.

And *look* at those stage set designs: there is Hardy's vision. The often-empty landscapes, used at the *front* of the stage, just as described in 'Why I Don't Write Plays', with characters grouped directly against it to suggest, rather than try to build, that distance, as in the lovely photograph group of *The Return of the Native*. The backdrops are often abstracted, perhaps scaled-up fragments of landscape paintings. There is the precise view of Kingston Maurward, with its 'Fane' or temple in front, which Beatty thinks Hardy worked on, given poll position. There is the wonderful range of many different types of trees, as separate flats, so that they could be re-grouped and ordered at will; and there is a lovely, empty seascape too. And there are many tiny, wonderful bits of furniture – milk churns, pails – of the sort Hardy drew himself for *Far from the Madding Crowd*. This is not a sideline; it is proper design direction work.

The sets for *The Woodlanders* and *Tess* designs look particularly good. There is a strange, huge Stonehenge (presumably for the front of the stage, and used with the lights down) and lovely, detailed, highly architectural (sometimes folding) ones of Wool Manor, including his own reproduced sketches of the d'Urberville women. These are fairly accomplished architectural watercolours, on which someone has spent a great deal of time. I cannot imagine anyone else would be allowed to make these. Tilley refused to make more after Hardy's death, and remember Hardy's description of the workings of the Chief Technicist: designing for others to make. Finally, he had found a way of working in three dimensions. And, of course, in the fourth dimension too.

Hardy and Tilley's model stage sets.

Hardy never let go of these theatricals. His last play, *The Famous Tragedy of the Queen of Cornwall* was another anticipatory experiment. 'The play's most striking characteristic was the centralising of actions on scene transitions, none of which involved actual changes of scenery.'[35] And, as we have seen, he immediately collaborated on the operatic adaptation too.

Amidst the general sense of mild local drama – the tangle of Bugler's intriguing but problematic celebrity status (and Florence's awkward attempts at intervening) – Hardy's involvement with the Players, and other performances, never stopped. His last outing was to a performance of *Tess* at Weymouth;[36] and as he grew older, performances were brought to him at Max Gate too.[37] Words, time, staging, performance; a native austerity and vision; a skill in enabling the practiced suspension of disbelief, design. With Gatrell's later work, *Thomas Hardy Writing Dress* in mind, I am wondering if the costume design for the Hardy Players should be considered too. A whole new process, which finally allowed him a way of working as a designer.

I am not sure that this was such a minor branch of interest for Hardy.[38] There was both local and national public interest, and Bugler, finally playing Tess to some acclaim, almost transferred to the West End. Perhaps most intimately of all, it was rehearsed, with Bugler playing Tess, at Woolbridge Manor – in front of those portraits, and with J.M. Barrie, Cockcroft and T.E. Lawrence in attendance. If Bugler was carried into that tomb, reality and fiction had indeed merged.

*

'When a man, not satisfied with the grounds of his own success, goes on and on, he becomes extraordinarily interesting to me ...' said Hardy, of Turner and Wagner. Exactly so. I suggest that in the later parts of his life, probably through the work on *Jude* and West Knighton, Hardy had rediscovered a heightened value in the actual making of things. Through the various work he did afterwards – in book designs, drawings and photography and the collaborative theatre designs, even the physical design of his later books and editions – he had regained a sense of not being just a 'literary architect' but being a *practising* one, in the various fields that his work now offered him. And that when he said 'if he had had his life again, he would live it as an architect in a small country town', he meant it (although probably as in 'if I had another lifetime now' rather than 'instead of the life I have had').

Perhaps, too, our typical insistence on creative work as a matter of individual, authored genius has stopped us from looking at many parts of Hardy's work as we should. Architecture is an essentially collaborative act, and architects themselves generally discuss and acknowledge the role of colleagues, employees, mentors, peers, contractors and clients (even if writers then simplify this to a matter of famous names). Creative work in architecture, at its best, is generally the result of a multiplication of talents; involving calling up, overseeing, and directing – and creatively assembling – the skills of others. Hardy describes this perfectly as being 'chief technicist' in A *Laodicean*, and that seems to be exactly what Hardy keeps doing.

For this remarkable late phase of Hardy's work is quite clearly part of his own, increasingly diverse shaping of his invention, in all kinds of media. He had finally found a way of working where he could manage his complete vision and he was clearly enjoying it. The 'small country town' was giving him back a wonderfully satisfying piece of design work to do.

22

A PARTIAL COMPLETION

The view of Wessex: Hardy's study.

So was Hardy a great architect? I have two answers: yes, absolutely; and it depends on what you mean. He was, I would say, a conceptual architect of extraordinary scope, and well in advance of his age. He developed one of the most famous, detailed and popular imaginary worlds of all time, using it deliberately to influence and shape the imaginations of readers well beyond the reach of architecture's peculiar publications. And he recognised it, developed it, used it, directly to help us reframe and recollect our relationship with a world we had largely left behind, helping us forward into a kinder relationship with the new one.

He was also a working architectural writer who, in fictional form, fully and directly engaged with the major architectural subjects of the day, taking issue against the prevailing view of the countryside, of the value of craftsmanship, of the nature of skilled intelligence, of the purposes of education, of the effects of work, of what buildings mean, how they are made and what they are for. He was thinking in the highest grounds of theory – and yet he carried his great polemic out to a vast, international audience – and all until now, more or less unrecognised.

He was also, directly and deliberately I would argue, the most influential writer on conservation there has ever been. He intentionally set out to inform public opinion of a great, vanishing and almost entirely underrated vernacular culture, and to set it firmly in social, human and imaginative terms. He used his great fictional realm, quite consciously, as a working part of the growth of the conservation movement – with an outreach which can only be guessed, and he certainly predicts the form and detail, high theory and everyday concerns of England's remarkable conservation culture.

If his work also anticipated the peculiar forms that radical architects a century later invented, it is because he used the same tools to do it: the complex cloud of skills of writing, drawing, publication, survey, comparison, technical knowledge, peculiar pictures and instinct that go to make up the projective imagination, and its working forms of 'enabling fictions' through which architects actually do their work, every day.

For architects it should be natural that his work is so predictive, that it deals with past and future: that is what architectural practice has been developed to do. And Hardy delivered his great imaginary-real project, in fictional form, to a vast and still active audience, with an outreach that most paper architects could only dream of. Right from the start, in 'How I Built Myself a House', Hardy was handing his specifically architecturally informed, constructed visions back to the public, to all of us.

Yet none of this remarkable, prescient architectural work has been recognised. He does not appear in Adrian Forty's *Words and Buildings*, a major book exploring architectural writing, books and language.[1] Indeed, Hardy's strengths are right in the middle of the gaps Forty describes in architecture's esoteric vocabulary: its only occasional interest in the vernacular and the human use of buildings; its general dismissal of descriptive writing (Hardy's and so many other novelists' great magic power). But the non-inclusion is striking when Forty regrets the omission of Proust's insights, or discusses Victor Hugo's phrase 'This Will Kill That' in *Notre Dame de Paris* (1832);[2] an idea 'which cannot, given the novel's great popularity – there were four different editions between 1833 and 1839 – be fairly calculated'.[3] Hardy, surely far more than Hugo, deserves at least such recognition in shaping our imaginative understanding of architectural thinking and its works.

There is a coda to this in Beatty's later edition of the Architectural Notebook. Victor Hugo himself visited Weymouth in 1899, and used many settings in and around Portland and Dorchester in his last novel.[4] Hardy was an admirer of Hugo, and wrote, for the centenary of his birth: 'His works are the cathedrals of literary architecture, his imagination adding greatness to the colossal and charm to the

Hardy's vision: *Wessex Poems* and his RIBA medal mounted on a mirror.

small.'[5] There can scarcely be clearer proof that Hardy thought novels were major players in the public idea of architecture; and that implicitly (as in placing Ruskin in the Preface to *Jude*), he was inviting comparison with his own work. And, indeed, challenging all of us as to whom the works of 'literary architecture' should be for.

The RIBA medal Hardy won for his essay is, incidentally, in the museum collection too, and is mounted on a little mirror lens, so one can read his name only in reflection. When he said the RIBA was 'an institution of which he never lost sight', he meant it. He must have kept it on his desk.

*

But did he design great buildings? Well, not really. I would say that he challenged the idea of everyday buildings being 'great'. Perversely, while he laid claim to the authorship of all Wessex – certainly not a modest claim – he also worked as part of the more or less nameless tide of craftsmen who have woven into the collective fabric of our world. He is roughly an anti-architect: an ambiguous title, coined and claimed by Cedric Price, the great 'poet king' of architecture, swimming against the tide of the architect's normal urge to build at almost all costs.

Hardy too was an unusual architectural thinker; exploring conscience and consciousness, vision and drains. He asserts the skilled but also essential human nature of both physical making and visionary imagination. In fiction, poetry, architectural criticism and built example, he is championing a human, irreverent, uneven tradition, over an idealised architectural one – even while he is claiming creative control of the whole concept through which we imagine it.

The conventions of literary research tend, like those of architecture, to insist on an individual creativity, when so much of our working process is more or less collaborative. Like many architects, Hardy seems both an absolute autocrat and a demanding but real collaborator; and increasingly, much of his work seems to be coming through those diffuse, unrecognised collaborations. These have not been sufficiently recognised as real creative work: collaborations with the people who Hardy credited almost too directly, like Florence with the *Life*. Hicks, Blomfield and his office, Crickmay, Emma, the various illustrators, publishers, Moule, Kegan Paul; Thomas Perkins, SPAB, his father and brother; Windle and New, Hermann Lea, J.M. Barrie, Granville-Barker, Henry Tilley, and many more. I believe further investigation might reveal more patches and fragments of creative work, perhaps of unexpected kinds. But my view is that Hardy had increasingly realised that his 'built' architectural work was a matter of a wider creative collaborative culture; and that it was made up of fragments – real fragments, collaboration, advice, influence, and new types of work, which he could, paradoxically, deliver through and because of his clearly authored, highly influential, imaginary project: Wessex.

*

This is partly a book about Thomas Hardy, and partly about how architects see things. As such, it is a self-fulfilling prophecy. Coming myself from a working culture of critical and speculative thought, a tradition where one constructs imaginary models of the world in architectural projects, I have naturally applied its methods to Hardy's work.

I have traced Hardy's life and work as I see it, as a working architectural writer. But I have been overwhelmed by evidence of familiar patterns – linking writing, building, drawing, vision, polemic, experiments in representation, drainage details and peculiar books – in the projective construction of a vast, complicated, imaginary, working, fully realised place. Having, almost unwillingly, allowed myself to imagine, on visiting Max Gate many years ago, that you could see Hardy as a conceptual architect, I have found Hardy ahead of me everywhere, in details, images, theory, fact, fiction and construction.

I am sure Hardy became aware of how profoundly his work was architectural, and that he kept re-engaging with it at all kinds of different levels. And that when he said that 'If he'd lived his life again, it would have been as an architect in a small country town', he meant it. It is only provocatively, if at all, a modest statement.

*

I am not suggesting this is a definitive reading of Wessex, which was, of its nature an evolving project, changing and shifting over time and with use, and already existing in a rich fabric of real and imagined, historic and polemic, written and drawn, built, photographed and imagined version; and there can be no definitive reading of Wessex, because as Hardy said, it can only really always exist in our own heads.

But I am arguing that architecture's native capacity for projective, practical, polemic, detailed and experimental thinking – what Robin Evans calls its 'enabling fictions';[6] the projected realities through which it works – provided both medium and method for Hardy's unique construction, maintenance and delivery of Wessex. His predictions of our own age's architectural ideas came because he was using our own projective skills to do it; albeit, a century ahead of the game.

As such, Wessex does not just give us a fully working model of the English countryside during the great change to urbanised life; it also shows how architects, as well as other, normal, creative human beings, imagine things. And how from that imagination, we are able to change, maintain, understand and see, what was, and might be, the real world.

NOTES

CHAPTER 1

1 Drabble, Margaret, 1979, 1984 edition, p. 139
2 Millgate, Michael, 1985, p. 371; Tomalin, Claire, 2006, p. 260
3 Millgate, Michael, 1985 p. 3
4 Fowles, John, 1984 p. 9
5 Fowles, John, 1984, p. 11
6 *Quis Noctat?* (What about night?) Installed after Hardy's death, but to his design
7 Oliver, Paul, et al., 1981
8 Millgate, Michael, 1985, p. 194
9 *A Laodicean*, 1881, p. 36
10 Beatty, Claudius, 1995, p. 31
11 Beatty, Claudius, 1966 (ed.), p. ix
12 *Later Years*, p. 262, quoted in Millgate, Michael, 1985, p. 102
13 Beatty, Claudius, 1991
14 Pugin, Augustus, 1836, p. 34
15 See Frogley, Alain, 1987 and Pettit, Charles, 2013 for a full discussion of this

CHAPTER 2

1 'The Ancient Cottages of England', 1927, pp. 13–16; Millgate, Michael, 1985, p. 192
2 *Life*, Wordsworth, 2007, (ed.), pp. 29–30
3 Pugin, Augustus, 1936, p. 34. See discussion of Dickens's *Martin Chuzzlewit* in Saint, Andrew, 1985, Chapter 3
4 *Life*, Wordsworth, 2007, (ed.), p. 28
5 Ibid.
6 *Life*, Wordsworth, 2007, (ed.), p. 33
7 Beatty, Claudius, 1991
8 Gittings, Robert, 2001, p. 89 and Millgate, Michael, p. 75. The other letter of introduction was to Benjamin Ferrey; it proved 'useless', but Ferrey appears again in this book
9 See Chapter 5
10 Pugin, Augustus, 1936, p. 34

11 Tomalin, Claire, 2006, p. 67
12 Saint, Andrew, 1985, Chapter 3
13 http://www.aaschool.ac.uk/AALIFE/LIBRARY/aahistory.php, last accessed 4 October 2017
14 Beatty, Claudius, 1966, 1995, p. 2
15 Saint, Andrew, 1985, Chapters 3, 5 and 7; MacEwen, Malcolm, 1974
16 Schad, John, 1997, p. xvii
17 Hunter, Michael, 1996, p. 2; Jokilehto, Jukka, 1999, p. 318
18 *Life*, Wordsworth, 2007, (ed.), p. 43
19 Hill, Jonathan, 2013, pp. 15–34
20 Beatty, Claudius, 1966, 2007, p. 23
21 *Life*, Wordsworth, 2007, (ed.), p. 38
22 Clark, Kenneth, 1964, p. 1
23 In the St Martin's Place office, before the move to the Adelphi
24 Ruskin, John, 1843–1860, 1894, pp. 354–355
25 *Life*, Wordsworth, 2007, (ed.), p. 39. He does not specify what is being read; many other passages would have been equally relevant
26 Beatty, Claudius, 1966, 2007, p. x
27 Beatty, Claudius, 1966, 2007, p. 28
28 van Schaik, Leon, 2005
29 Garbett, Edward, 1850, p. v
30 van Schaik, Leon, 2005; and Fraser, Murray and Hill, Jonathan, 2013
31 Quoting Joshua Reynolds's *Discourse* v1; Garbett, Edward, 1850, p. 120
32 Batchelor, John, 2001, p. xi
33 Powers, Alan, 2002, Chapter 12
34 Hill, Jonathan, 2013, p. 15
35 'How I Built Myself a House', 1861
36 'How I Built Myself a House', 1861, pp. 162–163
37 Ibid.
38 Forty, Adrian, 2000, p. 31
39 *Life*, Wordsworth, 2007, (ed.), Chapter 3, p. 48
40 Beatty, Claudius, 1995, p. 4

41 Beatty says he must have known the building well, though it is not mentioned in the *Life*. Beatty, 2007, pp. 20–21

42 Forty, Adrian, 2000, p. x

43 *Life*, Wordsworth, 2007, (ed.), p. 78

44 Ibid.

45 Beatty, Claudius, 1966, 2007, p. vii

46 Beatty, Claudius, 2007, p. 14

47 *Life*, Wordsworth, 2007, (ed.), p. 55

48 Ruskin, John, 1849, 1889, p. 189

49 See Stanford's map, 1862

50 Perhaps he was prompted by the bodies found on that site, as well as by another period of active architectural work

51 *Life*, Wordsworth, 2007, (ed.), p. 43

52 *Life*, Wordsworth, 2007, (ed.), p. 54

53 *Life*, Wordsworth, 2007, (ed.), p. 48

54 Ibid.

55 Millgate, Michael, 1982, pp. 76, 79–80

56 Beatty, Claudius, 1995, p. x

57 *Life*, Wordsworth, 2007, (ed.), p. 374

58 Beatty, Claudius, 1966, 2007, p. 32

59 *Life*, Wordsworth, 2007, (ed.), p. 62

60 Ibid.

61 'Memories of Church Restoration' and *Life*, 1906, p. 81

62 *Life*, Wordsworth, 2007, (ed.), Chapter 4

CHAPTER 3

1 Hands, T., in Page, N. (ed.), 2000, pp. 14–19

2 *Tess of the d'Urbervilles*, 1891, 1974, p. 449

3 Evans, Robin, 1986, 1997, p. 165

4 See Forty, Adrian, *Words and Buildings*, 2000

5 *Desperate Remedies*, 1871, 1890, p. 7

6 *Desperate Remedies*, 1871, 1890, p. 8

7 Gatrell, Simon, 2016, email to the author

8 For instance, Beach, Joseph Warren, *The Technique of Thomas Hardy*, 1922; Lodge, David, 'Thomas Hardy as a Cinematic Novelist', in *Thomas Hardy After Fifty Years*, ed. Lance St. John Butler, 1977; Grundy, Joan, 'Cinematic Arts', in her *Hardy and the Sister Arts*, 1979; Wright, T.R., *Thomas Hardy on Screen*, Cambridge University Press, 2006

9 See, for instance, the AD Architecture and Film series, Academy-Wiley; Vidler, Anthony, *Warped Space: Art, Architecture and Anxiety*, MIT Press, 2000 and many others

10 1862 International Great Exhibition, Wikipedia entry, https://en.wikipedia.org/wiki/1862_International_Exhibition, last accessed 4 October 2017

11 Herbert, Stephen, 27, http://www.stephenherbert.co.uk/wheelZOETROPEpart1.htm#fn27, last accessed 4 October 2017

12 *Life*, Wordsworth, 2007, (ed.), p. 43

13 *Desperate Remedies*, 1871, 1890, p. 13

14 *Desperate Remedies*, 1871, 1890, pp. 109–114

15 *Desperate Remedies*, 1871, 1890, p. 83

16 *Desperate Remedies*, 1871, 1990, p. 185

17 *Desperate Remedies*, 1871, 1890, p. 299

18 Beatty, Claudius, 1966, 2007, p. 25

19 *Desperate Remedies*, 1871, 1890, p. 72

20 The plan of the house used as a model for Eustacias's in *The Return of the Native* (held in the Dorset County Museum) looks like other presentation drawings done in hindsight for possible publication purposes

21 *Desperate Remedies*, 1871, 1890, p. 141

22 Millgate, Michael, 1994, p. 42

23 *Under The Greenwood Tree*, p. 7

24 Ruskin, John, 1894, p. 299

25 Yeazell, Ruth Bernard, 2009, p. 31

26 *Life*, Wordsworth, 2007, (ed.), pp. 47–49; it also related to Benjamin Ferrey. Hardy had friends working in his office; Millgate, Michael, 1985, p. 76

27 Camera lenses, drawing conventions and human eye all construct and frame pictures differently; direct overlays like this come from tracing or copying in some way

28 Ruskin, John, 1849, 1889, p. 44

29 *A Pair of Blue Eyes*, 1873, 1986, p. 272

30 Millgate, Michael, 1985, p. 446

31 Nussbaum, Emily, 2012

32 Derrida, Jacques, 1985

33 There's an interesting discussion of Hardy's proximity to Derrida in John Schad's introduction to *A Laodicean*, but without any mention that Derrida's work was so closely connected with a particular form of highly influential post-modern architectural practice

34 Quoted in Forty, Adrian, 2000, p. 31

CHAPTER 4

1 Plietzsch, Birgit, 2004, pp. 170–171

2 Alan Bennett, in *The History Boys*, has his teacher misunderstand this, describing Hardy's poem 'Drummer Hodge'

3 *Far from the Madding Crowd*, Macmillan, 1961, 1874, pp. 18–19

4 *Far from the Madding Crowd*, Macmillan, 1961, 1874, p. 163

5 Ruskin, John, 1849, p. 101

6 Ruskin, John, 1843, Chapter ii; Batchelor, John, 2001, p. 58

7   *Far from the Madding Crowd*, Macmillan, 1961, 1874, pp. 205–207

8   Tomalin, Claire, 2006, p. 131. Piers Dudgeon's book is a gripping argument describing Barrie's own use of imaginary places. Dudgeon, Piers, 2009

9   Beatty, Claudius, 1995, pp. 21–22

10 Evans, Robin, 1995, p. 370

11 Forty, Adrian, 2000, p. 20

12 *Far from the Madding Crowd*, Macmillan, 1961, 1874, p. 173

13 Allen, Isabel, 2006

14 Bragg, Melvin, et al., 2006

15 Plietzsch, Birgit, 2004, pp. 135, 204–205; Gatrell, Simon, 2003, p. 22

16 Gatrell, Simon, 2003, p. 22

17 Gatrell, Simon, 2003, p. 245

18 Dugdale, F. to Clodd, E.; Millgate, Michael, 1985, p. 168

19 *The Nation*, James, Henry, 24 December 1874

20 Plietzsch, Birgit, 2004, p. 199

CHAPTER 5

1   For example, Gattrell, Simon. 1986, finds this discussion into lesser novels 'unjustifiable', p. 70

2   Tomalin, Claire, 2006, p. 147

3   Dolin, Tim, 1997, *The Hand of Ethelberta*, 1876, 1997, p. xxix

4   *The Hand of Ethelberta*, 1876, 1997, p. 225

5   *The Hand of Ethelberta*, 1876, 1997, p. 125

6   *The Hand of Ethelberta*, 1876, 1997, p. 326

7   In *The True Principles of Pointed or Christian Architecture*, Pugin says: 'that there should be no features about a building which are not necessary for convenience, construction or propriety.' Forty, Adrian, 2000, pp. 297–298

8   *The Hand of Ethelberta*, 1876, 1997, pp. 296–297

9   Ruskin, John, 1849, p. 85

10 Ruskin, John, 1849, p. 34

11 Beatty, Claudius, 1966, 1980, pp. 185; http://list.english-heritage.org.uk/resultsingle.aspx?uid=1000719, last accessed 4 October 2017

12 *The Hand of Ethelberta*, 1876, 1997, p. 296

13 *The Hand of Ethelberta*, 1876, 1997, pp. 267–268

14 *The Trumpet Major*, 1880, 1997, pp. 155–157

15 Tomalin, Claire, 2006, pp. 184–187

16 *A Laodicean*, 1881, 1997, p. 18

17 *A Laodicean*, 1881, 1997, p. 29

18 *A Laodicean*, 1881, 1997, p. 35

19 *A Laodicean*, 1881, 1997, p. 60

20 Ruskin, John, 1849, p. 385

21 *A Laodicean*, 1881, 1997, pp. 101–102; Beatty, Claudius, 1995, p. 36

22 *A Laodicean*, 1881, 1997, p. 83; Beatty, Claudius, 1995, p. 37

23 *A Laodicean*, 1881, 1997, pp. 122–123

24 Schad, John, 1997

25 *A Laodicean*, 1881, 1997, p. 89

26 *A Laodicean*, 1881, 1997, p. 77

27 *A Laodicean*, 1881, 1997, p. 61

28 Schad, John, 1997

29 For instance, the Royal Melbourne Institute of Technology PhD by Practice. Until now, most research has concentrated on critical theories rather than accounts of actual practice such as this

30 Interestingly, these correspond to John Evelyn's four categories: the ingenious architect, the architect of words, the client and the supervising architect. Forty, Adrian, 2000, pp. 11–12

31 *A Laodicean*, 1881, 1997, pp. 122–123

32 *A Laodicean*, 1881, 1997, pp. 124–129

33 van Schaik, Leon, 2005, 2011

34 Beatty, 1966, p. 268; *A Laodicean*, 2007, p. 282

35 *A Laodicean*, 1881, 1997, p. 186

36 *A Laodicean*, 1881, 1997, Introduction

37 Beatty, Claudius, 1995, p. 7

38 *Two on a Tower*, 1882, 1999, p. 3

39 *Two on a Tower*, 1882, 1999, p. 5

40 *Two on a Tower*, 1882, 1999, p. 55

41 *Two on a Tower*, 1882, 1999, p. 226

42 Ibid.

CHAPTER 6

1   *The Return of the Native*, 1878, 1999, p. 9

2   *The Return of the Native*, 1878, 1999, pp. 10–11

3   *The Return of the Native*, 1878, 1999, p. 355

4   Purdy, 27, *Athenaeum*, 23 November 1878, p. 654; in Millgate, Michael, 1985, p. 198

5   Lodge, David, 1974, pp. 248–249

6   Millgate, Michael, 1985, p. 197

7   Ormond, Leonée, 2000, p. 376

8   *Letters* vi, p. 61

9   Or with the *Imperial Gazetteer of England and Wales*, 1870–1872

10 See Hill, Jonathan, 2013, for an analytical overview of this

11 Tomalin, Claire, 2006, p. 170

12 As mentioned, he drew a little plan, probably in hindsight, of the original of Eustacia's house. In the Dorset County Museum

13 In the Dorset County Museum

14 In his historical seafaring Aubrey–Maturin novels

CHAPTER 7

1 Beatty, Claudius, 1991, Introduction
2 *Life*, Wordsworth, 2007, (ed.), p. 48
3 Beatty, Claudius, 1991, Introduction
4 Kemp, Martin, 1991
5 I am indebted to Richard Difford for introducing me to Kemp's book
6 Beatty, Claudius, 1963, p. 379
7 As mentioned, Hardy remained friends with Perkins (a fellow conservation campaigner) and often cycled the seventeen miles to read the lesson, cycling back once with Emma from a harvest supper, by moonlight
8 http://www.dorset-churches.org.uk/turnworth.html, last accessed 4 October 2017
9 Beatty, Claudius, 1991
10 Smithson, Alison, 'Patio and Pavilion', 1956
11 Smithson, Alison, *AS in DS: An Eye on the Road*, 1983
12 Venturi, Robert, Scott Brown, Denise and Izenour, Stephen, 1972, 1977, p. 3
13 In *Sexuality and Space*, 1992 and *Privacy and Publicity*, 1994
14 Colomina, Beatriz, 1992, p. 100
15 Forty, Adrian, 2000, p. 31
16 De Smet, Catherine, 2005, p. 8
17 De Smet, Catherine, 2005, p. 67
18 De Smet, Catherine, 2005, pp. 86–87
19 Brewster, David, 1843
20 See for instance, Fraser, Murray, and Hill, Jonathan, 2013

CHAPTER 8

1 This varies in different cultures, but is widely used in leading international schools
2 Lanherne, The Avenue, Wimborne (now 16 Avenue Road); Millgate, Michael 1985, p. 22
3 Gatrell, Simon, 2003, Chapter 3
4 Author's Preface to *Far from the Madding Crowd*, 1912 edition. Orel, Harold, 1966, 1967, pp. 9–11
5 See for instance, Millgate, Michael, 1985, p. 217
6 Plietzsch, Birgit, 2004, p. 135
7 'The Dorsetshire Labourer', 1883; Orel, Harold, 1966, 1967, pp. 168–191
8 The rural labourer, about to be given the vote, was of fresh interest to the magazine-reading middle class
9 *The Woodlanders*, 1887, 1974, p. 154
10 'The Dorsetshire Labourer', 1883
11 'The Dorsetshire Labourer', 1883; Orel, Harold, 1966, 1967, pp. 172–173

12 *The Society of Dorset Men in London*, 1907; Orel, Harold, 1966, 1967
13 'Some Romano-British Relics Found at Max Gate, Dorchester'. The paper was presented in 1884 but published in 1885. Orel, Harold, 1966, 1967, pp. 191–195
14 *The Mayor of Casterbridge*, 1886, pp. 73–74
15 *Life*, 2007, p. 168; Taylor, Richard, 1979, p. xiv
16 Forty, Adrian, 2000, p. 203
17 Gatrell, Simon, 2003, p. 102
18 'Some Romano-British Relics Found at Max Gate, Dorchester', 1885. Orel, Harold, 1966, 1967, pp. 191–195
19 *Supercrit* #5, www.supercrits.com
20 June 1882. In Millgate, Michael, p. 234
21 Smithson, Alison, 'Patio and Pavilion', 1956
22 Sklair, Leslie, 2017
23 van Schaik, 2005
24 Millgate, Michael, 1985, p. 234
25 Millgate, Michael, 1985, p. 227
26 Millgate, Michael, 1985, p. 227, p. 234
27 *Two on a Tower*, 1882, 1999, p. 68
28 *Two on a Tower*, 1882, 1999, p. 77
29 http://www.catchersofthelight.com/catchers/post/2012/06/09/Comet-Detective-History-of-Astrophotography, last accessed 4 October 2017
30 Berger, John, 1972, 1977, p. 18
31 Millgate, Michael, 1985, p. 224

CHAPTER 9

1 Millgate, Michael, 1982, 1985, p. 248
2 Ibid.
3 Millgate, Michael, 1982, 1985, p. 240
4 Millgate, Michael, 1982, 1985, p. 242
5 *The Mayor of Casterbridge*, 1886, pp. 141–142
6 *The Mayor of Casterbridge*, 1886, pp. 7–8
7 'Some Romano-British Relics Found at Max Gate, Dorchester', 1885. Orel, Harold, 1966, 1967, pp. 191–195
8 *The Mayor of Casterbridge*, 1886, pp. 31–32
9 Draper, Jo, 2001, p. 49
10 *The Mayor of Casterbridge*, 1886, p. 32
11 Ibid.
12 Ruskin, John, 1851, vol. 1, p. 37
13 Ruskin, John, (1843–60) 1894, V ('The Two Boyhoods'); Batchelor, John, 2001, pp. 374–375
14 *The Mayor of Casterbridge*, 1886, p. 33
15 Ibid.
16 *The Mayor of Casterbridge*, 1886, p. 34
17 Stringer, Peter, 1960
18 Murphy, Keith, Iversson, Jonas and Lymer, Gustav, 2012

19 Reynolds, Joshua, quoted in Garbett, Edward, 1850, p. 49
20 *The Mayor of Casterbridge*, 1886, p. 6
21 Millgate, Michael, 1982, 1985, p. 248
22 'Some Romano-British Relics Found at Max Gate, Dorchester', 1885. Orel, Harold, 1966, 1967, pp. 191–195
23 Forty, Adrian, 2000, p. 20
24 MacEwen, Malcolm, 1974
25 *On the Occasion of the Presentation of the Freedom of Dorchester*, 1910. Reprinted in Orel, Harold, 1966, 1967
26 Ibid.

CHAPTER 10

1 SPAB website. Available at http://www.spab.org.uk/what-is-spab-/history-of-the-spab/, last accessed 4 October 2017
2 Hardy died on 11 January, 1928
3 Kegan Paul, Charles to Marks, N., 15 July 1881; Beatty, Claudius, 1995, p. 9
4 Hardy, T. to Vinall, C.G., 20 October 1881; Beatty, Claudius, 1995, p. 9
5 Miele, Christopher, 1996, in Hunter, Michael, 1996, p. 21
6 Beatty, Claudius, 1995, p. 9
7 Beatty, Claudius, 1995, p. 10
8 Kegan Paul, Charles, 1899, pp. 13–16, in Beatty, Claudius, 1995, p. 7
9 Saint, Andrew, 1996, p. 115
10 Hunter, Michael, 1996, p. 1
11 Forty, Adrian, 2000, p. 203
12 Ruskin, John, 1849, 1889, p. 184
13 Ruskin, John, 1849, 1889, p. 101
14 *The Mayor of Casterbridge*, 1886, p. 331
15 Plietzsch, Birgit, 2004, p. 86
16 Woodforde, John, 1969, p. 9
17 Surveyed for the Report on the Sanitary Conditions of the Labouring Population, 1842; Woodforde, John, 1969, p. 2
18 Pevsner, Nikolaus, 1968
19 In later editions. See discussion of The White Horse
20 http://www.dorsetlife.co.uk/2008/09/dorset-pub-stroll-4/, last accessed 4 October 2017
21 *The Mayor of Casterbridge*, 1886, p. 45
22 Ibid.
23 http://www.dorsetlife.co.uk/2008/09/dorset-pub-stroll-4/, last accessed 4 October 2017
24 *The Mayor of Casterbridge*, 1886, p. 283
25 Stringer, Peter, 1980, pp. 176–186
26 *On the Occasion of the Presentation of the Freedom of Dorchester*, 1910; Beatty, 1966, p. 38
27 Beatty, Claudius, 1995, pp. 10–19
28 He was visiting to develop ideas for *Tess*
29 Beatty, Claudius, 1995, p. 15 (citing Millgate)
30 Beatty, Claudius, 1995, p. 20
31 Beatty, Claudius, 1995, p. 23
32 E.g. SAVE's alternative developments for Mansion House or the Royal Opera House
33 Draper, Jo, 2011; SPAB 1898; Beatty, Claudius, 1995, p. 25
34 Beatty, Claudius, 1995, p. 31
35 Beatty, Claudius, 1995, pp. 25–26
36 Wheeler, Michael, 1995, p. 125
37 Beatty, Claudius, 1995, p. 45
38 *A Laodicean*, 1881, p. 57
39 Hunter, Michael, 1996, p. 7

CHAPTER 11

1 Millgate, Michael, 1985, p. 257
2 Beatty, Claudius, 1966, 2007, p. ix
3 Ibid.
4 *The Mayor of Casterbridge*, 1886, p. 84
5 According to Andrew Leah, another former resident
6 Rattenbury, Kester, *Invention or Discovery? Building Design*, 2006 http://www.bdonline.co.uk/invention-or-discovery?/3070337.article, last accessed 4 October 2017
7 Fellow-Townsmen, in *Wessex Tales*, p. 126, dated 1880
8 In a letter to Clodd, 1892. Millgate, Michael, p. 323
9 https://www.academia.edu/28005390/_A_Merely_Realistic_Dream-Country_The_Gothic_Revival_in_Hampshire_and_Wiltshire, last accessed 4 October 2017
10 Piper, John, 1945
11 https://www.nationaltrust.org.uk/red-house/features/red-house-and-william-morris, last accessed 4 October 2017
12 Millgate, Michael, 1982, 1985, p. 263
13 Millgate, Michael, 1982, 1985, p. 260
14 Sklair, Leslie, 2017
15 Piper, John, 1945
16 https://www.nationaltrust.org.uk/red-house/features/red-house-and-william-morris, last accessed 4 October 2017

CHAPTER 12

1 *The Woodlanders*, 1887, 1974, p. 122
2 *The Woodlanders*, 1887, 1974, pp. 16–18
3 *The Woodlanders*, 1887, 1974, p. 122
4 *The Woodlanders*, 1887, 1974, pp. 16–18
5 *The Woodlanders*, 1887, 1974, p. 83
6 Forster, E.M., 1939, pp. 679–680

7   *The Woodlanders*, 1887, 1974, p. 174
8   *The Woodlanders*, 1887, 1974, p. 83
9   *The Woodlanders*, 1887, 1974, p. 78
10 *The Woodlanders*, 1887, 1974, pp. 234–235
11 Garbett, Edward, 1850, p. 81
12 *The Woodlanders*, 1887, 1974, p. 226
13 *The Woodlanders*, 1887, 1974, Chapter 5
14 Also known as Villard de Honnecourt, which is the listing under which the Bibliothèque Nationale holds the original. de Honnecourt, Villard, *Album de Dessins et Croquis*, 13th century, http://visualiseur. bnf.fr/ark:/12148/btv1b10509412z/f8.image. r=villarddehonnecourt, last accessed 4 October 2017. Beatty says Hardy 'almost certainly' studied the English translation, published 1859. Beatty, Claudius, 1960, 2004, p. 330; 1995, p. 59
15 Beatty, Claudius, 1960, 2004, pp. 329–332
16 *The Woodlanders*, 1887, 1974, p. 39
17 *The Woodlanders*, 1887, 1974, pp. 54–55
18 *The Woodlanders*, 1887, 1974, p. 88
19 Pinion, F.B., 1968, p. 395
20 Turnworth House: *England's Lost Country Houses*, http://www.lostheritage.org.uk/houses/ lh_dorset_turnworthhouse_info_gallery.html, last accessed 4 October 2017
21 *The Woodlanders*, 1887, 1974, p. 215
22 *The Woodlanders*, 1887, 1974, p. 94
23 *The Woodlanders*, 1887, 1974, p. 253
24 *The Woodlanders*, 'Preface', 1912. Reprinted in Orel, Harold, 1966, 1967, pp. 19–21

CHAPTER 13

1   As early as 1886, *Vanity Fair* 'came closest to understanding the new links that Hardy was making in public between elements of his creative world'. *Vanity Fair*, 4 September 1886; Gatrell, Simon, 2003, p. 52
2   Hardy, T. to Marston, E., 1888, in Purdy and Millgate collected letters
3   Dickens, Charles, 1842–1844; Saint, Andrew, Chapter 3
4   These examples are principally about the circulation around a building; better explained by diagram (as Koolhaas does) than photographs
5   Sklair, Leslie, 2017, pp. 111, 122–125
6   Reprinted in Orel, Harold (ed.), 1966, 1967, pp. 110–125
7   Keith, W.J., 1969, p. 80
8   Stoneman, Patsy, 2002, p. 216
9   Dudgeon, Piers, 2009
10 Ashby-Rudd, Philip and Trehane, Emma, http://www.victorianweb.org/authors/ barrie/2.html, last accessed 4 October 2017
11 The first two full-length tourist guidebooks came in 1894: Annie Macdonnell; *Thomas Hardy* (which included her own map) and Lionel Johnson, *The Art of Thomas Hardy*. They were followed by Bertram Windle and Edmund New (with their own, stylish fully authorised map), *The Wessex of Thomas Hardy*, 1902; Wilkinson Sherren, *The Wessex of Romance*, 1902; Charles G. Harper, *The Hardy Country*, 1904; Hermann Lea, *The Wessex Country of Thomas Hardy's Novels and Poems*, 1905; Sir Frederick Treves, *Highways and Byways of Wessex*, 1906; Clive Holland, *Wessex*, 1906 (maps by Walter Tyndale); F. Outwin Saxelby, *A Thomas Hardy Dictionary*, 1911; Hermann Lea *Thomas Hardy's Wessex*, 1912
12 Keith, W.J., 1969, p. 88
13 Keith, W.J., 1969, p. 80
14 Plietzsch also follows this line, although she notes 'some similarity' with the *Bookman*. Plietzsch, Birgit, 2004, p. 223
15 The *Bookman*, 1891. It is fair to point out that Millgate, perhaps the most scrupulous and reliable authority on Hardy, says that Hardy declined to produce a map, but 'supplied the information on which a map could be based'. Millgate, Michael, 1985, p. 317. My own belief that Hardy himself drew the original map is drawn from the consistent graphic quality of this with other maps, including the sketch map of *Tess*: and the 'information' was the map
16 Gatrell, Simon, 2003, p. 94; 14 August 1891. Dorset County Museum (H4750)
17 Plietzsch, Birgit, 2004, p. 234
18 Other intriguing stylised maps may be seen on the Thomas Hardy Association website, http://www.thethomashardyassociation.org/ images/maps/wessexmaps.htm, last accessed 4 October 2017
19 Rattenbury and Hardingham, 2008
20 Windle, Bertram, *The Wessex of Thomas Hardy*, illustrated by Edmund New, John Lane, The Bodley Head, London and New York, 1902
21 Dorset County Museum (H5921)
22 *Letters* ii, p. 131, in Gatrell, Simon, 2003, p. 96
23 Millgate, Michael, 1985, pp. 421–422. The paintings were later published as Tyndale, Walter, A&C Black, London, n.d., https://archive.org/stream/ hardycountrywate00tynduoft#page/n49/ mode/2up, last accessed 4 October 2017
24 Fowles, John, 1984, p. 23
25 Gatrell, Simon, 2003, p. xvi

26 Gatrell, Simon, 2003, p. 173
27 Powers, Alan, 2002, is an interesting study of the peculiarities of architectural publications
28 Gatrell, Simon, 2003, p. 173
29 Gatrell, Simon, 2003, pp. 71–72
30 The Fondation Le Corbusier, too, maintains strict copyright controls over images of even *built* buildings, let alone the drawings, photographs, films and books from which Le Corbusier built his seminal work

CHAPTER 14

1   *Later Years*, pp. 143–146; Beatty, Claudius, 1966, 2007, p. 38
2   Andrew Leah validates this
3   Andrew and Marilyn Leah are former residents of Max Gate and Leah is a Vice President of the Thomas Hardy Society
4   Gatrell, Simon, 2003, p. 188
5   https://www.facebook.com/BBCBerkshire/videos/10154934976252936/, last accessed 4 October 2017
6   Hawkins, Desmond, 1983, Macmillan, p. 17
7   Beatty, Claudius, 1966, p. 31
8   Larkin, Steve, '*Interiorities in Oral Cultural Landscape*', unpublished PhD by Practice, RMIT, 2017
9   Beatty, Claudius, 1966, p. 31
10 In a letter to the DCM, Beatty believed the farm unbuilt or demolished, should be credited to Hardy's brother Henry, because of its poor drawing quality. I am less sure; those drawings are unfinished and would have been roughs for tracing over; Hardy's drawing quality *was* variable
11 Beatty, Claudius, 1966, p. 41
12 *The Ancient Cottages of England*, 1927. Orel, Harold, 1966, 1967, pp. 13–16
13 Hardy, T., 1927, pp. 13–16
14 South West Sustainable Land Use Initiative, 2004. http://www.self-willed-land.org.uk/articles/DorsetHeath2.pdf, last accessed 4 October 2017
15 Passing beyond Bhompston, a model for Blooms-End, photographed by Lea
16 Beatty, Claudius, 1960, 2004, p. x
17 *The Builder*, 26 May 1894, p. 411; Beatty, Claudius, pp. 41–43, *Notebook*
18 Beatty, Claudius, 1966, p. 32
19 'Memories of Church Restoration'. In Beatty, Claudius, 1995, p. 76. Beatty seems to think these are effectively 'forgeries', which is clearly not the case; 1966, 2007
20 It is written in his copy of the history book (Hutchins) which is in the Dorset County Museum
21 Beatty, Claudius, 1995, p. 76
22 'Memories of Church Restoration', Beatty, 1995, p. 77
23 *Jude the Obscure*, 1896, 1974, p. 104

CHAPTER 15

1   Millgate, Michael, 1985, p. 35
2   Email from Andrew Leah to the author, 22 May 2017
3   Plietzsch, Birgit, 2004, pp. 178–180
4   Part Six, *The Captive*, translated by C.K. Scott Moncrieff, 1929, p. 514
5   Beatty, Claudius, 1963, 2004 p. 394
6   'Dorset in London', 1908–1909; Orel, Harold, 1966, 1967, p. 220
7   Rattenbury, Kester, 2016, pp. 73–79
8   Robin Evans and the PhD by Practice model developed by RMIT are notable exceptions
9   Even 'realistic' or conventional projects, which we often think 'normal', do the same, projecting detailed worked-out pictures of something that does not exist. The extreme, fantasy form sometimes used to teach students, I would argue, is partly to teach architects the skills they will need on site: the ability to keep the whole shifting idea of the building in mind; to deal with the inevitable problems; and to improvise solutions in practice – just as Hardy described
10 Beatty, Claudius, 1963, 2004, p. x
11 The popularity of the PhD by Practice amongst working architects who have no need for academic qualifications is a measure of how highly this is valued as a means of improving your work
12 *Tess of the d'Urbervilles*, 1891, 1974
13 Eagleton, Terry in *Jude the Obscure*, 1896, 1974, pp. 9–10

CHAPTER 16

1   Gatrell, Simon, 2003, p. 61
2   Pettit, Charles, 2013, p. 14
3   *Tess of the d'Urbervilles*, 1891, 1974, p. 40
4   *Tess of the d'Urbervilles*, 1891, 1974, p. 65
5   Hardy says the separation of the worker from home also acts *against* the means of the society's advancement: education for all. The children of nomadic fieldworkers, who changed schools regularly, were found to

be years behind their contemporaries. 'The Dorsetshire Labourer', 1883, p. 182

6 *Tess of the d'Urbervilles*, 1891, 1974, pp. 66–67

7 *Tess of the d'Urbervilles*, 1891, 1974, p. 142

8 The serial was rejected by Mowbray Morris for *Macmillan's Magazine*: 'too much succulence' Wellesley, Mary, 2015

9 *Tess of the d'Urbervilles*, 1891, 1974, p. 189

10 *Tess of the d'Urbervilles*, 1891, 1974, p. 412

11 Ibid.

12 *Tess of the d'Urbervilles*, 1891, 1974, pp. 156–157

13 *Tess of the d'Urbervilles*, 1891, 1974, p. 331

14 Hardy quotes this bit of Lear for us in his 1892 preface to the second edition: 'As flies to wanton boys are we to the Gods/ They kill us for their sport'

15 As written to Bertram Windle; see Chapter 13

16 Viner, Linda, 2002, p. 26

17 Draper, Jo, 2013. http://www.dorsetlife. co.uk/2013/10/the-lost-buildings-of-lyscombe/, last accessed 4 October 2017

18 Viner, Linda, 2002, pp. 7–14

19 Lea, Hermann, 1913, 1977, p. 4, p. 26

20 Lea, Hermann, 1913, 1977, p. 26

21 Burton-Page, Tony, 'More to it than a brown loaf', *Dorset Life*, August, 2000, http://www. dorsetlife.co.uk/2009/08/more-to-it-than-a-brown-loaf/, last accessed 4 October 2017

22 In *Far from the Madding Crowd*, 1874, 1961, p. 374

23 Viner, Linda, 2002, p. 10. However, there is a map of vanished villages in Lea's book

24 *Tess of the d'Urbervilles*, 1891, 1974, p. 444

25 *Tess of the d'Urbervilles*, 1891, 1974, pp. 227–228

26 *Tess of the d'Urbervilles*, 1891, 1974, p. 426

27 Ibid.

28 *Tess of the d'Urbervilles*, 1891, 1974, p. 163

29 Descriptions of *modern* environments in English nineteenth-century novels are often overlooked. Architectural theorists prefer European or Russian accounts of alienated modernity, and ignore those by Wilkie Collins in *The Woman in White* or Dickens's less famous works: *Dombey and Son*; the hallucinatory *Mugby Junction*; many parts of *The Un-Commercial Traveller*

30 Bird Wright, Sarah, 2002, p. 238

31 *Tess of the d'Urbervilles*, 1891, 1974, pp. 20–21

CHAPTER 17

1 *Jude the Obscure*, 1896, 1974, p. 1

2 Gittings, Robert, 2001, p. 439

3 For example, 'when read selectively, Ruskin's work will yield almost any political position'; Batchelor, John, 2001, p. x

4 Ruskin, John, 1870, p. 5

5 Beatty, Claudius, 1995, p. 4

6 Bird Wright, Sarah, 2002, p. 238

7 *Jude the Obscure*, 1896, 1974, pp. 30–31

8 Lea, Hermann, 1913, 1977, p. 61

9 Ruskin, John (1843–60), 1894, *Modern Painters*, Vol V, p. 191, opening of 'The Two Boyhoods', Works Vii, pp. 374–375

10 Beatty, Claudius, 2004, p. 381

11 *Jude the Obscure*, 1896, 1974, p. 41

12 *Life*, 2007, p. 185

13 *Jude the Obscure*, 1896, 1974, p. 42

14 This is from John Donne's Sermon XIV

15 *Jude the Obscure*, 1896, 1974, p. 45

16 *Jude the Obscure*, 1896, 1974, pp. 98–99

17 *Jude the Obscure*, 1896, 1974, p. 103

18 Batchelor, John, 2001 p. xi

19 *Jude the Obscure*, 1896, 1974, p. 103

20 Ruskin, John, 1849, 1889, pp. 309–311

21 'Researching Design, Designing Research', ADAPT-r conference, Aarhus, 2015

22 *Jude the Obscure*, 1896, 1974, p. 104

23 Ruskin was giving lectures to students in Cambridge around the time Hardy was working in Oxford and wondering about his career

24 *Jude the Obscure*, 1896, 1974, p. 108

25 Batchelor, John, 2001, p. 80

26 *Jude the Obscure*, 1896, 1974, p. 156

27 McWilliam, Neil, 1978, p. 25

28 Ibid.

29 Beatty, Claudius, 2007, pp. 20–21

30 McWilliam, Neil, 1978, p. 26

31 Millgate, Michael, 1985, p. 346, http://thomas hardysfiction.blogspot.co.uk/2011_10_01_ archive.html, last accessed 4 October 2017

32 He stayed with the family in August 1895; he had one of his later crushes on Pitt Rivers' daughter, Agnes Grove. Pitt River's own remarkable collection within the Oxford Museum would have helped keep this in mind

33 Pets in the Max Gate pet cemetery include Kiddlewinkcompoops, Moss and the 'Famous Dog Wessex'

34 Wilde, Oscar, 1909, in Wilde, Oscar, *Miscellanies*, Methuen, London, 1908, p. 29

35 Hardy describes this specifically, although it is scarcely mentioned in the book. Beatty, Claudius, p. 1963, 2004, p. 381

36 Beatty links this phase of work with Theale; a striking church by Edward Garbett; probably the father of Hardy's favourite architectural author

37 *Jude the Obscure*, 1896, 1974, p. 319
38 Ruskin, John, 1867, in Batchelor, John, 2001, p. 220
39 *Jude the Obscure*, 1896, 1974, pp. 153–154
40 Batchelor, John, 2001, p. 79
41 See, for example, Marshall Berman's *All That is Solid Melts into Air*, 1982
42 *Jude the Obscure*, 1896, 1974, p. 348

CHAPTER 18

1 Millgate, Michael, 1985, p. 310
2 Graves, Robert, 1957
3 Dalziel, Pamela, 1997, p. 390
4 Letter to F. Henniker, 22 September 1898, in Dalziel, Pamela, 1997, pp. 390–400
5 Dalziel, Pamela, 1997, p. 391
6 *Letters* ii, p. 212; Dalziel, Pamela, 1997, p. 391
7 Ibid.
8 *Letters* ii, p. 214, pp. 153–154; Dalziel, Pamela, 1997, p. 392
9 Dalziel, Pamela, 1997, p. 390
10 Ruskin, John, 1849, 1889, p. 189
11 Wilson, Keith, 'Hardy and the Ethics of Looking', *The Hardy Society Journal*, vol. 7, no. 1, Spring 2011, pp. 38–48
12 Tschumi, Bernard, *The Manhattan Transcripts*, 1976–1981, www.tschumi.com/projects/18/, last accessed 4 October 2017
13 van den Berghe, Jo, PhD, RMIT 2012; Eeckhout, Riet, PhD RMIT, 2015 etc
14 Shires, Linda, 2015, p. 199
15 Shires, Linda, 2015, p. 210
16 Tomalin, Clare, 2007, p. 281
17 Dalziel, Pamela, 1997, p. 392
18 de Smet, Catherine, 2005, p. 67
19 Dalziel, Pamela, 1997, p. 392
20 Ibid.
21 Millgate, Michael, 1985, p. 310
22 Gatrell, Simon, 2003, pp. 71–72
23 Preface to *Tess of the d'Urbervilles*, in Orel, Harold, 1966, 1967, p. 9
24 Preface to *The Trumpet Major*, 1912
25 Preface, *Far from the Madding Crowd*, 1874, in Orel, Harold, 1966, 1967, p. 45
26 Fowles, John, 1984, p. 23
27 Plietzsch, Birgit, 2004, p. 248
28 Gatrell, Simon, in Page, Norman, 2000, p. 244
29 Millgate, Michael, 1985, pp. 422–3
30 It is thought Hardy was emulating the New York Editions of Henry James's novels, but Hardy had always directed his illustrators, and he was certainly no stranger to photography

31 These are full-length films: *London*, 1994; *Robinson in Space*, 1997
32 The drawings may be found on the Archigram Archival Project website: http://archigram. westminster.ac.uk/project.php?id=236, last accessed 4 October 2017, and a video of Webb discussing the project at http:// unit01greenwich.wordpress.com/2013/10/09/ mike-webbs-temple-island/, last accessed 4 October 2017
33 Email, Michael Webb to Kester Rattenbury, Tuesday, 2 September 2014; I assume this is a joke (it was written late at night), but even so, it shows how architects think

CHAPTER 19

1 Millgate, Michael, 1984, p. 323
2 The same bias afflicts Hardy editors who have voted (not unanimously) to use the first volume form for the new Complete Editions, despite Hardy's own continued re-workings)
3 Tomalin, Claire, 2006, p. 308
4 FitzHerbert, Claudia, 2011
5 Dudgeon, Piers, 2009
6 Forster, E.M., 1908, Chapter XVIII
7 Sassoon, Siegfried, 1921, (ed.) Hart-Davis, Rupert, 1981 p. 43
8 Bachelard, Gaston, 1958, p. 3
9 Siza, Alvaro, *Complete Works*, Phaidon, 2006

CHAPTER 20

1 Rattenbury, Kester, 2002, Chapter 11
2 Beatty, Claudius, 1995, p. 31
3 'Memories of Church Restoration'; Beatty, Claudius, 1995, p. 76
4 Beatty, Claudius, 1995, p. 27
5 Beatty, Claudius, 1995, pp. 28–29
6 Beatty, Claudius, 1995, p. 30
7 Hardy, T. to Boulter, S., 1903. Quoted in full in Beatty, Claudius, 1995, p. 31
8 Beatty, Claudius, 1995, p. 31
9 Perkins, T. to Turner, T., 1903. Quoted in full, Beatty, Claudius, 1995, p. 29
10 Beatty, Claudius, 1995, p. 73
11 Beatty, Claudius, 1995, p. 33
12 Beatty, Claudius, 1995, p. 36
13 Ibid.
14 Beatty, Claudius, 1995, pp. 42–49
15 Beatty, Claudius, 1995, p. 44
16 Hardy, T. to Turner, T., 7 February 1910; Beatty, Claudius, 1995, p. 44
17 Quoted in full, Beatty, Claudius, 1995, p. 45

18 Beatty, Claudius, 1995, p. 45
19 'Audi Alterum Partem', *Dorset County Chronicle*, 24 March 1910. Quoted in full, Beatty, Claudius, 1995, p. 46
20 Beatty, Claudius, 1995, pp. 52–57
21 Gatrell, Simon, 2003, p. 178
22 'Shall Stonehenge Go?' An Interview reported in the *Daily Chronicle*, August 24, 1899, p. 3. Orel, Harold, 1966, 1967, pp. 196–201
23 Beatty, Claudius, 1995, pp. 25–28
24 AR Powys; Beatty, Claudius, 1995, p. 60
25 Rattenbury, Kester, 2002, pp. 147–148
26 Stamp, Gavin, in Hunter, Michael, 1996, pp. 77–78
27 Saint, Andrew, in Hunter, Michael, 1996, p. 125
28 Stamp, Gavin, in Hunter, Michael, 1996, p. 97
29 Rattenbury, Kester, 2002, pp. 141–149
30 Rattenbury, Kester, 2002, pp. 136–155
31 Rattenbury, Kester, 2002, pp. 139–140
32 Jokilehto, Jukka, 1999
33 Beatty, Claudius, 1995, p. 72
34 Beatty, Claudius, 1995, p. 73
35 Ibid.
36 Forty, Adrian, 2000, p. 212
37 Jokilehto, Jukka, 1999, p. 216
38 Perhaps there is even a connection with some of the complex ideas of Cesare Brandi (1906–1988); Jokilehto, Jukka, 1999, pp. 228–237
39 Jokilehto, Jukka, 1999, p. 216
40 Denslagen, Wim, 2009, p. 209
41 Hunter, Michael, 1996, p. 2
42 Forty, Adrian, 2000, p. 218

CHAPTER 21

1 Beatty, Claudius, 1991
2 Simon Gatrell, email to the author
3 'The Dynasts, A Rejoinder', in Orel, Harold, 1966, 1967, pp. 142–143
4 *Life*, Wordsworth, 2007, (ed.), p. 310
5 Pettit, Charles, 2013, pp. 4–6
6 Ibid.
7 Charles Pettit's paper discusses this in detail
8 *Life*, Wordsworth, 2007, (ed.), p. 185
9 Wilson, Keith, 1995, p. 1, p. 20
10 'Why I Don't Write Plays', 1892, *Pall Mall Gazette*, 31 August. In Orel, Harold, 1966, 1967, p. 139
11 Wilson, Keith, 1995, Chapter 2, p. 17

12 'A British "Théâtre Libre"', *Weekly Comedy*, 30 November 1889, p. 7. In Wilson, Keith, 1995, p. 16
13 The play is based on John Berger's *Pig Earth*, describing the bitterness and hope of peasant life in France at the early twentieth century. Berger's *Ways of Seeing*, a television series and book of 1972 constructing visual arguments, is yet another key architectural text covering ideas discussed throughout this book
14 Wilson, Keith, 1995, p. 62
15 Wilson, Keith, 1995, pp. 68–69
16 Wilson, Keith, 1995, p. 9
17 Wilson, Keith, 1995, p. 3
18 Wilson, Keith, 1995, p. 158
19 Millgate, Michael, 1985, p. 456 and p. 510
20 Wilson, Keith, 1995, p. 71
21 *The Times*, 19 November 1908
22 *The Dynasts*, 1904
23 Wilson, Keith, 1995, p. 126
24 Wain, John, 1965, Introduction
25 *Morning Post*, 26 November 1914
26 *Morning Post*, 26 November 1914
27 Ashby-Rudd, Philip and Trehane, Emma, http://www.victorianweb.org/authors/barrie/2.html, last accessed 4 October 2017
28 'The Dynasts, A Rejoinder', *The Times Lit. Sup.*, 5 February 1904, pp. 36–37; Orel, Harold, 1966, 1967, pp. 142–143
29 Wilson, Keith, 1995, p. 99
30 Maurice Colbourn to Thomas Hardy, 8 December 1919, DCM. Wilson, Keith, 1995
31 Wilson, Keith, 1995, pp. 97–98
32 Wilson, Keith, 1995, p. 103
33 Ibid.
34 Wilson, Keith, 1995, p. 107
35 Wilson, Keith, 1995, p. 124
36 Plietzsch, Birgit, 2004, p. 236
37 Wilson, Keith, 1995, p. 110
38 Wilson, Keith, 1995, p. 107

CHAPTER 22

1 Forty, Adrian, 2000
2 Victor Hugo's *Notre Dame de Paris* was first published in 1831; 'Ceci Tuera Cela' was an extra chapter added in the second edition. Forty, Adrian, 2000, p. 74
3 Ibid.
4 The Portland stone runs under the channel to Caen
5 Beatty, Claudius, *Notebook*, 1966, p. 51
6 Evans, Robin, 1986, 1997, p. 154

SELECTIVE BIBLIOGRAPHY

WRITINGS BY HARDY

'How I Built Myself a House', *Chambers Journal*, 18 March 1861. Also in Orel, Harold (ed.), (1966) 1967, pp. 159–167

Desperate Remedies: A Novel (New Wessex Edition), Macmillan, London, (1871) 1980, 1986

Under the Greenwood Tree: A Rural Painting of the Dutch School, Penguin, London, (1872) 1998

A Pair of Blue Eyes, Penguin, London, (1873) 1986

Far from the Madding Crowd, Macmillan, London, (1874) 1961

The Hand of Ethelberta: A Comedy in Chapters, Penguin, London, (1876) 1997

The Return of the Native, Penguin, London, (1878) 1999

The Trumpet Major, Penguin, London, (1880) 2006

A Laodicean: Or, The Castle of the de Stancys, Penguin, Harmondsworth, (1881) 1997

Two on a Tower: A Romance, Penguin, London, (1882) 1999

'The Dorsetshire Labourer', in *Longmans Magazine*, July 1883, pp. 252–269. Also in Orel, Harold (ed.), (1966) 1967, pp. 168–191

'Some Romano-British Relics Found at Max Gate, Dorchester.' A speech read at the Dorchester meeting of the Dorset Natural History and Antiquarian Field Club in 1885, published 1890. In Orel, Harold (ed.), (1966) 1967, pp. 191–195

The Mayor of Casterbridge: A Story of a Man of Character, Macmillan, London, (1886) 1963

The Woodlanders, Macmillan, London, (1887) 1974

'The Profitable Reading of Fiction', in *Forum*, New York, March 1888, pp. 57–70. In Orel, Harold (ed.), (1966) 1967, pp. 110–125

Wessex Tales (vol. 1), Macmillan, London, 1888, pp. 127–247

Tess of the d'Urbervilles: A Pure Woman Faithfully Presented, Macmillan, London, (1891) 1974

'The Science of Fiction', in *New Review*, April 1891, pp. 315–319

'Why I Don't Write Plays', in *Pall Mall Gazette*, 31 August 1892. Also in Orel, Harold (ed.), (1966) 1967, pp. 19–21

Jude the Obscure, Macmillan, London, (1896) 1974

The Well-Beloved, Oxford University Press, Oxford, (1897) 1998

Wessex Poems, Harper and Brothers, London, 1898

The Dynasts: a drama of the Napoleonic wars, in three parts, nineteen acts & one hundred and thirty scenes, Macmillan, London, published in parts: 1904, 1906 and 1908, http://www.gutenberg.org/files/4043/4043-h/4043-h.htm#link2H_PART1, last accessed 4 October 2017

'The Dynasts, A Rejoinder', in *The Times Literary Supplement*, 5 February 1904, pp. 36–37. In Orel, Harold (ed.), (1966) 1967, pp. 142–143

'Memories of Church Restoration', 1906. Variorum edition, in Beatty, Claudius, 1995, pp. 72–83. Also in Orel, Harold (ed.), (1966) 1967, pp. 203–218

'Dorset in London', *The Society of Dorset Men in London: Year-Book 1908–9*, pp. 3–4. Also in Orel, Harold (ed.), (1966) 1967, pp. 74–75

'General Preface to the Novels and Poems', 1895, 1912. In many editions; also in Orel, Harold (ed.) (1966) 1967, pp. 44–50

'The Ancient Cottages of England', in *The Preservation of Ancient Cottages*, London, 1927, pp. 13–16. Also in *Journal of the Royal Society of Arts* (18 March 1927), pp. 424–429; and Orel, Harold (ed.), (1966) 1967, pp. 233–323. Also available at https://www.jstor.org/stable/i40064877, last accessed 4 October 2017

The Life of Thomas Hardy, 1840–1928 with Hardy, Florence (This edition brings together *The Early Life of Thomas Hardy, 1840–1891*, Florence Hardy 1928; and *The Later Years of Thomas Hardy, 1892–1928*, Florence Hardy 1930), Wordsworth, Hertfordshire, 2007

The Architectural Notebook of Thomas Hardy, Beatty, Claudius (ed.), Dorset Natural History and Archaeological Society, Dorchester, 1966, 1995, 2007

Thomas Hardy's Personal Writings: Prefaces, Literary Opinions, Reminiscences, Orel, Harold (ed.), Macmillan, London, (1966) UK edition, 1967

The Collected Letters of Thomas Hardy, Purdy, Richard Little and Millgate, Michael (eds), Clarendon Press, Oxford, 1978–2012

Selected Poems, Thomas, Harry (ed.), Penguin, Harmondsworth, 1995

WRITINGS ABOUT HARDY

Beach, Joseph Warren, *The Technique of Thomas Hardy*, University of Chicago Press, Chicago, 1922

Beatty, Claudius, 'The Particular Part Played by Architecture in the Life and Work of Thomas Hardy (With Particular Reference to the Novels).' PhD thesis, University of London by Claudius J.P. Beatty, 1963. Together with *A Biography of Thomas Hardy as An Architect*, 1980, Plush Publishing, Dorset, 2004

Beatty, Claudius, 'Introduction' *The Architectural Notebook of Thomas Hardy*, Beatty, Claudius (ed.) Dorset Natural History and Archaeological Society, Dorchester, 1966, 1995, 2007

Beatty, Claudius (ed.), *Thomas Hardy: Conservation Architect; His Work for the Society for the Protection of Ancient Buildings, With a Variorum Edition of 'Memories of Church Restoration'* (1906), Dorset Natural History and Archaeological Society, Dorchester, 1995

Beatty, Claudius, *Thomas Hardy and the Restoration of Rampisham Church, Dorset: A Discussion*, University of Oslo, Creeds [Privately Printed], Bridport, Dorset, 1991

Bird Wright, Sarah, *Thomas Hardy A to Z: The Essential Reference to his Life and Work*, Facts on File, New York, 2002

Dalziel, Pamela, 'Drawings and Withdrawings: The Vicissitudes of Thomas Hardy's Wessex', in *Studies in Bibliography*, vol. 50, The Bibliographical Society, University of Virginia, 1997, pp. 390–400

Dalziel, Pamela, 'Illustrations', in Page, Norman (ed.), *Oxford Reader's Companion to Hardy*, Oxford University Press, Oxford, 2000, pp. 204–209

Dalziel, Pamela, 'The Return of the Native', in *Oxford Reader's Companion to Hardy*, Oxford University Press, Oxford, 2000, pp. 374–380

Dorset County Museum: http://www.dorsetcountymuseum.org/history, last accessed 4 October 2017

Draper, Jo, *Thomas Hardy: A Life in Pictures*, Dovecote Press, Wimborne, 1989

Draper, Jo, *Dorchester Past and Present*, Phillimore & Co., Chichester, 2001

Draper, Jo, 'The Temporary Requirements of Mere Fashion', *Dorset Life*, January 2011. http://www.dorsetlife.co.uk/2011/01/%E2%80%98the-temporary-requirements-of-mere-fashion%E2%80%99/, last accessed 4 October 2017

Eagleton, Terry, 'Introduction', *Jude the Obscure*, Macmillan, London, 1974, pp. 9–20

FitzHerbert, Claudia 'The House that Hardy Built' *The Telegraph*, 2011. http://www.telegraph.co.uk/culture/books/bookreviews/8434460/The-House-that-Hardy-built.html, last accessed 4 October 2017

Forster, E.M., 'Woodlanders in Devi', in *New Statesman*, London, 6 May 1939, p. 680. Quoted in Furbank, P.N., 1974

Fowles, John, and Draper, Jo, *Thomas Hardy's England*, Jonathan Cape, London, 1984

Frogley, Alain, 'Vaughan Williams and Thomas Hardy: "Tess" and the Slow Movement of the Ninth Symphony', *Music & Letters*, 68(1) (January 1987): 42–59. http://www.jstor.org/stable/736401, last accessed 4 October 2017

Furbank, P.N., 'Introduction', *The Woodlanders*, Macmillan, London, 1974, pp. 11–23

Gatrell, Simon, 'Middling Hardy', in Page, Norman (ed.), *Thomas Hardy Annual*, No. 4, Macmillan, London, 1986, pp. 70–90

Gatrell, Simon, *Hardy the Creator: A Textual Biography*, Clarendon Press, Oxford, 1988

Gatrell, Simon, *Thomas Hardy and the Proper Study of Mankind*, Macmillan, Basingstoke, 1993

Gatrell, Simon, *Thomas Hardy's Vision of Wessex*, Palgrave Macmillan, Basingstoke, 2003

Gatrell, Simon and Lea, Hermann in Page, Norman (ed.), *Oxford Reader's Companion to Hardy*, Oxford University Press, Oxford, 2000, p. 244

Gittings, R., *Young Thomas Hardy* (1975) and *The Older Hardy* (1978), combined as *Thomas Hardy*: Penguin, London, 2001

Grundy, Joan, 'Cinematic Arts', in her *Hardy and the Sister Arts*, Palgrave Macmillan, London, 1979

Hands, Tim, 'Dramatizations', in Page, Norman (ed.) *The Oxford Reader's Companion to Hardy*, Oxford University Press, Oxford, 2001, pp. 14–19

Hawkins, Desmond, *Hardy's Wessex*, Macmillan, London, 1983

Ingham, Patricia, *Authors in Context: Thomas Hardy*, Oxford University Press, Oxford, 2003

James, Henry, Review of *Far from the Madding Crowd*, *The Nation*, 24 December 1874

Kay-Robinson, Denys, *The Landscapes of Thomas Hardy*, Webb & Bower, Tiverton, 1984

Keith, W.J., 'Thomas Hardy and the Literary Pilgrims', in *Nineteenth-Century Fiction*, 24(1) (June 1969): 80–92. http://www.jstor.org/stable/2932353, last accessed 4 October 2017

Keith, W.J., 'Thomas Hardy', *Regions of the Imagination: The Development of British Rural Fiction*, University of Toronto, Toronto, Buffalo and London, 1988, pp. 85–108

Lea, Hermann, *Thomas Hardy Through the Camera's Eye* (with an introduction by Richard Curle), The Toucan Press, Beaminster, Dorset, 1964

Lea, Hermann, *Thomas Hardy's Wessex*, London, Macmillan, (1913) 1969, 1977

Lea, Hermann, *The Hardy Guides, Touring Companion of Thomas Hardy*, Volumes 1 and 2, ed. Gregory Stevens Cox, Penguin, Harmondsworth (1966), 1986

Lodge, David, 'Introduction', *The Woodlanders*, Macmillan, London, 1974, pp. 9–30

Lodge, David, 'Thomas Hardy and Cinematographic Form', in *NOVEL: A Forum on Fiction*, 7(3) (Spring 1974): 246–254. http://www.jstor.org/stable/1345416, last accessed 4 October 2017

Lodge, David, 'Thomas Hardy as a Cinematic Novelist', in *Thomas Hardy After Fifty Years*, ed. Lance St. John Butler, Palgrave Macmillan, London, 1977

Millgate, Michael (ed.), *The Life and Work of Thomas Hardy, 1840–1928*, Macmillan, London, 1984

Millgate, Michael, *Thomas Hardy: A Biography*, Oxford University Press, Oxford, (1982) 1985

Millgate, Michael, *Hardy's Wessex Today: The Lea/Jesty photographic collection introduced by Michael Millgate*, Mellstock Press, Belper, 1990

Millgate, Michael, *Thomas Hardy: His Career as a Novelist*, Palgrave Macmillan, Basingstoke, (1971) 1994

Nussbaum, Emily, 'Tune in Next Week: The Curious Power of the Cliffhanger', in *The New Yorker*, New York, 30 July 2012. http://www.newyorker.com/magazine/2012/07/30/tune-in-next-week, last accessed 4 October 2017

Page, Norman, *The Oxford Reader's Companion to Hardy*, Oxford University Press, Oxford, 2000

Pettit, Charles, 'Literature into Music: Music Inspired by the Works of Thomas Hardy', *The Hardy Review*, XV–ii (Autumn 2013): 37–52. Reproduced in Robin Milford Trust website, http://www.robinmilfordtrust.org.uk/Hardy1.pdf, last accessed 4 October 2017

Pinion, F.B., *A Hardy Companion: A Guide to the Works of Thomas Hardy and their Background*, Macmillan, London, Melbourne, Toronto, St. Martin's Press, New York, 1968

Plietzsch, Birgit, *The Novels of Thomas Hardy as a Product of Nineteenth-Century Social, Economic, and Cultural Change*, Tenea Verlag, Berlin, 2004

Richardson, Albert, 'The Master Craftsman', in *The Builder*, CXXXIV(4433), 20 January 1928. Also in Beatty, Claudius, 1963 (2004), p. 431

Sassoon, Siegfried, *Siegfried Sassoon: Diaries 1920–1922*, ed. Rupert Hart-Davis, Faber & Faber, London 1981

Schad, John, 'Introduction', *A Laodicean*, Penguin, Harmondsworth, 1997

Shires, Linda M., 'Matter, Consciousness, and the Human in *Wessex Poems*', in *Studies in English Literature 1500–1900*, 55(4) (Autumn 2015): 899–924

Stringer, Peter, 'Models of Man in Casterbridge and Milton Keynes', in Byron Mikellides (ed.), *Architecture for People*, Studio Vista, London, 1960, pp. 176–184

Taylor, Richard (ed.), *The Personal Notebooks of Thomas Hardy*, Palgrave Macmillan, Basingstoke, 1979

The Thomas Hardy Association: http://www.thethomashardyassociation.org, last accessed 4 October 2017

Thomas Hardy Society: www.hardysociety.org, last accessed 4 October 2017

Tomalin, Claire, *Thomas Hardy: The Time-Torn Man*, Viking Penguin, London, 2006

Tyndale, Walter: *Hardy County Water-Colours*, A&C Black, London 19-- (First Edition is undated)

Victorian Web: http://www.victorianweb.org/authors/hardy/artov.html, last accessed 4 October 2017

Wain, John, 'Introduction', in *The Dynasts: An Epic-Drama of the War with Napoleon*, by Thomas Hardy, St. Martin's Press, New York, 1965, pp. v–xix

Wellesley, Mary, 'Too Much Succulence', *London Review of Books*, 23 June 2015. https://www.lrb.co.uk/blog/2015/06/23/mary-wellesley/too-much-succulence/, last accessed 4 October 2017

Wilson, Keith, *A Companion to Thomas Hardy*, John Wiley & Sons, London, 2009

Wilson, Keith, 'Hardy and the Ethics of Looking', *The Hardy Society Journal*, vol. 7, no. 1, Spring 2011

Wilson, Keith, *Thomas Hardy on Stage*, Palgrave Macmillan, London, (1994) 1995

Windle, Bertram, *The Wessex of Thomas Hardy*, illustrated by Edmund New, John Lane, The Bodley Head, London and New York 1902

Wright, T.R., *Thomas Hardy on Screen*, Cambridge University Press, Cambridge, 2006

WRITINGS ABOUT ARCHITECTURE

Allen, Isabel, 'Creating Space Out of Text: Perspectives on Domestic Regency Architecture or Three Essays on the Picturesque', in Madge, James and Peckham, Andrew (eds), *Narrating Architecture: A Retrospective Anthology*, Routledge, London, 2006, pp. 203–226

Archigram Archival Project, 'Temple Island' by Michael Webb, unfinished project of 112 images, http://archigram.westminster.ac.uk/, last accessed 4 October 2017

Bachelard, Gaston, *The Poetics of Space*, Presses Universitaires de France, 1958

Batchelor, John, *John Ruskin, No Wealth but Life*, Pimlico, London, 2001

Berman, Marshall, *All That Is Solid Melts into Air: The Experience of Modernity*, Simon and Schuster, New York, 1982

Bottoms, Edward, '"AA History": Abridged version of an introductory lecture to Archives For London & the Twentieth Century Society', February 2010. AA Archives, http://www.aaschool.ac.uk/AALIFE/LIBRARY/aahistory.php, last accessed 4 October 2017

Clark, Kenneth, *Ruskin Today*, Penguin, Harmondsworth, 1966

Colomina, Beatriz (ed.), *Sexuality and Space*, Princeton Architectural Press, New York, 1992

Colomina, Beatriz, *Privacy and Publicity: Modern Architecture as Mass Media*, MIT Press, Cambridge, Mass., 1994

Day, Michael, *Dorset Churches*, www.dorset-churches.org.uk, last accessed 4 October 2017

de Honnecourt, Villard, *Album de Dessins et Croquis*, thirteenth century, 14 http://visualiseur.bnf.fr/ark:/12148/btv1b10509412z/f8.image.r=villarddehonnecourt, last accessed 4 Ocober 2017

De Smet, Catherine, *Le Corbusier: Architect of Books*, Lars Muller, Zurich, 2005

Denslagen, Wim, *Romantic Modernism: Nostalgia in the World of Conservation*, Amsterdam University Press, Amsterdam, 2009

Derrida, Jacques, 'Point de Folie: Maintenant, l'Architecture', in Tschumi, Bernard, *La Case Vide: La Villette*, AA Publications, London, 1985

Evans, Robin, *The Projective Cast*, MIT Press, Cambridge, Mass., 1995

Evans, Robin, *Translations from Drawings to Buildings and Other Essays*, Architectural Association, London, 1997

Forty, Adrian, *Words and Buildings: A Vocabulary of Modern Architecture*, Thames and Hudson, London, 2000

Fraser, Murray and Hill, Jonathan (eds), *Design Research in Architecture: An Overview*, Ashgate, Farnham, 2013

Garbett, Edward Lacy, *The Principles of Design in Architecture as Deductible from Nature and Exemplified in the Works of Greek and Gothic Architects. Mr Weale's New Series of Rudimentary Work for Beginners*, John Weale, London, 1850

Hardingham, Samantha (ed.) and Price, Cedric, *Cedric Price: Opera*, Academy-Wiley, Chichester, 2003

Hardingham, Samantha and Rattenbury, Kester, *Supercrit #4: Bernard Tschumi: Parc de la Villette*, Routledge, London, 2011

THE WESSEX PROJECT

THE WESSEX PROJECT

Hill, Jonathan, *Architecture: The Subject is Matter*, Routledge, London, 2001

Hill, Jonathan, 'Design Theory – the first 500 years', in Fraser, Murray et al. (eds), *Design Research in Architecture: An Overview*, Routledge, London, 2013

Holbrook, Tom, *Expanding Disciplinarity in Architectural Practice: Designing from the Room to the City*, Routledge, London, 2016

Hunter, Michael, 'The Fitful Rise of British Preservation', in Hunter, Michael (ed.), *Preserving the Past: The Rise of Heritage in Modern Britain*, Alan Sutton Publishing, Stroud, 1996, pp. 6–10

Hunter, Michael (ed.), *Preserving the Past: The Rise of Heritage in Modern Britain*, Alan Sutton Publishing, Stroud, 1996

Jokilehto, Jukka, *A History of Architectural Conservation*, Butterworth Heinemann, Oxford, 1999

Kelso, Paul, 'Architect's copycat claim pure fantasy, says judge', *The Guardian*, 3 November 2001. https://www.theguardian.com/uk/2001/nov/03/arts.highereducation, last accessed 4 October 2017

Koolhaas, Rem, *Delirious New York: A Retroactive Manifesto for Manhattan*, Oxford University Press, Oxford, 1978

Koolhaas, Rem, *Content*, Taschen, Cologne, 2004

Le Corbusier, *Vers Une Architecture* (*Towards a New Architecture*), The Architectural Press, London, (1923); first English translation 1927

MacEwen, Malcolm, *Crisis in Architecture*, RIBA Publications, London, 1974

McWilliam, Neil, 'A Microcosm of the Universe: The Building of the University Museum, Oxford', *Oxford Art Journal*, 1(1) (1978): 23–27. http://www.jstor.org/stable/1360082, last accessed 4 October 2017

Miele, Christopher, 'The First Conservation Militants: William Morris and the Society for the Protection of Ancient Buildings', in Hunter, Michael (ed.), *Preserving the Past: The Rise of Heritage in Modern Britain*, Alan Sutton Publishing, Stroud, 1996, pp. 17–37

Murphy, Keith, Ivarsson, Jonas and Lymer, Gustav, 'Embodied Reasoning in Architectural Critique', in *Design Studies*, 33(6) (2012): 530–556

Oliver, Paul, Bentley, Ian and Davis, Ian, *Dunroamin: The Suburban Semi and its Enemies*, Barrie & Jenkins, London, 1981

Pevsner, Nikolaus, 'The Architectural Setting of Jane Austen's Novels', in *Journal of the Warburg and Courtauld Institutes*, 31 (1968): 404–422. Available at http://www.jstor.org/stable/750649, last accessed 4 October 2017

Piper, John, 'St Marie's Grange: The First Home of A.W.N. Pugin', *Architectural Review* (October 1945). https://www.architectural-review.com/rethink/viewpoints/1945-october-st-maries-grange-by-john-piper/8604214.article, last accessed 4 October 2017

Powers, Alan, 'The Architectural Book: Image and Accident', in Rattenbury, Kester, *This Is Not Architecture: Media Constructions*, Routledge, London, 2002

Pugin, A.W.N., *Contrasts, Or the Parallel Between Noble Edifices of the Fourteenth and Fifteenth Century and Those of the Present Day, Shewing the Present Decay of Taste, Accompanied by Appropriate Text*. Privately Printed, London and Salisbury, 1836

Pugin Society, 'A Merely Realistic Dream-Country: The Gothic Revival in Hampshire and Wiltshire', The Pugin Society Summer Study Tour, 2016. https://www.academia.edu/28005390/_A_Merely_Realistic_Dream_Country_The_Gothic_Revival_in_Hampshire_and_Wiltshire, last accessed 4 October 2017

Rattenbury, Kester, *This Is Not Architecture*, Media Constructions, Routledge, London, 2002

Rattenbury, Kester and Hardingham, Samantha: *Supercrit #2, Robert Venturi and Denise Scott Brown: Learning From Las Vegas*, Routledge, London 2007

Rattenbury, Kester, 'Ghosts in the Machine', in *Supercrit #5, Rem Koolhaas, Delirious New York*, www.supercrits.com, November 2013

Rattenbury, Kester, 'Revealing Secrets', in *The Architectural Review*, 2015. http://www.architectural-education.club/revealing_secrets_kester_rattenbury, last accessed 4 October 2017

Rattenbury, Kester, 'The Thing Itself', in Heron, Katharine and Hamman, Clare (eds), *Adapt-r*, exhibition catalogue, University of Westminster, London, 2016, pp. 73–80

Ruskin, John, *Modern Painters*, Estes and Lauriat, Boston, (1843–60) 1894

Ruskin, John, *The Seven Lamps of Architecture* (6th edition), George Allen, Orpington, (1849) 1889

250

Ruskin, John, *The Stones of Venice*, Smith, Elder & Co., London: volume 1, 1851; volume 2, 1853; volume 3, 1853

Saint, Andrew, *The Image of the Architect*, Yale University Press, London and New Haven, Conn., 1985

Saint, Andrew, 'How Listing Happened', in Hunter, Michael (ed.), *Preserving the Past: The Rise of Heritage in Modern Britain*, Alan Sutton Publishing, Stroud, 1996, pp. 115–133

Sklair, Leslie, *The Icon Project: Architecture, Cities and Capitalist Globalization*, Oxford University Press, Oxford, 2017

Smithson, Alison, *AS in DS: An Eye on the Road*, Delft University Press, Delft, Netherlands, 1983; Lars Müller Publishers, Zurich, 2001

Smithson, Alison, 'Patio and Pavilion', Essay for *This is Tomorrow* exhibition, Institute of Contemporary Arts, 1956. See *Patio and Pavilion Reconstructed*, AA Files part 47, 2002, 37–44

The Society for the Protection of Ancient Buildings, 'An Extract of a Tiny Portion of The Society for The Protection of Ancient Building's Work Over the Last 125 Years'. http://www.spab.org.uk/what-is-spab-/history-of-the-spab/, last accessed 4 October 2017

Stamp, Gavin, 'The Art of Keeping One Jump Ahead: Conservation Societies in the Twentieth Century', in Hunter, Michael (ed.), *Preserving the Past: The Rise of Heritage in Modern Britain*, Alan Sutton Publishing, Stroud, 1996, pp. 77–98

Tschumi, Bernard, *The Manhattan Transcripts*, Academy Editions, London, 1981

Tschumi, Bernard, *Cinegramme Folie: Le Parc de la Villette*, Princeton Architectural Press, Princeton, N.J., 1988

Tschumi, Bernard, *Event Cities*, MIT Press, Cambridge, Mass., 1994

van den Berghe, Jo, 'Theatre of Operations, or The Construction site as Architectural Design', PhD by Design, Royal Melbourne Institute of Technology, 2012

van Schaik, Leon, *Mastering Architecture: Becoming a Creative Innovator in Practice*, Wiley, Chichester, 2005

van Schaik, Leon with Johnson, Anna, *The Pink Book: By Practice, By Invitation Design Practice Research at RMIT, 1986–2011*, sixpointsixone, Melbourne, 2011

van Schaik, Leon and Blythe, Richard, 'What If Design Practice Matters?', in Fraser, Murray et al. (eds), *Design Research in Architecture: An Overview*, Ashgate, Farnham, 2013

van Schaik, Martin and Macel, Otakar (eds), *Exit Utopia: Architectural Provocations, 1956–1976*, Prestel, Munich, 2004

Vesely, Dalibor, 'In Defence of Architecture', in *Compendium: The Work of the University of Cambridge Department of Architecture*, University of Cambridge Martin Centre, Cambridge, 2006, pp. 28–33

Venturi, Robert, Scott Brown, Denise and Izenour, Steven, *Learning From Las Vegas: The Forgotten Symbolism of Architectural Form*, MIT Press, Cambridge, Mass., (1972) revised edition, 1977

Vidler, Anthony, *The Architectural Uncanny, Essays in the Modern Unhomely*, MIT Press, Cambridge, Mass., (1992) 1994

Vidler, Anthony, *Warped Space: Art, Architecture and Anxiety in Modern Culture*, MIT Press, Cambridge, Mass., (2000) 2002

Wigglesworth, Sarah (ed.), *Around and About Stock Orchard Street*, Routledge, Abingdon, 2011

Wilde, Oscar, 'Art and the Handicraftsman', in Ross, Robert (ed.), *Essays and Lectures*, Methuen & Co., London, 1909

Woodforde, John, *The Truth About Cottages*, Routledge and Kegan Paul, London, 1969

OTHER COMPARATIVE AND CONTEXTUAL SOURCES

Ashby-Rudd, Philip, and Trehane, Emma: 'Never-Land, Lulworth Cove and the Intellectual Circles of J. M. Barrie, Thomas Hardy, Alfred Fripp, Sir Frederick Treves and Gerald Du Maurier'. Victorianweb, http://www.victorianweb.org/authors/barrie/2.html, undated, last accessed 4 October 2017

Bachelard, Gaston, *The Poetics of Space*, Beacon Press, Boston, (1958, in English 1964) 1994

Barthes, Roland, *Camera Lucida: Reflections on Photography*, translated by Richard Howard, Vintage, London, (1980) 1993

Benjamin, Walter, *Illuminations: Essays and Reflections*, ed. Hannah Arendt, Schocken, New York, (1955) 1969

Berger, John, *Ways of Seeing*, BBC and Penguin Books, London, (1971) 1972

Bragg, Melvin et al., 'The Great Exhibition of 1851', *In Our Time*, BBC Radio 4, broadcast 27 April 2006. http://www.bbc.co.uk/programmes/p003c19x, last accessed 4 October 2017

Brewster, David, *Letters on Natural Magic*, Harper and Brothers, New York, 1843

Dickens, Charles, *Life and Adventures of Martin Chuzzlewit*, Wordsworth Editions, Hertfordshire, (1843) 1997

Dickens, Charles, *Dombey and Son*, Wordsworth Editions, Hertfordshire, (1848) 1995

Dickens, Charles, *Bleak House*, Wordsworth Editions, Hertfordshire, (1853) 1993

Drabble, Margaret, *A Writer's Britain: Landscape in Literature, Photographed by Jorge Lewinski*, Thames and Hudson, London, (1979) 1984, 1987, p. 139

Draper, Jo, 'The Lost Buildings of Lyscombe', *Dorset Life*, October 2013. http://www.dorsetlife.co.uk/2013/10/the-lost-buildings-of-lyscombe/, last accessed 4 October 2017

Dudgeon, Piers, *Captivated: J.M. Barrie, Daphne du Maurier and the Dark Side of Neverland*, Vintage, London, 2009

Eliot, George, *Middlemarch*, Oxford World's Classics, Oxford, (1871) 1997

Forster, E.M., *A Room with a View*, Penguin Classics, London, (1908) 2012

Forster, E.M., *Howard's End*, Penguin Classics, London, (1910) 2012

Forster, E.M., 'Woodlanders on Devi', New Statesman and Nation, 6 May 1938, pp. 679–680

Goodman, Nelson, *Ways of Worldmaking*, Hackett Publishing Company, Indianapolis, 1978

Herbert, Stephen, 'From Daedalum to Zoetrope', undated. http://www.stephenherbert.co.uk/wheelZOETROPEpart1.htm#fn24 278, 279, last accessed 4 October 2017

Kemp, Martin, *The Science of Art*, Yale University, New Haven, Conn., 1991

Mitchell, W.J.T., 'Image X Text', in Amihay, Ofra and Walsh, Lauren (eds), *The Future of Text and Image: Collected Essays on Literary and Visual Conjunctures*, Cambridge Scholars Publishing, Newcastle upon Tyne, 2012, pp. 1–11

South West Sustainable Land Use Initiative, 'The Dorset Heathland Project: Hardy's Egdon Heath and Urban Heath's LIFE Project', Forum for the Future, October 2004. http://www.self-willed-land.org.uk/articles/DorsetHeath2.pdf, last accessed 4 October 2017

Viner, Linda, *Lost Villages: Discover Dorset*, Dovecote Press, Wimborne, 2002

Yeazell, Ruth Bernard, *Art of the Everyday: Dutch Painting and the Realist Novel*, Princeton University Press, Princeton, N.J., 2009

INDEX